THE
FEDERALIST SYSTEM

ALEXANDER HAMILTON

[From the portrait by Weimar, in the N. Y. City Hall]

THE
FEDERALIST SYSTEM

1789–1801

BY

JOHN SPENCER BASSETT, Ph.D.

PROFESSOR OF HISTORY, TRINITY COLLEGE

WITH MAPS

COOPER SQUARE PUBLISHERS, INC.
NEW YORK
1968

Originally Published 1906
Published by Cooper Square Publishers, Inc.
59 Fourth Avenue, New York, N. Y. 10003
Library of Congress Catalog Card No. 68-19308

Printed in the United States of America
by Noble Offset Printers, Inc., New York, N. Y. 10003

TO

THE MEMORY OF

HERBERT BAXTER ADAMS

INSTRUCTOR AND FRIEND

CONTENTS

CONTENTS

MAPS

EDITOR'S INTRODUCTION

WITH the present volume the *American Nation* passes to the continuous narrative history of the United States under an enduring federal government. From this point till 1860 event follows event and year ushers in year in continuous and orderly fashion. Nevertheless, although the separate history of the commonwealths is for the most part merged into that of the nation, the national history grows steadily more complex: while the colonies had no separate international relations or independent economic policy or extended geographical field, under the new Constitution foreign relations became an exciting cause of fluctuation in politics, economic welfare was a staple of discussion in Congress, and a new group of western communities powerfully reacted upon the other parts of the Union.

The year 1789, at which this volume begins, is not an exact delimitation: the influences which brought about the new federal constitution, and which are described in McLaughlin's *Confederation and Constitution* (Vol. X.), were still required to set the new government into operation; and hence Professor

Bassett's first three chapters are devoted to an account of the creation of the machinery of government, the erection of a stable financial system, and the sudden appearance of rival political parties. The years from 1789 to 1793 make up a period of construction hardly less important and less permanent in its results than the years from 1787 to 1789.

Having thus seen the substructure securely laid, the author next attacks, in chapters iv.–vii., the complicated subject of a national foreign policy, taking up in succession the relations with England, Spain, and France. These powers, all of them occupying American colonies in the neighborhood of the United States, two of them holding strips of territory claimed by this country, were brought into complex relations among themselves by the outbreak of European wars in 1793. It has been the province of the author to unravel the threads of American diplomacy and to show where the interests of the United States lay and how they were subserved by Washington's administration.

Chapters viii. and ix. describe the contentions with England which were terminated for the time by the Jay treaty, and the political difficulties which came upon Washington in his second administration. Chapters x. to xiii. are devoted to a study of social and economic conditions during the period of Federalist supremacy, including one chapter on slavery. This general treatment may be read in connection with chapter vi. in McLaughlin's *Confederation and Constitution*, and also with chapter vi. of Channing's *Jeffersonian System*. The remainder of the volume, chapters xiv. to xix., follows the progress of the difficulties with France up to the point of actual war, and the consequent dissensions within the Federal party. It includes chapters on the alien and sedition laws and their counterpart, the Virginia and Kentucky resolutions. The Critical Essay on Authorities deals particularly with the voluminous materials on biography and the collected works of the statesmen of the period.

The special function of this volume in the *American Nation* series is to describe the foundations of the present American party system and its application to the extremely difficult problems of that time. Such a study necessarily involves an effort to penetrate the character and discover the real motives of a group of giants: in any list of America's half-dozen greatest statesmen, the names of Washington, Hamilton, and Jefferson invariably appear; for those were the three men who most clearly expressed and most strongly influenced the American people of their time. The volume also distinguishes the causes of friction with foreign powers, especially the questions of neutral trade and neutral rights, in a period when many of the present principles governing American international relations were first enounced. In a single sentence, the province of the

book is to show how, from 1789 to 1801, the American
people faced a new Constitution, a new party system,
and a new set of problems, yet contrived to make
their government effective and to transmit it un-
impaired.

AUTHOR'S PREFACE

ON its political side this volume treats of three principal facts: the successful establishment of the government under the Constitution, the organization of the Republican party on the basis of popular government, and the steady adherence of the government to a policy of neutrality at a time when we were threatened with serious foreign complications. The first achievement was chiefly due to Hamilton, the second to Jefferson, and the third to Washington, first, and, after his presidency, to John Adams.

To these cardinal features of the history of the time I have added some chapters on social and economic conditions. I have discussed at some length the progress of the anti-slavery cause in the country, because of its relation to the growth of sectionalism. In these chapters, as well as in those on political affairs, my endeavor has been to write from the stand-point of the men of the time. The men of the day were very human and practical, and they had definite views of the needs of the present and prospects of the future. They believed earnestly in some ideals which to the men of to-day seem strange and in some cases grotesque. But they were average men, and, in spite of their passionate outbursts, their foreign sympathies, and their political sensitiveness, they met the problems before them as capable Americans. They had the good sense to approve of Hamilton's organization of the government, Washington's fidelity to neutrality, Jefferson's confidence in democracy, and Adams's unwillingness to bring on an X Y Z war. American self-government was never better justified than during the first three national administrations.

The difficulties in the preparation of this volume have been to a large extent offset by the sympathy and assistance of my friends. To Professor Albert Bushnell Hart, editor of the series; Mr. Frederic Bancroft, of Washington; Mr. Herbert Putnam, Librarian of Congress, and his ever-courteous assistant, Dr. Ainsworth R. Spofford; and Professor Andrew C. McLaughlin, of the University of Michigan, I am indebted for valuable help; to Mr. Worthington C. Ford, chief of the Manuscripts Division of the Library of Congress, I owe a peculiar debt of gratitude. To all I make my sincere acknowledgments.

JOHN SPENCER BASSETT.

THE
FEDERALIST SYSTEM

CHAPTER I

LAUNCHING THE NEW GOVERNMENT
(1789–1791)

THE winter of 1788–1789 saw the dissolution in the United States of an inefficient form of government and the inauguration in its stead of a stronger union. Much that transpired in the preceding years showed that the change was necessary. The heavy debt of the nation was running up and thus begetting contempt for America abroad and serious discontent at home. The states were growing openly jealous of one another, and it seemed likely that the breaches which had been made would become wider rather than narrower. There were serious foreign problems which the older authorities had not been able to settle, among them the execution of the British treaty of 1783, and the right to navigate the Mississippi River. The weakness of the central authority was evident to all, and to none more than to those who attempted to exercise it. England also was fully conscious of how things were going, and felt a lively satisfaction in a hope of taking back singly the colonies lost through their united resistance. Out of these dangers there was no other way than to create a government strong enough to manage the finances, restrain local antagonisms, and uphold the national dignity abroad. Such a way was found in the constitution which was framed in the summer of 1787 and adopted in the twelve months following.[1]

The old government went out of existence quietly. While the constitutional convention was sitting, Congress, then in session in New York, rallied enough strength to pass, July 13, 1787, the Northwest Ordinance, one of the most important of its enactments. After that it sank into supineness, feeling, no doubt, that it ought to attempt no matter of moment till the issue of the convention was decided. When in the summer of 1788 adoption became certain, the members of Congress began to steal away from New York City in order to take some steps at their homes towards the organization of the new government. One matter, however, aroused their interest: they spent two months debating the location of a permanent capital. No agreement could be made on the point, and it was dropped, after first ordering that the new Congress should meet in New York.

[1] Cf. McLaughlin, *Confederation and Constitution* (*Am. Nation*, X.), chaps. xii.–xviii.

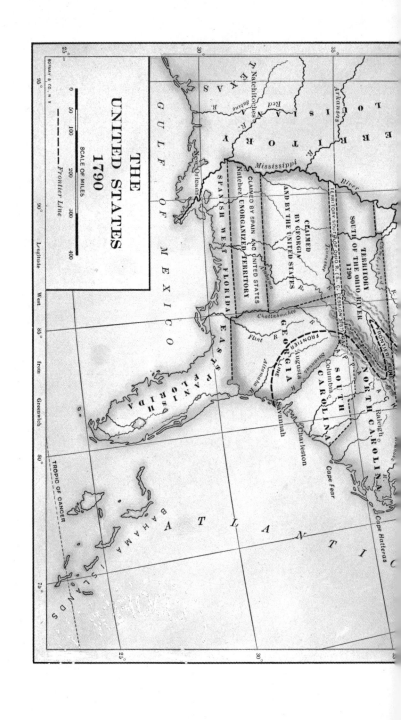

THE
UNITED STATES
1790

SCALE OF MILES

0   50   100   200   300   400

—— Frontier Line

Bormay & Co., N.Y.

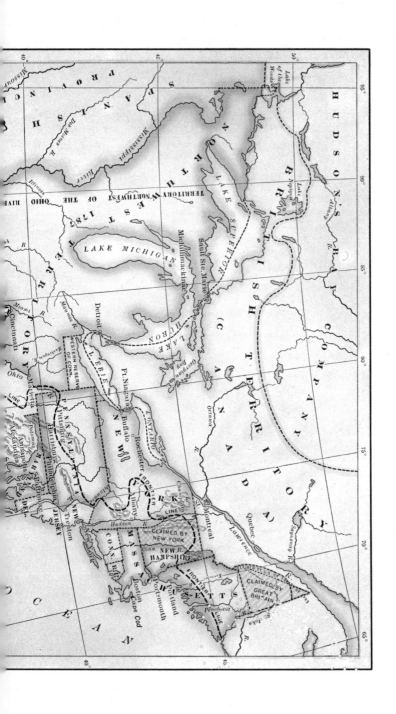

The Confederation rendered important service to the nation. Weak as it seemed, it was as strong as the nature of the situation warranted when it was formed. It took time and the peril of disintegration and foreign interference to induce the states to surrender an additional portion of their individuality and to form that "more perfect union" which at the close of 1788 was about to be placed in power. Perhaps at no other time in American history was there as rapid an advance in the nationalizing forces.

The president of the Continental Congress, on July 2, 1788, rose in his seat and announced that nine states had ratified the Constitution of the United States, and that it behooved the body before him to take steps to put the new government into operation. The Congress took the matter into consideration, and ordered that the states should choose presidential electors on the first Wednesday in January, 1789; that the electors should vote for president and vice-president on the first Wednesday in February; and that the new Congress should assemble in New York on the first Wednesday in March.[1] Thus the old government bowed its youthful successor to the scene of action.

For president, all eyes turned to Washington. Never was a rich personal character worth more to a nation than Washington's now proved to be. His name gave strength to the Union at home and abroad. In Europe, even in England, he was highly

[1] McMaster, *With the Fathers*, 150–152.

esteemed for honor, sagacity, and mental balance. In America he was trusted as the one force who could command the respect of both of the parties which had violently disputed about the adoption of the Constitution. His election was unanimous.

Washington hesitated before he made up his mind to accept the presidency. He had a genuine love of retirement; he had served his country so long that he needed rest for a strong body which had already begun to show the effects of fatigue; his private affairs were in want of his supervision; he had a strong personal attachment for the fine old mansion of Mount Vernon; and he had been so active in securing the adoption of the Constitution that he feared that people would say, if he now became president, that he had been seeking his own advancement. To many friends he urged these things as reasons why he should not receive the honor they proposed for him; but all insisted that he was necessary to the success of the Union, and he ceased to object.

For vice-president it was felt that a New England man ought to be taken, lest sectional jealousy should crop out in the very beginning. Hancock and Samuel Adams, whose past services had made them pre-eminent among New-Englanders, had recently been anti-Federalists, and it was thought unwise to put into high office men who had opposed the Union. The choice fell, therefore, on John Adams. He was a scholarly man, a patriot, and a

Federalist. He had served many years as American minister in Europe, where his exclusive tastes had been stimulated by association with cultivated people. He was not in close sympathy with American democracy. His enemies declared that he was squeamish, unsocial, and priggish; and his friends have not denied that he was lacking in tact, sympathy, and resourcefulness. Yet he was honest and above party trickery. In his writings he seemed to approve of the dominance of "the rich, the well-born, and the capable." [1] Consequently, he was proclaimed by his opponents an aristocrat and a monarchist.

The first Wednesday in March, 1789, was the fourth of the month. It was the day for the meeting of Congress. In New York there had been much hurrying of workmen lest the fine City Hall at the corner of Wall and Nassau streets should not be ready for the use of the expected body; but the day came without a Congress. Of the twenty-two senators only nine were in their seats, and of the fifty-nine representatives only thirteen were present. The short period which had elapsed since their election, the unseasonable time of the year, and the difficulties of the roads were given as excuses for the delay. But to Washington, chafing at Mount Vernon, it seemed due to a lack of interest in the government, and it made him a little apprehensive of the future. [2] It was not till April 2 that the

---

[1] John Adams, *Works*, IV., 290.
[2] Madison, *Writings* (Congress ed.), I., 458.

House had a quorum and began to transact business, and not till April 5 that the Senate was organized, John Langdon, of New Hampshire, being chosen president *pro tempore*.   April 6 the electoral returns were counted and messengers sent to notify Washington and Adams that they were elected president and vice-president respectively of the United States of America.

Adams set out from Braintree, Massachusetts, at once.   He was given an ovation as he went up to the seat of government; for he was to the people the first visible embodiment of the power and dignity of the new government, and their joy was unrestrained.   He arrived in New York on April 22, repeated the oath of office, and took his seat as presiding officer of the Senate.

Charles Thomson, since 1774 the secretary of the Continental Congress, the messenger to Washington, arrived at Mount Vernon on April 14.   In the drawing-room of the old mansion, while the family stood around, he presented the letter of Congress announcing Washington's election.   Two days later the president-elect set out for New York.   A mile from his home he was met by an escort from Alexandria; at the Potomac's bank he was turned over by these to an escort from Georgetown; and thus he was passed on by Georgetown to Baltimore, thence to Philadelphia, thence through New Jersey to New York; so that he was never, during the whole journey, without a suitable guard of honor.   Chil-

dren and women strewed flowers in his road, the
dignitaries of the towns through which he passed
met him with speeches, from which he was led
away to dinners, and at the dock on Manhattan
Island he was received with the wildest expressions of joy.[1]

Congress had already concerned itself about the
inauguration. Ceremonies in general were giving
that body much trouble, and the Senate especially
was disposed to take for itself much of the dignity
of the old colonial council, which had in most of the
colonies acted as the upper house of the legislatures.
Among the disputed matters was the manner in
which the Senate should receive a messenger from
the House. A plan marked by elaborate formality
was reported to the Senate, and was tabled because
it was objectionable to the House and to some of
the senators as well. Meanwhile, April 30, the day
fixed for inauguration, arrived.

The occasion was made a holiday in the city.
At 9 A.M. all the church-bells in New York were
rung, and the people assembled to pray for the
government which was about to be inaugurated.
From the churches throngs turned to the City Hall,
where the two Houses of Congress met at eleven
o'clock. The Senate was particularly conscious of
its importance, and the face of every member wore
an air of expectancy; but none of them knew just
how to take the part assigned to them. John Adams

---

[1] Marshall, *Washington*, V., 153–167.

was much excited. "Gentlemen," he said, with a nervous air, "I wish for the direction of the Senate. The president will, I suppose, address the Congress. How shall I behave? How shall we receive it? Shall it be standing or sitting?" [1]

Thereupon men fell to discussing. Adams, Izard, of South Carolina, and Lee, of Virginia, instinctively came back to the only precedent they knew, the king addressing Parliament. But Charles Carroll, of Carrollton, pertinently observed that the custom of Parliament was nothing to an American legislature. Here the wordy discussion was interrupted by the announcement that a messenger from the Lower House was at the door to say that the representatives were about to join the Senate in order to witness the coming ceremonies.

This produced a new confusion; for how should a messenger be received? There was a hurried consultation; some one moved to take up the report of the committee on receiving communications, a new debate was started, and the anxieties of the vice-president were left unsatisfied. Then more words were spent. Suddenly it was whispered that the representatives were at the door. Let them wait— the debate went on. The situation was becoming ludicrous, when by some chance the door was opened and the expectant Lower House crowded in and took seats without any announcement. They sat on one side of the broad aisle which ran from the chair of

[1] Maclay, *Journal*, 7–9; *Annals of Cong.*, 1 Cong., 23, 29–31.

the presiding officer to the door, and the Senate
sat on the other.

For a moment there was a pause: men had forgotten what came next. Then it was remembered
that it was time for the appearance of Washington;
but the committee on ceremonial, who had arranged to go for him, had neglected that duty in
order to take part in the wrangle over ceremony.
Hastily taking their hats, they thrust themselves
through the expectant crowds in the streets and
hurried to the residence of the president - elect.
The two Houses awaited their return for over an
hour, gazing silently at one another across the
central aisle.[1]

Finally the shouts of the multitude told of the
approach of Washington. A moment later he entered the chamber. His tall, solemn figure was clad
in a suit of deep brown, with white stockings; a
sword was at his side, and his hair was dressed in a
bag-wig. In his face there was a slight trace of
embarrassment, but he walked firmly down the
room, bowing to the right and the left, and took a
seat by the side of the vice-president. In a moment Adams arose and said to Washington that
the oath of office should now be administered. Out
to the balcony which overlooked the street passed
the parties concerned, and there Livingston, chan-
cellor of the state of New York, administered the
prescribed oath. A second later he turned to the

[1] Maclay, *Journal*, 7–9.

crowd and shouted, "Long live George Washington, president of the United States!" and the vast throng re-echoed his words.[1]

Within the Senate chamber, a few minutes later, the president read his inaugural address. He was visibly agitated, as one not trained to public speaking. His words voiced the simple virtues, for which he was pre-eminent. He pleaded that "local prejudices" and "party animosities" should be forgotten, that harmony and magnanimity should continually be practised, and he implored the blessings of Heaven on the new government. He stressed an idea which was rarely absent from the most patriotic men of his day, the fact that the eyes of the world were watching us to see what we should make of our experiment of liberty. He did not know that six days later at Versailles there was going to be inaugurated another great movement in government, another experiment in liberty. The address delivered, the entire Congress went on foot to St. Paul's church where they heard prayers.

These scenes were characteristic of the times and the men who participated in them. A new state had been hewn from the side of an old one; it needed time to find itself, to develop its own purposes, and to discard the ideals which had dominated it in former days. The men into whose hands were thrust its destiny were to have many struggles among themselves before they should hammer out a

[1] McMaster, *With the Fathers*, 176.

national policy. It was a conflict in which personal
reputations were made and lost, in which party
hatreds were nourished, in which the cruder ideals
of society were to attack the higher ideals, and in
which there was to be, nevertheless, a continual
progress towards a powerful organization of democracy.

The first duties of the government were those of
organization. Congress had to provide for all the
ordinary tasks of government and many of the
extraordinary ones. The provision of a revenue,
the creation of great executive departments, the
establishment of a judicial system, the regulation of
foreign intercourse, and the adjustment of an intricate system of subordinate administration were
only a few of the things which demanded immediate
attention. The president had duties equally numerous. He must fill the great offices with the men
best fitted to administer them and most likely to
satisfy the various local prejudices which might
prove a menace to the new government. With the
advice of these he must fill a multitude of lower
offices with the same care and wisdom. Each step
taken, either by the legislature or the executive,
must be carefully watched lest it give to some
organ powers which might in future prove to be too
great or too small, and lest it be twisted into an
undesirable precedent. The slow and measured
steps by which the men of the day proceeded have
at times been pronounced pedantic. They were

rather the outcome of the extreme caution of men who were zealously guarding the ideals which they believed to be right, and the tenacity with which these ideals were defended ought to be held as one of the best things of the day.

The first care of Congress was to provide a revenue. The initiative under the Constitution was in the House, which on April 8, 1789, proceeded to a discussion. Madison, the chief author of the Constitution, whom the hostility of the Virginia anti-Federalists had kept out of the Senate, appeared as leader in the great measures before the representatives. He enjoyed at that time the intimate confidence of Washington, and went hand in hand with Hamilton, in conjunction with whom he had given the world, with some aid from Jay, the best-written defence of the principles of the Union. It was he who led the first great debate in the American Congress.

The organization of the new Congress was simple. The Senate chose its president *pro tempore*, elected its secretary and other officers, and awaited business from the other House. It was disposed to look on itself as an upper, or revising, branch of the legislature, somewhat like the old colonial councils. It believed itself, also, to be entitled to higher respect and greater remuneration than the lower House. It began its business in secret sessions with much chatter about titles and ceremonies.[1]   In the House

[1] Kerr, *Origin and Development of the U. S. Senate*, 38, 92.

of Representatives proceedings from the first were
more business-like. For speaker, Frederick A. Muhlenberg, of Pennsylvania, was chosen, a man who
had made a reputation for presiding over a delibera-
tive body. It was not till 1791 that the office became a political affair. The speaker had much
power, although he had not through the appointment of many standing committees the authority
which he later obtained. Most of the business was
done, as in the old Congress, in the committee of
the whole, the chairman of which was appointed
by the speaker.[1]

No sooner had Madison proposed his scheme of
taxation than there appeared a division of sentiment which was destined to play a great part in the
future debates of Congress. It was desired by him
and many others that a revenue bill suitable to the
present year should be passed quickly, so that it
might be made to apply to the spring importations.
Such an act, it seemed, ought to be passed in a few
days. But the trading classes of Philadelphia,
New York, Baltimore, and other places rallied
against the measure; for, in anticipation of such a
tariff, they had already ordered large quantities of
goods from Europe, and strove to delay the bill till
their ships had come to port. They fought so well
that the first tariff bill was not approved till July 4,
and it contained a clause to defer its operation till

[1] Hart, *Am. Hist. told by Contemporaries*, III., chap. xii.; Fol-
lett, *Speaker of the House*, 137.

August 1.   Some people considered this sheer trickery, and later remembered it as the first instance
of a series in which the action of government turned
in favor of the moneyed class.   They observed that
the merchants were shrewd enough to raise the
prices of goods in expectation of the new tariff, so
that, while the delay cost the treasury the benefit of
taxes, the people were, nevertheless, forced to pay
them to the merchants.   One of the critics declared
that by this means the revenue was diminished a
million and a quarter.[1]

The tariff was hurried out of the way to make
opportunity for the consideration of the great departments of government.   May 19, 1789, the House
took up the matter and decided that there should
be created departments of foreign affairs, treasury,
and war.   Bills for each were then considered, and
July 27 a state department was created, August 7 a
war department, and September 2 a treasury department.   In the judiciary bill, which passed
September 24, provision was made for an attorney-
general.   It was not intended that this officer
should rank as one of the great executive heads, but
the very nature of his duties was such that he was
soon brought within that classification.[2]

The Constitution provided for no official advisers
of the president.   Some persons feared that this
function would be assumed by the Senate, and they

[1] Maclay, *Journal*, 46.
[2] *Annals of Cong.*, 1 Cong., 368, 2132, 2158, 2174, 2182.

thought that this union of executive and legislative powers would be a menace to liberty. It was, however, not the Senate, but the heads of the departments which took the position of a presidential council. Washington had little experience in administrative affairs, and leaned on the men who knew more about them than he. The secretaries and the attorney-general were freely consulted; they were assembled frequently for the consideration of general matters, and when Washington was absent from the seat of government they were given a temporary control of the public business, subject to the president's oversight.

For secretary of state, Washington turned to Jefferson, then minister of the old government in Paris. Next to Franklin, who was weak with age, and Adams, who was vice-president, Jefferson was the American most successful in dealing with foreign courts. He possessed mental acuteness, social capacity, and cosmopolitan tastes — all qualities proper for one who must deal with the representatives of foreign nations in America. His service in Paris, also, had acquainted him with the habits of diplomacy, and this could not fail to be serviceable in forming the practices of the new department. He was in good repute in France, and this was important; for it seemed to most Americans that the young republic must for some time keep close under the strong wing which had in the recent crisis so well protected it.

The appointment was tendered to Jefferson in a letter dated October 13, 1789. At that time he had already left Paris for a temporary visit in Virginia. He received the offer soon after he arrived at Norfolk, and wrote, December 15, to say that he preferred to return to France, but that if Washington considered his services necessary to the success of the administration he would sacrifice his inclination and accept. Between the two men a cordial friendship existed, and Jefferson, although he criticised some minor points in the Constitution, was loyal to the government erected under it. Washington did not, in his reply, make a definite decision; but Jefferson thought that his inclinations were plainly discernible, and in February, 1790, he accepted the proffered office. As soon as his personal affairs were in order he set out for the north, going by way of Richmond; and on March 21, 1790, he was at New York. John Jay, head of foreign affairs under the old Congress, had retained the place till the new secretary should arrive. He now turned over the papers of his office and became, according to his own choice, the first chief-justice of the United States.[1]

For secretary of the treasury, Washington chose Alexander Hamilton, and the selection had the approval of all the supporters of the Union. At that time he had not developed those principles of gov-

[1] Jefferson, *Writings* (Ford's ed.), V., 143, 148, 149, 151; Washington, *Writings* (Ford's ed.), XI., 439, 467.

ernment which later made him a signal of party dissension. To Washington, who had known him well in the Revolutionary army, he recommended himself by his strong mind, practical energy, fascinating personality, and frank and forceful patriotism. He was known to be an adept in the science of finance as then understood; and the chaotic condition in which this branch of the public business was left by the impotent Confederation demanded a master-hand to restore it to order.

For secretary of war, Washington chose General Henry Knox, of Massachusetts, then holding over in a like office under the Confederation; and for attorney - general, Edmund Randolph, of Virginia. Knox was a man of fair ability, quite equal to the task of looking after an army which numbered no more than 840 men, together with the supervision of public lands and the watching of the Indians on the frontiers. Randolph was influential in Virginia, where he had been governor; he was a good lawyer and a popular man of fashion. Unfortunately, neither of the two was a man of strong personality; it was their fate to fall at times into the hands of one or the other of the two forceful characters who held the leading places under Washington. These four men made up the president's cabinet.

During the debate on the law to create the office of secretary of state, the question of the right of removal from office came up. Some members thought that it was incident to the appointing power, and others declared that it gave too much authority into the hands of the president. The decision was in favor of the former contention, and the principle became established that the president might remove all officers whom he appointed.[1]

In the mean time, Congress was proceeding to its own tasks. Many other things remained to be done before the government was fairly launched, among them the establishment of a federal judiciary system. The Constitution had declared that there should be a supreme court and subordinate federal courts, all of which were to be constituted by Congress. The determination of the organization, jurisdiction, and powers of these courts was a very difficult matter. The greatest care must be taken to define the respective rights of states and of the Union, lest the one should encroach on what was deemed the just sphere of the other. Two schools of ideas, national and state rights, came out strongly in the debates. The latter, jealous lest the subordinate federal courts should prove more that equal rivals with the state courts, declared openly against the proposed system of lower federal courts. Was it not enough, they said, to give to the state courts cognizance of all subordinate cases under the federal law, with appeal to the higher court? But the men who believed that the Union should be strong enough to take care of itself insisted that the federal

[1] Hart, *Actual Government*, 282–285; Fish, in Am. Hist. Assoc., *Report* 1899, I., 67–86.

law should have an entirely distinct system of courts, and they were able to carry the two Houses of Congress. A chief-justice and five associates were to hold the supreme court, below which were created four circuit and thirteen district courts.[1]

Other matters vital to the organization of the government were the erection of light-houses, the fixing of salaries for the various officers of government, the designation of a form of territorial government, the making of appropriations for ordinary expenses, the regulation of shipping, the formulation of an Indian policy, and the establishment of a post-office. All were duly provided for by appropriate statutes, and on September 29, 1789, Congress adjourned till January. It had been a laborious session. The members had performed a duty which many wise men predicted could not be successfully accomplished. They took all their powers under an instrument which was full of compromises, and which had never been interpreted by competent authority. Yet they did their work so well that it pleased the people to whom it was referred, secured the approval of posterity, and is in considerable parts still in force.

One of the most important matters which came before this Congress was the amendments to the Constitution suggested in the state conventions, in order to win to the support of the Constitution

[1] *U. S. Statutes at Large*, I., 73.

some delegates who were halting between their hopes and fears.[1]

When in Congress days and weeks passed without any action on these amendments, it seemed that the distrust of the anti-Federalists was justified. In Virginia, where Patrick Henry, the most implacable of the anti-Federalist flock, was supreme, this state of affairs was deeply resented. He had been able to defeat the great Madison for the Senate, and to press him so hard in the race for the House that it was only by announcing that he would support the amendments in good faith that Madison came in ahead of his opponent. When, therefore, it began to be whispered about in Virginia that Madison, the leader of the House, had done nothing to redeem his promise, unfavorable murmurings arose.[2]

Then Madison bestirred himself. Seventy-eight amendments had been offered by various states. From these he selected a certain number which, on June 8, he asked the House to consider. Two weeks later he got his motion referred to a committee. The House with evident unwillingness decided, on August 22, to recommend seventeen amendments for adoption by the states. This number was reduced to twelve by the Senate, and of these ten were ratified by the states.

---

[1] See McLaughlin, *Confederation and Constitution* (*Am. Nation*, X.), chap. xvii.

[2] Henry, *Henry*, II., 423–430, III., 399, 416, 421; Madison, *Writings* (Congress ed.), I., 448; Rowland, *Mason*, II., 318–323.

When the anti-Federalists saw the amendments framed by Congress, they felt added disappointment. They had demanded in the conventions certain changes in the organs of government and certain guarantees of right as well, such as were embodied in many state bills of rights. But Madison and the Congress sedulously cut out all the suggested changes in the powers of government, and the amendments as submitted were merely a supplementary bill of rights. To the majority of the people the question had already lost much of its significance; but there was a respectable minority who considered themselves foully dealt with, and the feeling remained as a source of bitterness in their memories for a long time. In Virginia the disappointed ones were numerous and put Madison in a rather uncomfortable situation; but he was adroit enough to win back his lost popularity when Hamilton's assumption scheme was proposed to Congress.[1]

In the autumn of 1789, Washington made a tour through New England, journeying as far north as Portsmouth, New Hampshire. In all places he was received with marked honor by the enthusiastic people. Reports of this trip kindled the ardor of patriots everywhere, and it served to deepen the general confidence in, and respect for, the government over which the popular idol presided. In Boston, John Hancock, governor of the common-

---

[1] *Annals of Cong.*, 1 Cong., 424–450, 660, 703; Maclay, *Journal*, 134; Henry, *Henry*, II., 444, III., 398.

wealth, tried by a half-disguised ruse to force Washington to call on him first, thinking thus to exemplify the greater dignity of the state as compared with the Union. Washington was of all men the last to sacrifice what he considered the just dignity of an office intrusted to him. He gave a plain intimation of his views, and Hancock dared not risk public opinion by ignoring them. To such high Federalists as Fisher Ames it did a world of good to see their old anti-Federalist antagonist, rich in worldly goods, proud in spirit, and tenacious of his political doctrines, standing, in spite of his gout, with cap in hand, at the door of the highest officer in the land.[1]

The strength of the Union was well illustrated in this same autumn when North Carolina, who had deferred her ratification of the Constitution in accordance with anti-Federalist plans, called another convention and declared for the Constitution by a vote of 193 to 75. Rhode Island held out till the next spring, but when Congress threatened to pass a bill to cut her off from the privileges of trade, she resisted no longer. Thus all the original thirteen that had fought side by side in the great struggle for independence were at length brought safely under the protection of the great federal state which had sprung up out of the blood which their sons had shed.

[1] Washington, *Writings* (Ford's ed.), XI., 444 *n.* 1; Fisher Ames, *Works*, I., 74.

The second session of Congress began shortly after New Year's, 1790. It enacted the chief parts of Hamilton's great project for fiscal reforms, a subject which is reserved for the next chapter. Of measures of less note which it adopted, a naturalization law, a census law, an act to fix the punishment of crimes against the United States, an act receiving Tennessee from North Carolina, an act organizing "The Territory South of the Ohio River," and a copyright law may be mentioned. A third session of Congress began on December 6, 1790, and continued till March 3, 1791. It was chiefly occupied by the discussion of Hamilton's projects.

During the recess of 1790, Washington made a journey to Rhode Island, where his presence went far to put in good temper many who were loath to accept the dominance of the Union. In the spring of 1791 he completed what many fancied an obligation by making a tour through the states south of Virginia. He went as far as Savannah, going by way of Newbern, Wilmington, and Charleston, and returning by way of Columbia, Charlotte, Salem, and Hillsboro. The whole distance—eighteen hundred miles from Mount Vernon and back to it — was covered in three months with his own horses, and with hardly a change in the itinerary which he had planned before leaving Philadelphia. It was a thing characteristic of the methodical Washington. He had been told that there was much discontent in the back parts of these states, but the warm

reception he received convinced him that the report was not true. He returned convinced that
the south was both satisfied and prosperous.[1]

[1] Washington, *Writings* (Ford's ed.), XII., 30, 35, 45, 48, 49;
Hamilton, *Works* (Hamilton's ed.), V., 472.

CHAPTER II

HAMILTON'S FINANCIAL SYSTEM
(1789–1791)

IN 1789 the most embarrassed feature of the national government was its finances. The Revolution had necessitated vast debts by both the general and state governments, the weak Confederation had been unable to pay even the interest on its part of these obligations, and many of the states had been unwilling, or unable, to do any better. The result was a prostrate credit at home and abroad. Over against these debts were great natural resources, capable, as any man of experience could see, of profitable manipulation, and holding the promise of splendid development in the future. The serious feature of the situation lay in the fact that the states had from colonial days been so used to careless management of their credit that it was not certain that they could now be brought to protect it in a satisfactory manner. One man there was who proved himself able to rouse the people to the necessary measures, and his name was Alexander Hamilton.

This remarkable statesman was a financier by nature. Before he was a mature man his mind was full of schemes for establishing the national credit. When he was only twenty-three years old he had projected a great national bank, which the Continental Congress did not feel authorized to charter.[1] He came into the treasury with the confidence of the business interests. He was well acquainted with the process by which English commerce had been able to extend itself into most parts of the world, and his ultimate purpose was to give our own relations a tendency in the same direction.

Hamilton's scheme had also a political purpose, which was more important than its financial side. He saw that by pursuing a strong fiscal policy he would draw to his party-following the moneyed classes. In this respect he profited by his knowledge of English history; for he knew that since the days of Walpole the wealthy part of the population had exercised a political influence out of proportion to its numbers. More than this, he calculated that a strong financial policy might be made to knit the nation together, and thus to aid in breaking down that separateness which he deeply deplored. If individuals held the obligations of the nation, they would sacrifice more to prevent its dissolution, and thus a national debt might be made a national blessing. It was an argument which men had heard for many years in England, where it had long since ceased to be believed that the public debt would ever be paid.

[1] Hamilton, *Works* (Hamilton's ed.), I., 116; cf. McLaughlin, *Confederation and Constitution* (*Am. Nation*, X.), chap. v.

We may get some valuable light on Hamilton's
financial views by considering those of his opponents.
Of all the men who criticised him the best financier
was Gallatin.   He did not come on the national arena
till 1795, but his views will do no injustice to the Republicans of 1791.   He would have the government
follow the careful policy of a thrifty business man:
let expenses be reduced to the lowest point and the
savings be carefully applied to the payment of debts.
Let debts be scrutinized closely before they are
paid.   Let everything be done deliberately and without éclat.   Gallatin was, therefore, economical, safe,
and cautious.   Hamilton was audacious, sagacious,
and brilliant.   The former counted on the well-tried
principles of thrift.   The latter counted on the rapid
development of the country, which he could fore-
see.   Had the policy of the former been followed
from the beginning the debt would have been paid
slowly and surely, and gradually we should have secured the confidence of the world.   By Hamilton's
brilliant plan our credit leaped at once into good
repute, but the payment of the debt was greatly
deferred.

The strongest criticism of Hamilton's project was
its extravagance.   His political ideas were partly
responsible for this, and the trying situation of
foreign affairs was also somewhat to blame; but
besides these two factors he was lacking in thrift.
To the charge of extravagance the best answer is
that the results he obtained for the nation were

worth all he paid for them.   It was a service not to be estimated in dollars that in a year we changed from a nation with no credit to one which could borrow on the same terms as the older and most responsible nations of Europe.

Hamilton entered office on September 11, 1789. Ten days later Congress asked him to prepare a report on the state of the finances.   In compliance he submitted to Congress at various times four principal reports: the first report on the public credit, January 14, 1790; the second report on the public credit, December 13, 1790; the report on the national bank, December 13, 1790; and the report on manufactures, December 5, 1791.   In these four documents, intimately connected by a common idea, his whole system was embraced.[1]

The first dealt with the payment of the debt. After some appropriate remarks about the nature of credit, the secretary summarized the state of the indebtedness.   To foreign creditors, chiefly to the French government, we owed, including arrears of interest, $11,710,378.   To domestic creditors we owed $42,414,085, including interest, and $2,000,000 of unliquidated claims and currency.   These debts Hamilton proposed to refund.

To this course there was not much objection in Congress or out of it; in fact, the Constitution provided that the United States must pay the debts of the old confederation; but there was everywhere difference

[1] Hamilton, *Works* (Hamilton's ed.), III., 1, 95, 106, 192.

of opinion as to how they should be settled.   Hamilton argued that to protect our credit they should be
paid to the holders at par; and he also made it clear
that it would be very difficult to make any distinction against the present holders in favor of the
original possessors.

In Congress, however, were many persons who did
not accept this idea.   The certificates of the debt
had depreciated till they were worth only twenty to
twenty-five cents on the dollar.   The first intimation
that they were to be funded at par caused many of
the shrewd money-dealers to buy them up as a
speculation, thus raising the price to forty or forty-
five per cent.   These speculators had always been
unpopular with the ordinary thrifty citizens, particularly with the farmers and planters of the south;
and to pay them what was nothing but a handsome
bonus on their speculation had the air of indorsing
their craftiness.   Those who put the public credit
above all else, and those who were intolerant of speculation, thus found themselves on opposite sides.
There was another group concerned—the speculators
themselves.   They were city people, financiers, con-
trolling some newspapers, and having alliances, as the
moneyed class ever has, with many of the most influential men in public life, including some members
of Congress itself.   The persistence with which this
small group stood by their leader, Hamilton, gave a
color to the charge of the Republicans that they were
corruptly selfish.

Throughout the first session, Madison was looked upon as the administration leader in the House, but he did not indorse this first measure of Hamilton's. Possibly he was influenced by the strong opposition to it on the part of the Virginians. He waited till much had been said in opposition and then he brought in a compromise measure. He proposed to pay the face value of the debt, but to allow the present owners only the market value at the time the discussion began, and to the original owners the difference between that sum and par. This measure was supported by all who opposed Hamilton's plan of payment.[1]

It was not difficult to show that it was impossible to ascertain who were the original holders of the debt. Many certificates had been issued to persons to whom the right to collect them had been assigned, or to agents, and of these complications the treasury books took no account. For the sake of such hair-splitting Congress did not think it worth while to tamper with the public credit, and it passed the bill essentially as proposed by Hamilton.

The old debt, accordingly, was to be exchanged for new bonds. Two-thirds of this debt was to bear interest at six per cent, from date of issue, and one-third was to bear interest at the same rate from 1801, and the arrears of interest were to be funded at three per cent. Before this it had been customary for the

---

[1] *Annals of Cong.*, 1 Cong., 1191, 1205-1412, 1417-1448.

government to issue its bonds redeemable at pleasure. But Hamilton provided that only two per cent. of those outstanding should be redeemable each year, a provision which gave color to the charge, freely made against him, that he wished to make the debt all but perpetual.[1]

The next feature of Hamilton's scheme in regard to the debt was unexpected, even by the keen-scented speculators. He proposed to assume for the national government all the unpaid debts incurred by the individual states on account of the recent struggle, a total estimated at $25,000,000; but he fixed on the sum of $21,500,000, and proposed to divide it as fairly as possible between the states in proportion to their indebtedness. For the amounts stated, the holders of adjusted claims against the states might receive new bonds from the national government. As a matter of fact, only $18,271,786.47 were assumed on this account. Another source of state assumption came from the balancing of accounts between the state and federal governments for money advanced. It was found that some of the former owed the latter $3,517,584, whereas the federal government owed the other states an equal sum. The government assumed $3,517,584 for these creditor states, trusting to their debtor sisters to reimburse it. Except for $200,000 which New York paid for certain harbor defences none of this sum was repaid to the government. The ultimate amount

[1] *U. S. Statutes at Large*, I., 138.

of debt, therefore, created by assumption, was more than \$21,500,000.[1]

Hamilton's argument in support of assumption was threefold: the state debts were incurred in the common defence, and they ought to be paid by all; if assumed, they would serve as a further cement of union; and by removing from the market a large quantity of American obligations of varying value, the credit of American securities would be strengthened.

The states which had the largest unpaid debts were naturally the most anxious for assumption. Of these Massachusetts, Connecticut, and South Carolina were most notable. On the other hand, the states having small debts were against the measure, and among them was Virginia, who had paid much of her Revolutionary debt through the sale of western lands. Assumption, therefore, meant that she would have to bear a large part of the burden of paying the debts of other states. All the speculating class, in Congress and out of it, were zealously in favor of the scheme; and while it was still being debated they were trying by all the means known to their class to buy up, even in the remote parts of the country, the old bonds at the depreciated values. Those persons, and there were many, who favored a strong central government, also declared for assumption.

---

[1] *U. S. Statutes at Large* (Peters's ed.), I., 142, 178; Dewey, *Financial Hist. of the U. S.*, 92.

In the wake of Virginia followed the states south of her, save South Carolina, while New England was for assumption. The middle states divided, the commercial parts going for and the agricultural parts against the measure.

The leader of the opposition was Madison. Loath to forsake Hamilton, he stood for a compromise in regard to the funding bill; but on the question of assumption he went over entirely. He was opposed to the Hamilton idea; Virginia was in revolt, his popularity was weakened by the matter of amendments, and the mighty Henry was watchful for a chance to destroy him. Under the circumstances, to favor assumption would have meant political death.[1]

The debate in Congress was the most exciting yet heard in that body. March 3, assumption won in committee of the whole by eight votes. Before it could pass the House formally the North Carolina delegation appeared, reversed the majority, and on April 26 it was defeated in the House. There was much sparring, during which the friends of the bill succeeded in keeping it alive till May 25, but on that day it was definitely rejected in the House. This had been the last of it had not Hamilton in his extremity made a deal with the southerners, which secured its passage.[2]

[1] Washington, *Writings* (Ford's ed.), XI., 483 *n.*; Henry, *Henry*, II., 455.

[2] Hunt, *Madison*, 184; *Annals of Cong.*, 1 Cong., 1412, 1545, 1614.

In 1788–1789 the location of the capital of the new nation was considered one of the most important measures before Congress. New York City would have been glad to be the capital. Pennsylvania desired it also and probably would have had it if her own representation had not been divided in accordance with their own private interests, so that they could not unite on the exact place. The matter led to an acrimonious but inconclusive debate in the first session of Congress.

It was taken up in the second session, and after some debate the choice settled down to one of two places, one somewhere in Pennsylvania, and the other on the Potomac near Georgetown. The southern states, including Maryland, were for the latter place, and the north favored the former, there being a small total majority for Pennsylvania.

This situation gave Hamilton an opportunity which he knew well how to use. He cared nothing about the location of the capital and the Virginians cared much about it. He accordingly proposed to Jefferson, then newly arrived in Philadelphia, that he would get some northern votes for a Potomac capital if Jefferson would get some Virginia votes for assumption. This idea, which, however, did not originate with Hamilton,[1] recommended itself to Jefferson, but with characteristic caution he chose to throw the responsibility for it on Madison. He invited Hamilton and Madison to dinner, and be-

[1] Maclay, *Journal*, 231, 233.

tween those two the terms were settled. The capital was ordered to remain in Philadelphia for ten years, and after that to be permanently in a district ten miles square on the Potomac, the exact spot to be selected by 'Washington.[1]

Jefferson later came to say much against the wisdom of assumption. At that time he sought to justify himself for the part he took in passing it into law by saying that he was new in the politics of the country and did not understand them; but his contemporary letters show that he was not much opposed to the measure,[2] and he had been in America ever since assumption had been proposed, most of the time in close connection with the Virginia politicians. It is evident that his objection to assumption was chiefly an after-thought, born of his later opposition to Hamilton.

One of the complaints of the Republicans, repeated frequently in the next few years, was that nearly half of the amount thus assumed was needlessly assumed. To this charge Gallatin gave his approval. In his *Sketch of the Finances* (1796), he argued: Each state was a part of the old government; but if the government owed certain sums to each of them, it was the same as if each state owed the other. Each was also a creditor of the others. Ascertain, therefore, what each state owed to, and was due from, each other state, make a mutual cancellation of

---

[1] Jefferson, *Writings* (Ford's ed.), I., 162, 163; V., 184, 185; VI., 172.　　　　　[2] *Ibid.*, V., 250.

equal sums, add up the remainders, and the sum
would be the true amount which ought to be assumed. By an intricate calculation Gallatin cancelled
out several millions and concluded that assumption
might have been consummated for $11,609,259.[1]

To this argument one need only say that the question was not one of state credits.   It was concerned
with the claims of individuals against the states.
Equalizing and cancelling out state claims would not
have paid all the individual creditors.   Therein was
the gist of the whole matter.   Hamilton desired to
substitute national credit for state credit, and the
best way of doing this was to assume the state debts
in their entirety.

December 13, 1790, Hamilton sent to Congress his
second report on the public credit and his report
on a national bank.   In the former he recommended
an increase of duties and an excise on the manufacture of spirituous liquors.   Both were designed to
raise money to pay the additional expenses on account of the new interest charges.   The excise encountered serious objection from those who were
suspicious of consolidating influences.   Hamilton
urged that it would increase the power of government to collect a tax directly from the individual.
The truth of this argument made it unpopular with
those who were jealous of the power of the government.   Although in the western parts of Pennsylvania, Virginia, Maryland, and North Carolina

[1] Gallatin, *Works*, III., 69.

spirituous liquor was one of the chief products, and
the excise was particularly unpopular, the measure
passed into law on March 3, 1791.   The prestige of
its author was at its highest point, and his confident
following had their way in Congress.

In the mean time they pressed for the bill to charter
a national bank; but against this measure the whole
Republican influence was thrown with great earnest-
ness.   There was no explicit warrant in the Constitution for such a bank, but Hamilton argued that
the right to establish one was implied in specific
clauses.   His followers supported him closely and
the bill became a law on February 25, 1791.   Washington watched the debates with interest, and he
was struck by the constitutional argument.   Before
he would sign the law he called on the members of
the cabinet for their opinions on the disputed points.
Jefferson and Randolph thought that it was unconstitutional, and Hamilton and Knox took the other
side.   The president was not clearly convinced but
signed the charter on the principle that where there
was equal division of opinion he would support the
officer in whose department the business under discussion fell.[1]

The bank which was thus incorporated had a capital stock of ten million dollars, one-fifth of which
was to belong to the government.   Its notes were re-
ceivable for all debts due the United States, three-
fourths of its private stock might be paid in national

[1] Mason, *Veto Power* (*Harvard Hist. Monographs*, I.), 25.

bonds, and branch offices might be established for discount and deposit. It was to be the depository of government funds, but it was not to lend more than one hundred thousand dollars to the treasury without the consent of Congress.[1]

The services of the bank to the infant government were important. It gave an easy and safe means of handling the public revenue, it provided a steady and ample currency, it was a wholesome restraint on the issue of state bank notes, and it offered facilities for the business of the country. But the favors it received from the government were equally important. Its monopoly of the public funds, and the receipt of its bills for government dues were substantial advantages. Keen - scented business men foresaw that it would be a profitable affair, and days before subscriptions for stock were received the rush to get its shares had become a mere scramble. In Philadelphia the amount offered to the public was subscribed in an hour after the books were opened. Within a year thereafter the stock was selling at fifty per cent. above par, much to the dismay of Hamilton, who feared inflation. Its average dividend for eighteen years was eight and one-half per cent., and the government stock was sold a few years after the date of the charter at a handsome profit.[2]

---

[1] *U. S. Statutes at Large*, I., 191.
[2] Knox, *History of Banking*, 39; Madison, *Writings* (Congress ed.), I., 538; King, *Life and Corresp. of King*, I., 402.

Three other features of Hamilton's financial system demand a consideration. (1) December 5, 1791, he sent to Congress his report on manufactures, in which he outlined the argument for protection. His broad reasoning rested on the necessity of a proper distribution of agriculture, manufactures, and commerce in a great and prosperous society; but it was many years before this feature of his policy was accepted by Congress. (2) A sinking-fund was a part of his funding scheme. It was conceived according to the prevalent idea of English financiers; but experience was to prove its inutility. Its history demonstrated the truth of the principle that "nothing pays a debt except clear income." [1] (3) Hamilton recommended the establishment of a mint, and Congress adopted the suggestion. The only point which roused debate was a proposition of Hamilton's to place on the coins the head of the president in whose administration they were issued. To the opposition this smacked too much of the practice in monarchies, where coins were adorned with the heads of sovereigns. It was finally agreed to stamp on the coins the head of the goddess of liberty.

[1] Adams, *Science of Finance*, 563.

CHAPTER III

FOUNDING THE REPUBLICAN PARTY

(1790–1792)

THE Federalist party of 1787–1788 was not the same as the Federalists of 1791: the former embraced all those who desired to save the country from the chaos of the government under the Articles of Confederation; the latter included those who supported Hamilton in his plans for conducting the affairs of the country. Many who acted with Hamilton in 1788 were not with him three years later; but this does not mean that if the old problems had to be faced again such men would be opposed to their former position. The problems of 1791 were new problems; they had to do, not with union or chaos, but with two clearly defined lines of internal policy.

After the completion of the ratification of the Constitution in 1788, anti-Federalism died, because its *raison d'être* was gone. Although a few threats were made later to dissolve the union, notably by Massachusetts when it seemed that assumption was defeated, such a policy received no serious support from any considerable number of men. In the first Congress there was not more than a handful of members who had been anti - Federalists.[1] Those who had supported that cause now attached themselves to one or the other of two new parties, most of them joining the Republican organization.

Thomas Jefferson was well adapted to head a militant democracy. His mental qualities were those which gave him mastery of the art of leading the people. He was intelligent, quick - witted, shrewd, imaginative, suspicious of despotism, and prejudiced. He was unawed by superior rank. He was a patient, skilful, and undiscouraged organizer of party, and a sagacious observer of the trend of public opinion. His very faults served to strengthen him for the political task which he was to assume. Had he possessed self-restraint and broad-mindedness he would hardly have been a popular leader in the conditions which surrounded him. He had an appreciation of literature, architecture, and science unusual in the New World, and thus gave to his political activity the crown of being a man of culture.

His task was a plain one. At bottom he proposed to build a democracy. Hamilton had rested his plan of government on the influence of the upper classes, a thing not difficult in England, where suffrage was restricted; but in a country which had a widely extended popular suffrage, only the effort to rouse the people was necessary in order to overthrow class influence. Thus reasoned Jefferson, and with

[1] Madison, *Writings* (Congress ed.), I., 459; Jefferson, *Writings* (Ford's ed.), VI., 3.

wisdom.   His new party was at first called "Democratic" and "Republican," but through the parti-
ality of his followers for French republicanism, the
latter term was permanently adopted.

The methods by which the Republican leaders
sought to rouse the people were not always becoming;
but it may be asserted that the appeals of their opponents were but little more temperate.   It was
the old story of popular agitation, a fight between the
"people" and the "aristocracy"; and in the end it
fulfilled all the hopes of those who planned it.
Popular feeling against England, gratitude towards
France, love of state autonomy, dislike of Tories,
prejudice against monarchy and wealth, impatience
of high taxes, jealousy of section against section, and
whatever other thing could serve a turn with the
people, all were marshalled in support of the Republican cause.   During the revolutionary period
party feeling had worked itself out on the Tories; now
there sprang up rivalries little less severe between
the two parties striving for political mastery in the
independent nation.

Jefferson and his associates were honest.   If they
adopted methods unworthy of intellectual men, it
was because they thought them justifiable under the
circumstances.   Their party was a great machine
in which were many parts.   Jefferson was not responsible for everything that a Republican editor
might say, although his sense of party expediency
might well tell him that he ought not to repudiate

the rash utterance of a subordinate which would
not have been approved by him in the first instance.

The Republicans were especially strong in the
south, where society was divided between a small
number of great planters and a much larger group of
small farmers. The former were usually Federalists;
but the latter were Republicans, although with them
there might act many people of means, who from one
or another motive preferred to identify themselves
with that party. To the rural south, which had
little in common with the commercial and manufacturing north, Hamilton's splendid system was a
matter of indifference. Moreover, this part of the
south, which is to say the majority of it, was Ar-
cadian; and when was Arcady practical or modern?
To these people it seemed that speculators and banks
and protected manufactures were snares and de-
lusions. They did not think that money could be
rightfully gained through the rise in the prices of
government bonds and bank stock. They decried
the whole class of speculators in securities, although
there was hardly a public man in the south who was
not concerned, frequently through government favor,
in speculations in land, the only other great com-
modity of uncertain and changing value.

Madison's split with Hamilton, which has already
been mentioned, opened the way for the unification
of Virginia; for to the young leader came the bulk of
the old anti-Federalists and many of the Federalists.
Jefferson gave his influence also. The one stalwart

anti-Federalist who would not co-operate was Patrick Henry, Madison's old antagonist, although Jefferson tried to bring him into the combination.[1] He hated the secretary of state savagely; and he was growing rich. It was as natural for him to readjust his party affiliation under new conditions as for Madison to do so. He remained neutral for some time, but in his last years he became an avowed Federalist.

The Republican leaders were early made to feel the necessity of the support of the press. Most of the papers were in the interest of the townspeople, or Federalists. John Fenno, editor of the *United States Gazette*, had been early taken under Hamilton's protection,[2] and followed the capital from New York to Philadelphia. To counteract his influence, Madison, Henry Lee, and Aaron Burr concerned themselves. Philip Freneau, one of the best known of the poets of the day, a native American of French descent, and a strong Republican, was in 1790 working on a New York paper, but he formed a purpose of setting up a newspaper of his own, perhaps in New Jersey. The three politicians mentioned had known Freneau at Princeton, when all were students there. They suggested his name to Jefferson, who agreed to give him the position of translating clerk in the department of state. The salary was only two hundred and fifty dollars, but it did not require all the services of the recipient; and Jefferson thought that it might be

[1] Henry, *Henry*, II., 549.
[2] King, *Life and Corresp. of King*, I., 357, 502.

something of an inducement to get Freneau to set up his proposed paper in Philadelphia. He offered to give certain favors, also, in regard to priority of news, derived from his foreign despatches, and Freneau accepted the proposition.[1]

In the autumn of 1791 the poet-politician was in Philadelphia and made his bow to the public as editor of the *National Gazette*, probably the most biting critic of public men and policies then existing in the United States. In poetry and in prose, with satire and with invective, he penetrated every weak point in the armor of the Federalists.

His regular weekly diversion was roasting Hamilton. Even Washington and Mrs. Washington suffered from his criticism. He objected to the monarchial ways of the president and to the court splendor which Mrs. President displayed. He was noisy, but powerful. His enemies called him a "barking cur," and they poured contempt on him and his whole tribe. Their disdain he returned with the good measure of the plebeian who feels the boot of the aristocrat. Jefferson saw the violent spirit which was springing up, and disapproved of it, but he was too wise to attempt to check it.[2]

The two parties were now fairly launched, and they did not fail to find matter over which they could

[1] Madison, *Writings* (Congress ed.), I., 369; Jefferson, *Writings* (Ford's ed.), V., 336; Randall, *Jefferson*, II., 74.

[2] Foreman, *Political Activity of Philip Freneau (Johns Hopkins University Studies*, XX.), 492–500.

dispute.   The two Adamses, father and son, gave the
occasion to one noticeable controversy.   The French
Revolution gave a decided stimulus to republicanism in America, and to check this tendency John
Adams, then in England, wrote *The Essays of Davila*,
a heavy discussion of the principles of government,
advocating a government in which the enlightened
classes should have the greatest influence.   The
book aroused much criticism from Adams's opponents, and he was pronounced an aristocrat and
finally a "monocrat."   His championship of titles
as necessary in order to secure respect for the
government was taken as proving the same tendency.

Republicanism was speedily put to the proof of
public discussion.   In 1791, Thomas Paine wrote his
Rights of Man, in reply to Burke's *Reflections on the
French Revolution*.   He published it in England,
and for doing so was declared an outlaw by the
English courts.   In reply to Paine's theories came
a piece signed "Publicola," in style so much like
"Davila" that the public concluded that it was
from the same pen.   Adams denied the authorship, and it was afterwards learned that the article
was by his son, John Quincy Adams.

Meanwhile some Republicans in Philadelphia decided to bring out an American edition of Paine's
pamphlet.   Jefferson had a copy of the English
edition in his possession, and on request sent it to
the publisher, with a note explaining his action.

He went further by remarking that he was glad to
see that Paine was going to be placed before the
American public, and that something ought to be
done to counteract some of the doctrines which
were being advocated in recent writings by persons
in high places, a plain reference to "Publicola." The
publisher, probably contrary to Jefferson's expecta-
tions or wishes, used this letter as an introduction to
his book.   Adams took the matter seriously, and
nothing that Jefferson could say would satisfy him.
It was long before the two men resumed cordial
relations.   The most important effect was the impression that the incident made on the public, by
calling attention to a hitherto undiscovered division
in the administration, and the tendency was to
put the secretary of state at the head of the new
party.

Another occasion of the appearance of party strife
was the apportionment bill, made necessary by the
census of 1790.   A bill was brought in to allow one
representative in Congress for every thirty thousand
inhabitants.   After it had passed the House, November 24, 1791, it was found that it would leave un-
represented certain large fractions in the north and
none in the south.   The Senate voted for a rival bill
which gave representatives to the large fractions,
and this led to the charge that the north got more
than its share.   The measure passed both Houses,
but Washington, after careful consideration, vetoed
it on constitutional grounds.   A new measure was

then adopted providing one representative for every thirty-three thousand. The extreme Federalists found satisfaction in the fact that at last it was proved that the president could veto a bill.

Relations between Jefferson and Hamilton by the spring of 1792 had become so strained that the inevitable outbreak was impending. Neither could disguise the distrust he felt for the other, and both participated in many little differences in the cabinet meetings. Hamilton was impetuous and disdained concealment, and the biting paragraphs of Freneau led him to move first. In July, 1792, a short letter signed "T. L." appeared in Fenno's paper, charging that Freneau was given government employment in order that he might the better abuse the administration. Freneau brusquely denied the charge, and countered by the hint that Fenno's government printing was more of a bonus than his own paltry salary. Then came a reply signed "An American," in which the attack against Freneau was repeated with considerable temper, and it was plainly charged that Jefferson had used his government patronage to support a political organ. Both of these letters were written by Hamilton, a proof that he had concluded that the time had come for an open rupture. Possibly the object for which he fought was to bring Washington over completely to the Federalist ranks; for Freneau's scurrilous attacks aroused the anger of the president, and if it could be made to appear that Jefferson supported Freneau, might it not weaken the confidence of Washington in the secretary of state? [1]

The controversy ran its course. Jefferson, according to his custom, remained silent; but numerous faithful adherents fought in his behalf. Aside from its political significance, the incident serves to illustrate the futility of Washington's plan for a bipartisan cabinet. It was to the credit of Jefferson that he saw the anomaly of his position and early proposed to retire from office.

Washington, however, was bent on maintaining the existing arrangement as long as possible. He believed that each month it continued more power was secured for the "experiment" of the new government. Before the explosion just mentioned he had seen the estrangement and planned to remedy it. Arriving at Mount Vernon in July, 1792, he talked freely with his neighbors, George Mason and others, about the situation, and from them he received a catalogue of the grievances of the discontented against Hamilton, a paper really drawn up by Jefferson. Washington sent it to Hamilton and asked him to reply to it.[2] This happened four days after the publication of the "T. L." letter, and it is not probable that it was related to the Freneau matter. Hamilton's reply justified himself against Jefferson.

---

[1] Foreman, *Political Activity of Philip Freneau* (*Johns Hopkins University Studies*, XX.), 43–63.

[2] Jefferson, *Writings* (Ford's ed.), VI., 101; Hamilton, *Works* (Hamilton's ed.), IV., 303; Washington, *Writings* (Ford's ed.), XII., 147.

Then the president wrote to both of the secretaries, with the plain purport of bringing about a reconciliation between them. Each responded by throwing the blame on the other. Jefferson offered to resign, and Hamilton suggested that both should quit the cabinet. But it was harmony and not a rupture in the government that Washington wanted, and the proffered resignations were not accepted. During the following autumn and winter there was no open conflict, but the spring of 1793 at once brought the question of neutrality, which made it impossible for things to go on in the old way.

A financial crisis which came early in 1792 was another source of political strength for the Republicans. Capitalists, enriched by dealing in government securities, were so infatuated that speculation became an epidemic. During 1791, United States bonds, stock in the bank, and other securities were steadily bid up, while hundreds of rash projects were launched by an enthusiastic public. Hamilton observed the process with dismay. He knew that the bubble must burst, and he feared that it would injure both the newly established bank and the public credit. He gave warning to some of the leaders of the movement, but without avail.[1] In the first months of the year the market turned. Cries of distress rose from those who saw ruin staring them in the face. Hamilton vainly tried to turn aside the danger by buying bonds from the public and thus

Hamilton, *Works* (Hamilton's ed.), V., 478.

relieving the money market. With the resources at hand he could do little. In two or three weeks stock in the bank fell from 120 to 74, and six-per-cent. government bonds dropped from 130 to 106.[1]

One of the worst sufferers was William Duer, formerly an assistant in the treasury department, but since 1790 the head of the column of Midas. He now found himself in a debtor's prison, from which he was said to have issued threats of terrible revelations if some people who had money did not secure his release. From the horde of speculators, great and small, and from the public generally, there now came a torrent of criticism for all who had been connected with the recent bubble. Hamilton was unjustly accused of some mysterious connection with its projectors. Many people would not believe in his innocence, and his opponents used the occasion to heap opprobrium on him and his financial system.

To these events bearing on the development of parties must be added the political significance of St. Clair's defeat.[2] This lamentable and inexcusable affair brought discredit to the American arms, in a region where they ought to have been easily successful. The Republicans did not hesitate to demand a congressional investigation, which the Federalists could not refuse. It acquitted St. Clair of blame; but Washington demanded his resignation,

[1] Hamilton, *Works* (Hamilton's ed.), V., 477, 480, 491, 498, 501, 502, 505. [2] See below, p. 63.

an action which only half relieved the hot indignation of the country.

From the preceding sketch of political conditions
in 1792 may be seen the hopes and chances with
which the Republicans entered the first presidential
campaign they ever waged. Their hopes were so
good that the Federalists felt much anxiety. If
Washington would not stand for re-election, what
could they hope under a leader like Adams, or any
other prominent Federalist. Could Washington be
persuaded to become a candidate? It was known
that he had declared against a second term, and in
the spring of 1792 he was considering the preparation of a farewell address like that which he issued
four years later. To the first advances of Hamilton
and others he returned a refusal. He consulted
with his friends. Jefferson, divided between his
political views and his friendship for his chief,
hesitated to give an answer, probably intending to
get the counsel of his friends; but he soon realized
the extent of the demand for Washington, and he
added his opinion to that of the other leaders, that
the president should accept another term. Although
he was longing for rest and retirement, Washington
consented. He later had many opportunities to desire that his decision had been otherwise.

The result of the election of 1792 was certain
after the second term had been decided upon. The
Republicans contented themselves with trying to
defeat Adams by bringing out George Clinton, of

New York; but Adams had 77 votes and his opponent only 50.   In the congressional elections they
had better success, securing a majority of the House
of Representatives which sat from 1793 to 1795. To
have won fifty votes for Clinton in an election
which was overshadowed by the name of Washington was no mean achievement for a party which
had just been organized.   Much of this result was
due to the excellent local organization which Jefferson and his followers in Congress had planned in
the beginning of the campaign.   From now on they
were able to carry on an agitation which could
reach every part of the country.[1]

---

[1] Illustrative extracts from writers of the time may be found
in Hart, *Am. Hist. told by Contemporaries*, III., §§ 83–91.

CHAPTER IV

ENGLAND AND THE NORTHWEST
(1789-1794)

THE boundary agreed upon in the treaty of peace with England gave to the United States all that part of the northwest which lay south of a line drawn through the Great Lakes and through a chain of watercourses to the Lake of the Woods, and eastward of the Mississippi, together with the right to navigate that great river. The fine country which was thus accorded to us was an object of great consideration to the British people of Canada. It was the source of an excellent fur supply, and the rich traders of Quebec and Detroit did not relish having to surrender it to a power which would divert the fur-trade to the Ohio. It was also the key to the upper tributaries of the Mississippi; and Canadian officials believed that, if a certain western part of it were retained permanently under the flag of their nation, it would be a stepping-stone to large territorial developments beyond the great river. Canadian interests, therefore, were against the formal surrender of this region, and a way was found to impress their ideals rather strongly on the government in London.[1]

This region was chiefly unsettled in 1789, but it was held in a military sense by the posts of Michilimackinac, Detroit, Fort Erie, Niagara, Oswego, Oswegatchie (on the St. Lawrence), and Point-au-Fer and Dutchman's Point (on Lake Champlain).[2] England still refused to surrender these posts, hoping, no doubt, that the chaotic government under the Confederation would never be able to demand them.[3]   In fact, there was a good pretence for holding them: the treaty of peace stipulated that the states should not interfere with the collection of debts which Americans had owed to British subjects at the outbreak of the Revolution, and that Congress should recommend to the states the repeal of certain severe laws against the Loyalists. The recommendations were duly made, but the states paid very little attention to them. The English claimed that they had agreed to the treaty because they were assured that such a recommendation would have a compelling moral force on the states. The Americans replied that the English must be supposed to know the powers of the Confederation, and that they could not have de-

[1] For the geography of this region, see Thwaites, *France in America* (*Am. Nation*, VII.), chap. xvi.

[2] *Am. State Paps., Foreign*, I., 190.

[3] See McLaughlin, *Confederation and Constitution* (*Am. Nation*, X.), chap. vi.; McLaughlin, *Western Posts and British Debts* (Am. Hist. Assoc., *Report* 1894), 413–444.

luded themselves as to the exact value of the promise.

Another cause of disagreement was the provision that the British would carry away no slaves from the places they then held; but it was alleged that in contravention of this they had taken away some thousands of negroes from New York and the southern ports, and no compensation had been paid. The Americans alleged that the failure to make restitution justified the states in disregarding the recommendations of Congress as to the Loyalists. Thus it happened that when the national government began we had a dispute with England over the execution of the treaty, each side charging the other with having first failed to keep its obligations. The truth of the matter was that each side had been wrong, and that each desired to put the blame on the other.

Two other matters served to vex our relations with the mother-country when Washington entered the presidency. First, never since our independence was acknowledged had England sent us a minister, though John Adams had been duly commissioned in 1785; and, secondly, England steadily refused to make a treaty of commerce. As coming from a foreign country, American trade was submitted to all the inconveniences of the British navigation laws, which seriously crippled the former trade with the West Indies, and complaint from New England was loud and insistent. It was believed by many that

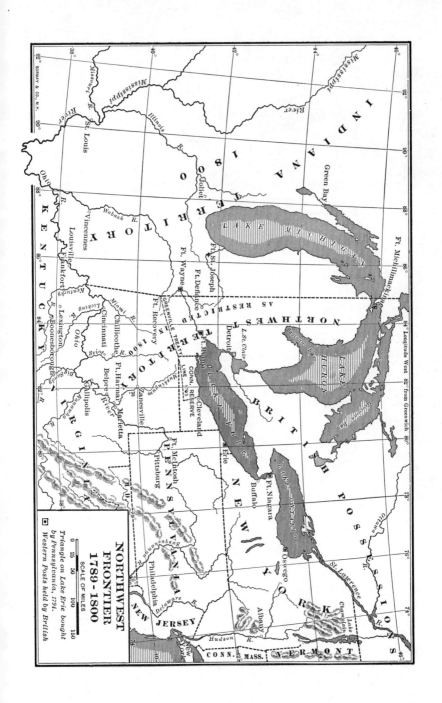

NORTHWEST
FRONTIER
1789 - 1800

SCALE OF MILES

0   25   50   100   150

☐ *Triangle on Lake Erie bought
by Pennsylvania, 1794.*

☐ *Western Posts held by British*

the purpose of this course was to make the states
feel as much as possible the inconveniences of separation, so that they might be the more willing to
come back to their old allegiance.

Washington early turned his thoughts to these
affairs. In the autumn of 1789 he authorized
Gouverneur Morris to go to London as an informal
agent to ascertain if the treaty would be executed,
and if a treaty of commerce would be made or a
minister sent. Morris waited patiently at the court
from March till December, with no other answer to
his inquiries than soft words and the assurance that
a minister would be sent. He was convinced that a
majority of the ministry were in favor of continuing
the existing policy; and the best suggestion he could
make was that we should threaten retaliation against
England and come closer to France, in order to
reach the British merchants, who really controlled
the situation.[1]

Before this report was made, Great Britain had
reason to think very carefully about her course in
America. In the autumn of 1789 a controversy
arose with Spain over trade on the northwest coast
of America. It lasted till the treaty of Nootka
Sound in 1790, and for some months it seemed that
war must begin. Some persons in England and some
in America hoped that in such an event the two

---

[1] Gouverneur Morris, *Diary* (Morris's ed.), I., 315, 327, 346,
370, 488; Jefferson, *Writings* (Ford's ed.), V., 224, 261; *Am.
State Paps., Foreign*, I., 121–127.

nations might be found acting together in mutual support. Whatever England may have thought of these plans, it was certainly good policy, in view of possible developments, to have a minister in Philadelphia.[1]

This controversy gave Washington much concern of another kind: if war should come between England and Spain, it could not be doubted that England would attack Louisiana from Canada. What ought to be our course if England should march through our territory to the upper Mississippi? To the inquiries of the president, Hamilton replied by suggesting that we co-operate with England against Spain; he was doubtful whether we should ever need the west bank of the great river. Jefferson argued that we ought to make an alliance with Spain and if possible draw France into it.[2] Fortunately, England and Spain settled their difficulty amicably, and it was not necessary for Washington to press the matter to a decision.

Early in 1790 there arrived in New York from Quebec a Major Beckwith, who announced that he was authorized to speak in an informal way for Lord Dorchester, the governor of Canada. His business was really to keep his superior informed of the progress of affairs in relation to the northwest and to

---

[1] Manning, *Nootka Sound Controversy* (Am. Hist. Assoc., *Report* 1904), 279–478.

[2] Hamilton, *Writings* (Hamilton's ed.), IV., 48–69; Jefferson, *Writings* (Ford's ed.), V., 199–203, 238.

act in other matters as an unrecognized diplomatic agent. Arriving before Jefferson entered office, he never transacted business with the secretary of state, but established relations with the secretary of the treasury.[1] In the autumn of 1791 he was superseded by Hammond, the regular minister from England; and thereupon the United States sent Thomas Pinckney to represent them in London.

Hammond and Jefferson at once fell into a profitless discussion as to the execution of the treaty. Each charged the nation of the other with first violating it, but still no steps were taken to put it into execution. On the question of a commercial treaty, Hammond had received no instructions, though he professed himself ready to discuss proposals to that effect subject to the approval of his government. It was evident that he came to continue the old policy of delay.

While these dilatory negotiations were going on, affairs on the northwestern boundary were assuming an aspect which threatened to produce serious relations with England. The Indians on the Maumee and Wabash rivers were in a state of ferment because of the advance of the white settlers across the Ohio. By a treaty at Fort Harmar in 1789, a certain large strip of land beyond this river was ceded; but the Indians claimed that it was secured by fraud from

---

[1] Jefferson, *Writings*, I., 173, V., 324; Hamilton, *Writings* (Hamilton's ed.), IV., 30-33; Madison, *Writings* (Congress ed.), I., 531-534.

a few of the tribes, and that it was not binding on all, and the treaty was the subject of prolonged discussion.

The British in Canada could not observe this dispute without taking a part in it. They had two reasons for desiring that the Indians be not disturbed in their lands: there was a rich fur-trade from this region to the St. Lawrence, and all those who were concerned in it feared that they would be undone if the Indians should come under the influence of the people who lived on the Ohio; moreover, the Canadian officials were deeply convinced that the western posts should never be given up, and the attacks which were threatened by the United States against the Indians they always construed into disguised attacks on the posts. Traders and officials, therefore, gave constant countenance to the grievances of the Indians, and distributed presents of ammunition and supplies among them. They claimed that their presents were only the supplies which they were accustomed to give in times of peace; but it is certain that they did not try to induce the Indians to use them peaceably. The assistance the savages were wont to receive in an unofficial way from the officials of Canada was little short of the aid given ordinarily to an open ally.

General Arthur St. Clair was appointed governor of the Northwest Territory in 1789. He was a man of good impulses, a successful subordinate, but not fitted to have supreme control in a delicate situation.

When he arrived on the Ohio he found that all indications pointed to an Indian war. His first act was to send General Harmar with about fifteen hundred men against the Indians on the Maumee. In this expedition a large number of huts were destroyed and a quantity of corn was burned; but the permanent effect on the savages was not great. Hard on Harmar's rear they followed as he returned to the south, and the scalping-parties infested the settlements as before.

Preparations were now made on a larger scale to chastise the Indians into obedience. In 1791 Congress voted two thousand troops to serve six months, and authorized the calling out of mounted militia. St. Clair proceeded to prepare for a stroke, but he was much delayed; the recruits sent him were levied from the idlers of the eastern cities, and the supplies came slowly and in scant quantities. Not till October 3, 1791, could he march with two thousand men out of Fort Washington at Cincinnati on the proposed campaign. By slow stages and with little caution he penetrated the northern forest, till on November 4 he found himself suddenly surrounded by the enemy. He had marched so carelessly that he was taken at complete disadvantage, and his scattered troops could not form a battle-line. Falling on every side, they fired with little effect at the concealed foe, till in desperation St. Clair ordered them to break through the circle which surrounded them and regain the road by which they had approached.

The command was obeyed; and the enemy gave up the chase in order to secure the plunder which had been left on the field. Only fifty of the fourteen hundred Americans in the fight were uninjured.

In Philadelphia the tidings caused consternation. It was the first war the new government had fought, and the result was inglorious. Washington, usually a man of much equanimity, gave himself up to a fit of violent rage when he heard of it. The opponents of the administration were inclined to carp, but both parties united in asking for an investigation. It was duly granted, and St. Clair was held guiltless of wrong-doing; but he resigned his military command, although he retained his civil governorship.

The Indians now became more active and daring than ever. They continued their raids into the settlements, and they boldly demanded that all the land north of the Ohio and west of the Muskingum should be left to them. Brant, the famous Mohawk, was acting in their behalf, visiting many tribes throughout the northwest, and urging that it was now time to stand together in behalf of their hunting-grounds. The British gave countenance to them and hinted rather broadly that it would be right to create a neutral zone running from Lake Ontario through the upper northwest to the Mississippi, to be surrendered to the savages in sovereignty and safeguarded as a buffer state. The manifest result of such a plan would be to put this buffer state into the hands of the British.

Anthony Wayne was next appointed to succeed to the command on the Ohio. He was ordered to prepare a sufficient force and subdue the hostiles. From the autumn of 1792 till late in 1793 he gave himself up to drilling the new army which he collected at Fort Washington. In the summer of 1793 an effort was made at negotiation, through the good offices of the Senecas. The only result was that the Maumees and the Wabash Indians agreed that they would hold a general council in the following year, and that in the mean time each side would confine itself to defensive measures. A great council was accordingly held at Sandusky in the summer of 1793. Washington sent commissioners to it, although few of his friends thought that any good could come of it. There were, however, many indications that the Indians would accept a compromise. But at the last moment the sentiment for conciliation was dissipated through the efforts of the British traders and of Simcoe, governor of lower Canada. The council broke up, and on October 7 Wayne moved with twenty-six hundred troops into the Indian country. He built Fort Greenville, about seventy-five miles north of Cincinnati, and took his forces into winter quarters there. The long and hard drill he was giving them was transforming them into veterans.

In the mean time, relations with the British were dangerously near the point of hostilities. The officials on the Canadian frontier expected that

Wayne would surely attack the retained posts. Detroit seemed to them to be his real objective. To protect it they sent a detachment to the rapids of the Maumee, sixty miles to the southward, where a fort was built and occupied. This action was entirely a violation of the treaty of 1783, for the spot was in no sense British territory. The excuse that it was a part of the defences of Detroit had but a semblance of truth. In America the effect was decided, and Washington, who was always for peace, ordered Wayne to reduce it if it stood in his way.

A still more aggravating circumstance was a speech which Dorchester, the governor of Canada, made in February, 1794, to a delegation of the hostile Indians. He told them that the United States had not kept their treaty, that the settlements in the disputed Northwest Territory were unauthorized, and that it was probable that the British and the Americans would be at war within a year, when the Indians might recover their lands with the improvements. This speech was widely circulated among the savages, where it made a deep impression. In Philadelphia it also caused much excitement. The partisans of England said that it was too absurd to be true, and the British minister tried to parry the effects of it by saying that if it had been uttered it was only a private speech; but the administration responded that the effects on the Indians were the same whether it was private or official. The English government was not so warlike as that of Canada, and rebuked Dorchester in private for his ill-advised words.

In June, 1794, Wayne was joined in his camp at Greenville by sixteen hundred mounted militia from Kentucky, and soon afterwards he began his advance. At the point where the Auglaise joins the Maumee he erected works which he called Fort Defiance. Proceeding down the Maumee, he came, on August 18, upon a band of thirteen hundred Indians assembled within two miles of the new British fort. They attacked him from a body of fallen timber which was overgrown with grass. His troops behaved excellently, charging with spirit, and the enemy retreated. The Indians seemed to have expected to be received into the forts, but its gates were not opened to them. They thereupon disappeared into the forest, and thus ended the battle of Fallen Timber.

Wayne remained in the vicinity destroying crops, huts, and other Indian property. He did not spare the effects of the traders, but he left the fort untouched. To assail it would have meant the outbreak of war with England. He soon began to receive advances from the Indians. To settle matters with them, he appointed a great council for making a permanent peace in the summer of 1795. At that meeting he was able to tell them that a treaty was about to be signed by which the posts were to be surrendered, and this made his negotiation easier. The treaty of Greenville, agreed to on August 4, established a boundary between the Indians and whites, beginning on the Ohio at a point opposite the mouth of the Kentucky River, running thence to Fort Recovery, thence eastward to the Muskingum, and following that river and the Cuyahoga to Lake Erie. The region south and east of it, together with sixteen small reservations on the other side of it, was ceded to the United States. With this treaty and with the surrender of the posts in 1796 the northwest became peaceful and secure.[1]

[1] Winsor, *Westward Movement*, chaps. xix., xx., xxii.; see also A. C. McLaughlin, *The Western Posts and British Debts* (Am. Hist. Assoc., *Report* 1894, p. 413).

CHAPTER V

SPAIN AND THE SOUTHWEST

(1789-1795)

WHILE England nursed the fancy that fortune might throw a part of the northwest into her hands, Spain had similar hopes as to the interior. Louisiana she had received from France in 1763, and Florida had been receded to her by England in 1783. She denied the validity of the secret article in the treaty between England and the United States in 1782, by which England agreed that if Florida returned to Spain the northern boundary should be the thirty-first degree of latitude. During the war Spain seized Natchez, the only fortified point in the disputed territory, and claimed that England had no right to cede the region, because she did not then possess it. England replied that if the seizure could be understood as an occupation of the whole province it did not transfer ownership unless it was so stipulated in the treaty which closed the war. The question was a pretty one, and gave promise of a lengthy entanglement between the oldest and the youngest powers then on the continent. England would, perhaps, have been glad to see them fighting lustily over the matter.

But Spain held tenaciously to the navigation of the Mississippi. Holding each bank for two hundred miles from its mouth, she was in a position to enforce her claim to the sole right of navigating it to the Gulf. To the Americans she would give an equal privilege on the river, or commercial concessions in South America, but she would not yield both favors. Jay's celebrated treaty of 1786 gave up the former and held to the latter. Its defeat in the old Congress did not remove from the minds of the western people the notion that they might be sacrificed to the interests of the east. Kentucky and other frontier regions were deeply dissatisfied, and undisguised plans for a separation from the east were considered.[1]

Spain watched from New Orleans with keen interest as this feeling developed. She hoped that it might be so turned that it would deliver these rich young communities into her own hands. She did not lack means and agents to carry her purposes into effect. Skilful agitators were subsidized to scatter favorable ideas, directly or indirectly, among the people. Of all these, the chief was James Wilkinson. He was long in the pay of the Spanish governor, furnishing information and manipulating public sentiment in the west in behalf of his employer; and he did not scruple to keep this up after he had become a high officer in the American army.[2]

[1] See McLaughlin, *Confederation and Constitution* (*Am. Nation*, **X.**), chap. vi.   [2] Winsor, *Westward Movement*, 356, 363, 369.

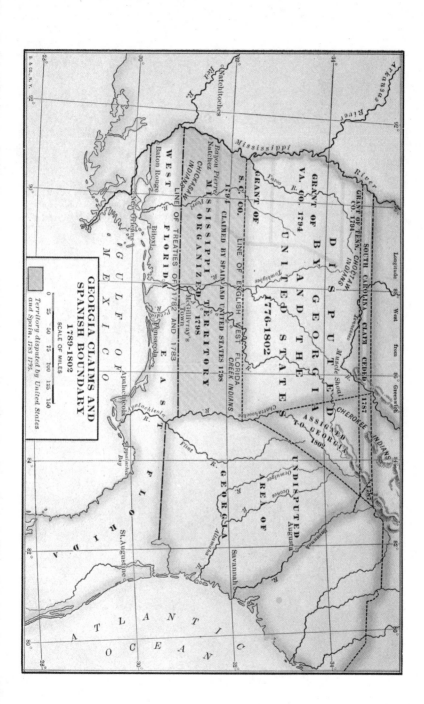

GEORGIA CLAIMS AND
SPANISH BOUNDARY
1789–1802

SCALE OF MILES

0   25   50   75   100   125   150

Territory disputed by United States
and Spain, 1783–1795.

In November, 1788, a convention was held in Kentucky to consider the interests of that region. Wilkinson got himself elected a member of it: he appeared with his hands full of Spanish gold, and sought to put the community in such a position that Congress would take some rash step which would justify an appeal to force on the part of Kentucky. His efforts were futile: instead of the passionate resolutions he favored, the convention made a temperate address to the Virginia assembly asking for separation.[1]

In Tennessee there was discontent also. Sevier, disappointed in the fall of the state of Franklin, was opening negotiations with Spanish authorities. Robertson, the father of the Cumberland settlements, was so well disposed to the same power that he called the new area in which his settlers were planted the District of Mero, after the governor of New Orleans.[2]

Fortunately, the threatened dangers were avoided. Virginia gave Kentucky the freedom which she desired, and North Carolina transferred Tennessee to the federal government in 1790. A territorial government was created for the region south of the Ohio, but this was a short-lived arrangement. In 1792, Kentucky was admitted into the Union. Tennessee was continued under territorial government till it became a state in 1796. The sentiment in favor of

[1] Winsor, *Westward Movement*, 369.
[2] Phelan, *Tennessee*, 165.

separation did not disappear at once, but it had passed its climax.[1]

The centre of plotting next shifted to the disputed region north of the thirty-first parallel. In December, 1789, the Georgia legislature granted large tracts of land here to three companies, known as the South Carolina, the Virginia, and the Tennessee companies. These grants lay along the Mississippi in order from north to south. To that part of this region which was claimed by Spain, Georgia had no clear title, for whatever right the Americans had to it was derived from England through the treaty of 1782; but the Georgians did not abide by this view of the case, claiming that, as this had been a part of their territory under their colonial government, before the crown had set it up as a part of West Florida, it was now the duty of the United States to hand it over to them again. The collapse of the schemes now launched prevented the development of a dispute between state and nation, but it was to appear in a more perplexing form nearly a decade later.[2]

The Tennessee Company actually sent settlers into what is now north Alabama, near the Muscle Shoals; but the federal authorities did not offer protection, and the Cherokees broke up the settlement.[3]   The

---

[1] Winsor, *Westward Movement*, 369; Shaler, *Kentucky*, chap. viii.

[2] Haskins, *Yazoo Land Companies* (Am. Hist. Assoc, *Papers*, V., 396); Harcourt *vs.* Gaillard, 12 Wheaton, 523.

[3] Haskins, *Yazoo Land Companies* (Am. Hist. Assoc., *Papers*, V., 413).

Virginia Company did not attempt to plant a settlement.

The South Carolina Company, however, went further, under Dr. James O'Fallon, who really acted for Wilkinson. He opened negotiations with the governor of New Orleans, and announced that he would soon have ten thousand men in the region in question, and was prepared to plant a community which should recognize the Spanish authority. To the people of Kentucky he declared that his enterprise was to plant a province which should become independent of Spain and join the Union as a state. Wilkinson assured the governor of New Orleans that the affair was in Spanish interest. By this double dealing it was without doubt the purpose of the projectors to get immunity from Spanish attacks and assistance from the Kentucky settlers, trusting to future developments to give the project whatever course future expediency should indicate.[1]

Washington gave the enterprise a death-blow when the news of it was carried to him. It was really an invasion of the national domain; it would be a dangerous interference with our relations with the Indians, and it would violate the neutrality which we were bound to observe towards Spain. He accordingly issued a proclamation warning the western people to have nothing to do with it. For this reason

[1] Pickett, *Alabama* (ed. of 1900), 408, 410, 443.

the enterprise failed in the beginning.   The charter
was repealed by Georgia.[1]

From the Spanish intrigues with the whites the
story turns to their intrigues with the Indians.   Near
the junction of the Coosa and Tallapoosa rivers, and
from there far up to the Georgia line, lived the Creeks,
a nation which could muster more than three thousand warriors; in the southern part of what is now
Mississippi lived the Choctaws with more than four
thousand warriors; around the head-waters of the
Tombigbee lived the Chickasaws, a very active tribe,
although it had only about two hundred and fifty
warriors; and in the mountains of Georgia and the
Carolinas lived the Cherokees with two thousand
five hundred warriors.[2]   Altogether they had about
ten thousand fighting men.   To unite these Indians
in opposition to the extension of the American power
was one of the dreams of Spain.   Over them she
had long exercised a strong influence through commerce and through the fact that she did not plant
outlying agricultural communities.   Wherever she
went among the savages, trading-posts and European goods followed; but in the wake of the man
from the northward farms, roads and fortified places
sprang up.   To the Indian the difference was essential.

In her relations with the Creeks—for her schemes,
the most important of all the tribes—Spain found a

[1] Haskins, *Yazoo Land Companies* (Am. Hist. Assoc., *Papers*,
V., 398–412).   [2] Pickett, *Alabama* (ed. of 1900), 125, 136.

valuable agent in Alexander McGillivray. He was
an able and unscrupulous half-breed who had a
great influence over the Creeks; a man of rare powers,
which he used in intrigues. He was a Tory during
the Revolution, and, some of his property having been
confiscated by the Whigs, he became an inveterate
enemy of the American cause. A powerful trading-
house in Florida paid him well for his influence with
the Indians, and the government of the province
made him a commissary, with a good salary attached. We shall see that he became also an American officer and received a large compensation.[1]

In 1784 the Spaniards made a treaty with the
Creeks. They took these Indians under their protection, and received the assurance that no white
man should come among the savages without a
Spanish permit, and that efforts should be made to
establish permanent peace with the other three great
tribes.[2]

Soon after this the settlers in Kentucky and
Tennessee began to be harried by Indian attacks.
There is good evidence that Spain set these on foot
in order to make life so dangerous for the frontiersmen that they would be glad to put themselves under
her power so as to stop the massacres. The new
government was no sooner organized than complaints came thick from these people: they asked for

[1] Pickett, *Alabama* (ed. of 1900), 344–346, 385–407; Winsor,
Westward Movement, 329, 346.
[2] Winsor, *Westward Movement*, 329; Phelan, *Tennessee*, 167.

protection; they showed that the Indians operated from Spanish territory; and they made it clear that something must be done or there would be a war which might involve Spain itself.

To avoid this, Washington resorted to diplomacy. A messenger was sent to the Creeks inviting them to a great council in New York in order to make a treaty of peace. McGillivray was not loath to accept any chance in which his greedy eyes saw personal advantage. He accepted the invitation and wrote to the Spanish governor saying that whatever treaty he might make he would not forsake Spain. In New York he was received with éclat. The government began by allowing him one hundred thousand dollars for the goods which the Whigs had confiscated.[1] They gave him the sole control of the trade among the Creeks; they made him a brigadier-general with a salary of twelve hundred dollars a year, and ceded back to the Creeks certain lands which Georgia had purchased from them. In return the Indians agreed to keep the peace.[2] McGillivray pocketed his gain and turned his feet homeward. He was hardly back on the Alabama before his scalping-parties were again marching against the settlers. In the art of double-dealing he was equalled by no one but the false Wilkinson himself. He claimed that he could not restrain his people from outrages, but that was only a subterfuge. Till his death in

---

[1] Pickett, *Alabama* (ed. of 1900), 367.
[2] Winsor, *Westward Movement*, 385.

February, 1793, he maintained his position of pretended friend and secret enemy.[1]

The people of the frontier were anxious to take into their own hands the task of protecting themselves; but the government was then conducting the long and unprofitable negotiation of Carmichael and Short, and gave strict orders that no movements should be made except for defence. To this the people replied that the only defence for the frontier was hard blows in the enemy's country. Blount, the governor of Tennessee, enforced his instructions, and the time wore on. At last the people would submit no longer. In 1793, Sevier gathered a band of men in east Tennessee, and marched against the Cherokees as far as the present Rome, Georgia, defeating them in two sharp engagements and destroying towns and property. The effect was salutary so far as that part of the frontier was concerned.[2] In 1794 the people on the Cumberland rose under Robertson and Major Ore and carried war into the towns of the Chickamaugas. These fierce and wily savages were surprised in their strongholds and slain without mercy. Such a blow was given that they were no longer a factor in the history of that region. Among their effects were found a Spanish commission made out to an Indian warrior, and other evidences of Spanish complicity in the recent outrages.[3] These two expeditions gave peace to the southwestern frontier.

[1] Roosevelt, *Winning of the West*, IV., 14, 125, 131, 132.
[2] Phelan, *Tennessee*, 150.   [3] *Ibid.*, 157–163.

Let us now turn to the diplomatic side of the question. Washington had been deeply impressed by the state of public opinion in the west in regard to the Jay-Gardoqui treaty. Although he thought that the westerners ought to wait patiently till they were so strong that their demand could not be refused, he realized that the situation was difficult. Jefferson more than he was in sympathy with the position of the west. He was, in fact, one of the first of our public men to realize the possibilities of this great section. He quickly caught at the opportunity which the Nootka Sound incident gave him to turn Spain towards a treaty. He sought to get the good offices of France in our behalf, with the object of acquiring Florida, as well as the navigation of the Mississippi, and in return proposed to guarantee the west bank of that river to Spain. The sudden settlement of the difficulties between Spain and England rendered all this useless.[1]

Jefferson then had recourse to ordinary methods of diplomacy. In 1791 he received an intimation from Spain that negotiations for a treaty would be revived. Short, who had been our *chargé* in Paris, was sent to join Carmichael, who held the same position in Madrid; and the two were constituted commissioners to negotiate a treaty. They were to treat concerning commerce, the navigation of the Mississippi, the Florida boundary, and the return

[1] Jefferson, *Writings* (Ford's ed.), V., 229, 314–316; *Am. State Paps., Foreign*, I., 247.

of fugitives.[1] After much of the usual Spanish delay, Gardoqui was appointed to negotiate in behalf of his country, and this boded no good. He took a blustering tone and began by offering to make a treaty essentially like that proposed in 1786; and from this position he would not budge. All through the year 1793 a fruitless exchange of views which could not be reconciled went on between the two sides. Finally, in January, 1794, Carmichael gave up the task and returned home, and this dissolved the commission.[2]

It was while these negotiations were going on that Genêt appeared in the United States. France was then at war with Spain, and one of his instructions was to endeavor to seize Louisiana and Florida from the frontiers of the United States. He planned three expeditions—one against East Florida from the Georgia border; one against Louisiana from the Carolina frontier; and one from Kentucky down the river to New Orleans. All of these were to be composed of adventurers from the states. To serve in the first and second expeditions more than three thousand men are said to have been recruited.[3] The authorities of South Carolina and Georgia were more or less cognizant of what was going on, but they made no effort to put a stop to it. These attempts

---

[1] *Am. State Paps., Foreign*, I., 252; Jefferson, *Writings* (Ford's ed.), V., 456.

[2] *Ibid.*, I., 259–263, 432–446.

[3] Am. Hist. Assoc., *Report* 1897, pp. 569–679.

languished when Genêt failed to furnish the money
he had promised. They collapsed utterly when he
was discredited by his government.

The third expedition was more promising still.
George Rogers Clark, the hero of the northwest in
Revolutionary days, was filled with the hope of
making another great stroke into hostile territory
ere he closed his earthly career. He dreamed of
opening the Mississippi, and had submitted plans to
that effect to the French government as early as
Christmas, 1792. To Genêt he accordingly offered
his services for an attack on New Orleans. The
offer was promptly accepted, Clark was made an
officer in the French army, and he was authorized
to command an Independent and Revolutionary
Legion to be raised in the western region. Commissions were sent to Kentucky, as well for the
whites who would serve in the proposed legion as for
the Indians who were to be auxiliaries. Genêt proposed to appoint Michaux, the botanist, who was
then in America, a French consul in Kentucky; but
Jefferson refused to recognize such an officer. The
secretary, however, gave Michaux a letter of introduction to the governor of Kentucky,[1] and the
botanist proceeded to negotiate covertly in the interest of the French. Jefferson reminded Genêt that
we were then conducting negotiations with Spain,
and he caused the Frenchman to understand that a
little explosion on the Mississippi might be welcomed

[1] Am. Hist. Assoc., *Report* 1896, pp. 971, 986, 990–996.

by the Americans as tending to convince Spain that it would be wise to make a treaty.[1]

In the west, French influence ran high. Democratic societies were organized in many parts of Kentucky and Tennessee, and French ideas took such a deep root that in the latter state as late as 1798 the first governor of the state was officially described as "Citizen Sevier." Clark's preparations were not secret, and finally his purposes were boldly announced in a Cincinnati paper. Washington had before this become alarmed at the prospect of having a breach of neutrality; he now determined to try to avert the threatened danger. Letters were sent to the governor of Kentucky to stop the proposed expedition. That dignitary moved slowly and to little purpose. The people saw in the juncture of circumstances an opportunity to settle for themselves the question of the use of the great river. What they would have done does not appear; for the arrival of a new minister in February, 1794, brought a reversal of French policy in this respect.[2]

But the incident had its effect. The United States had come to see how much the west was being alienated, and Spain was realizing what a

---

[1] Jefferson, *Writings* (Ford's ed.), I., 235; VI., 158–161; Am. Hist. Assoc., *Report* 1903, II., 222; Roosevelt, *Winning of the West*, IV., 178–183.

[2] Turner, *Origin of Genêt's Projected Attack* (*Am. Hist. Rev.*, III., 650), and *Correspondence of Clark and Genêt* (Am. Hist. Assoc., *Report* 1896, p. 930); Ogg, *Opening the Mississippi*, 421–459.

complete overthrow of her power would follow a serious attempt of the frontiersmen to right their own wrongs. Our own government was, therefore, stimulated to renewed negotiations, and Spain was brought to accept the wisdom of meeting us in a friendly spirit. The upshot of the matter was that Thomas Pinckney, our minister to England, was shifted in November, 1794, to Madrid and instructed to make a treaty if possible. He was directed to limit his negotiations to boundaries and the navigation of the river. At the head of the Spanish ministry was Godoy, a progressive statesman, who, from having just concluded a satisfactory peace with France, had been hailed as "the Prince of Peace." He was willing to prove himself further worthy of the title by settling the long-debated question with the United States. The fact that in the Jay treaty, which was about to be definitely ratified, we had made a long step towards friendship with England, had also a strong influence on his mind. Pinckney's negotiations went on with smoothness for a time. At last, however, it seemed that the old spirit had taken possession of the Spaniards. He could make no progress in his diplomacy. In disgust he gave fair warning that he should be compelled to break off the business and return to his country empty-handed. At this his opponents became reasonable; the threads of diplomacy were taken up again, and on October 27, 1795, a satisfactory treaty was signed in Madrid. It settled the

boundary of West Florida at the thirty-first degree
of latitude, from the Mississippi to the Appalachi-
cola; it gave the Americans the right to use the river;
and it allowed them the right of deposit for their
products in the city of New Orleans.   This was all
that the western people had ever demanded.   They
now saw the door to the markets of the world opened
to them.   With the acquisition of that privilege all
danger from Spanish intrigue and western treason
passed away.[1]

[1] *Am. State Paps., Foreign*, I., 533-549; Pinckney, *Thomas Pinckney*, 124-137; Rives, *Spain and the United States in 1795* (*Am. Hist. Rev.*, IV., 70-79).

CHAPTER VI

NEUTRALITY AND THE MISSION OF GENÊT
(1793)

IN the beginning of our national existence we were bound to two great European nations: to England by ties of consanguinity, commerce, ideals, and long habit, to which no afterglow of war could blind thoughtful men; to France by a sense of gratitude for past assistance and by certain special treaty concessions. Two treaties of 1778 existed with the latter nation, one a treaty of amity and commerce, the other a treaty of alliance. The former provided for mutual trade privileges, regulated contraband, prohibited visitation and search of the ships of either nation by those of the other, and established free West Indian ports. It gave full privileges for each nation to take into the ports of the other the prizes of its privateers, and forbade the ports of either nation to the captors of prizes from the other. Subjects of either nation must not serve against the other, and no foreign nation should fit out privateers in the ports of either nation against the commerce of the other. The treaty of alliance pledged each contracting nation to guarantee the integrity of the territory of the other so long as the treaty should last. Thus we were bound to receive French, and not to receive English, prizes in our ports; not to allow England to fit out privateers against France in our waters; and to defend France's title to her West Indian possessions should England seize them. France, however, did not call on us for a strict performance of our treaties, and she made that an excuse for not observing strictly her obligations towards us. A consular convention of 1788 defined the rights of merchants and other citizens of one nation resident in the territory of the other.[1]

It was not to the interest of the country to be bound to any foreign power; but our position as a new and defenceless state, as well as the difficult position in which foreign affairs at that time threw us, made the wisest Americans content to submit their nation to a degree of subordination for a time, in the hope that events would bring the ability and the occasion to assert complete independence. This thought is the true explanation of our foreign relations for the first twenty-five years of the federal government.

In 1793 a very exciting incident began to divide us from France, and relations steadily grew worse till 1798. A long series of injuries and a second war were necessary to destroy our dependence on England. The proclamation of the French republic,

---

[1] *U. S. Treaties and Conventions*, 296, 307, 316; cf. Hart, *Am. Hist. told by Contemporaries*, III., §§ 93–98.

and the execution of Louis XVI. (January, 1793), created great enthusiasm in America. A wave of republicanism swept over the country as far north as New England. French songs were sung, titles were decried, "citizen" and "citess" began to be used, and tri-colored cockades were worn in all companies. The Federalists scoffed at all this, but they were impotent to stem the popular movement. Early in April, 1793, came news of another kind. War was declared between France on the one side and England and Spain on the other. The more thoughtful portion of the community foresaw the serious possibilities for our government, but the populace shouted the more for France and liberty. It was enough for them that somebody was fighting our old enemy.

In this situation both Jefferson and Hamilton turned at once to thoughts of neutrality; and to Washington, who was then at Mount Vernon, they opened their minds. The president hurried back to Philadelphia, a cabinet meeting was called, at which the situation was reviewed, and a proclamation of neutrality was ordered to issue. Hamilton, who had long regretted the French treaties, thought this a good chance to get them repealed. In the coming struggle they must necessarily, through the special privileges they gave the French in our ports, bring us into disagreement with England. But Jefferson and Randolph objected, and that part of the matter was postponed.

The proclamation issued on April 23 nowhere used the word "neutrality," but simply declared that we were at peace with both France and England, and warned all citizens to abstain from acts of hostility. Jefferson and Hamilton were always on the watch for political results, whatever the matter before them. The proclamation, therefore, was no sooner issued than the former began carping at it in his letters to his friends, on the ground that as the right to declare peace and war was reserved to Congress, the executive had no power to settle the matter in favor of peace without consulting the legislature. This was a good Republican suggestion, for that party had a majority in the House.

Hamilton, also, thought of the interest of his own party. In a series of powerful letters in the Federalist papers he defended, over the signature of "Pacificus," the principles of the proclamation against the criticism of the Republican editors. He never wrought with a more effective hand, for Jefferson winced deeply and turned at length to Madison. "For God's sake, my dear sir," he exclaimed, "take up your pen, . . . and cut him to pieces in the face of the public."[1] Madison did his best under the name "Helvidius." He said that it was a most grating task,[2] and the paper itself showed how little the author threw his soul into it.

April 8, 1793, two weeks before the proclama-

---

[1] Jefferson, *Writings* (Ford's ed.), VI., 338.
[2] Madison, *Writings* (Congress ed.), I., 588.

tion was issued, there arrived at Charleston, Genêt, the minister of the newly established French republic. He had been minister to Russia, where he got into difficulties through his republicanism, a circumstance which seemed to his superiors to recommend him for the vacant post in America. In her struggle with the combined European monarchs, France had need of the great republic in the west.

The ardent Frenchman burned to draw the United States into France's war against England, and his instructions appear to have been framed with the same intent. He was ordered to send bands of adventurous Americans against Spain, who was believed to be about to declare for England, in Florida and Louisiana, and against England herself in Canada; to offer us free trade with the French West Indies if we would continue to guarantee French rights there; and to protest against the armament of British ships in American waters and against the admission into our ports of French ships taken by English vessels as prizes. He understood that he was to equip privateers in American waters, and for this purpose brought over two hundred and fifty blank letters of marque. If the United States lent themselves to these plans, England would hardly fail to consider them a party to the war. Among his instructions, however, were matters of a more peaceable nature: he was to negotiate a new treaty of commerce, to secure large quantities of supplies,

and to cultivate American friendship;[1] but these
pacific injunctions were lost sight of in his heedless
attempt to bring the others to pass.

Genêt came to America in the frigate *L'Ambusçade*,
bound for Philadelphia; but contrary winds brought
her to Charleston, where he decided to continue his
journey by land, ostensibly to see the president at
Mount Vernon. Two other reasons probably had
something to do with the change of his route: he
learned that two British frigates were cruising off
New York and Philadelphia on the lookout for him;
and he wanted to make an appeal to the people of
the south on his way northward.

His reception in Charleston was an ovation.   The
rich planters and merchants, the backbone of the
Federalist faction, held back; but the rest of the
population were in ecstasies.   Mangourit, the French
consul, introduced him to Governor Moultrie, the
Revolutionary hero. Leading citizens pressed round
him, to all of whom he smiled, bowed, and said things
that pleased them.   That a foreign minister should
be so accessible to all who came, pleased them greatly.   His ten days' stay in the city was marked by
every feature of a personal triumph.[2]

But these days were not all given to social affairs.
Although he was not yet an accredited minister, not
having presented his credentials, he undertook to
discharge some of the most important business com-

---

[1] Am. Hist. Assoc., *Report* 1903, II., 202–211.
[2] *Ibid.*, 211–213.

mitted to him. He commissioned four privateers, manned chiefly by Amercans, and sent them out to attack the British commerce along our coast; he appointed consuls and gave them admiralty jurisdiction for the condemnation of prizes; he even went so far as to arrange for an expedition of American adventurers to be organized on the Georgia frontier in order to attack the Spaniards. In all of these proceedings he consulted Moultrie and declared that he had the governor's approval. On April 18 he set out for Philadelphia.

Two routes offered themselves to his march: one along the coast passed through a region controlled by large planters; another to the westward traversed a region settled by small farmers, among whom there was supposed to be much dissatisfaction with government on account of the excise. He chose the latter, not without design. His progress was a continued ovation. "The good American farmers," he said, "who have received me in their arms and under their modest roofs, have offered me much grain and corn. I have in my hands offers of more than six hundred thousand barrels."[1] At Salisbury, John Steele, a Federalist congressman, described his appearance: "a good person, fine ruddy complexion," he said; "quite active, and seems always in a bustle, more like a busy man than a man of business."[2] Genêt

---

[1] Am. Hist. Assoc., *Report* 1903, II., 215; Hazen, *Am. Opinion of French Revolution*, 176.

[2] Hamilton, *Writings* (Hamilton's ed.), V., 561.

rode into Philadelphia on May 16, escorted by thousands of the people, who had gone out to meet him. On the same day a delegation of merchants went in a body to thank Washington for the neutrality proclamation, which meant so much to their business.

All this glory might have turned a weaker head than Genêt's. Everywhere he was told that the people were with him. He had not reached the city before there began to arrive congratulatory addresses from all parts of the country. He took them as the people's reply to the neutrality proclamation. "You could appreciate the value," he wrote to his superior in Paris, "of the declarations of neutrality which have been made if you knew the enthusiasm and the entire devotion of our friends in the United States."[1]

Washington was unmoved by the clamor. He knew how much depended on neutrality, and he did not flinch in his determination. On May 18 he received Genêt with formal dignity. It was the first bit of homely dealing which the Frenchman had met in America, but he was in no frame of mind to profit by it. He had come a great distance to carry on a delicate piece of negotiation, but he was about to range against him the only man through whom he could hope to accomplish his task. His ideas about Washington are interesting: "this old man," as he called him, was not what history had painted him. The president, he added, impeded him at every turn, could not forgive him his success with the people,

[1] Am. Hist. Assoc., *Report* 1903, II., 214, 216.

and was thus about to force him "to press secretly
the convening of Congress." [1] From that time it
was a prime idea with Genêt that he could override
the executive.   Much of his folly was no doubt suggested to him by the enthusiastic Republicans to
whom he surrendered himself; but not all of that
party were devoid of wisdom, and it is known that
he received moderate advice from some of them. [2]
His inability to distinguish the sane from the erratic
is enough evidence of his own weakness.

The negotiation of a new commercial treaty, which
was the most prominent feature of his instructions,
was hardly suggested to the government before all
his attention was taken up with difficulties arising from the arming of the privateers.   From the
stipulations of the treaty of 1778, [3] Genet deduced
two important principles: that, since an enemy of
France was forbidden to fit out privateers in our
ports, the privilege was intended to be reserved to
the French; and that, if French privateers might
bring their prizes into our ports, they might also
sell them there. [4]

The problem was not an easy one.   Hamilton,
who desired heartily to be rid of the French connection, would yield nothing to our former friend.
Jefferson would yield all that would not involve us in

[1] Am. Hist. Assoc., *Report* 1903, II., 217.
[2] Jefferson, *Writings* (Ford's ed.), VI., 323.
[3] See above, p. 84.
[4] *U. S. Treaties and Conventions*, 296.

war with England. Washington held the balance.
His actions leaned to France, as if to give her no
excuse to say that we had been guilty of bad faith.
After much debate it was decided that we could not
forbid France to license her privateers in our ports,
as this was in keeping with the international practice
of the day, but that vessels thus commissioned must
leave our waters and not send their prizes back.
To do otherwise would put us in the position of
furnishing a base of operations against England.
In accordance with this determination, Genêt was
informed that he must send the new privateers out
of our waters.[1] About the prizes already taken, nothing was said, although Hamilton desired that they
should be given up. To the decision Genêt gave unwilling compliance. To his own government he reported that he had armed fourteen privateers, which
took more than eighty rich prizes, and that only the
opposition of the American government kept him
from arming many more.[2]

This happened early in June, and for a short time
there was some prospect of a calm, of which Wash-
ington took advantage to make a necessary visit to
Virginia. He was soon recalled by a most alarming
incident. Early in July it was learned that *The
Little Sarah*, a prize which had been sent in by a
French national ship, was being armed for the sea.
Genêt's purpose, which he carefully disguised, was

---

[1] *Am. State Paps., Foreign*, I., 150.
[2] Am. Hist. Assoc., *Report* 1903, II., 253.

to send her to close the mouth of the Mississippi and to co-operate with an expedition from Kentucky;[1] but it was assumed that she was to be a privateer. Loud complaint was made. The governor of Pennsylvania sent Dallas, his secretary of state, to interview the minister to know if the ship would go to sea. Genêt flew into a rage and uttered many complaints of his treatment by the administration. Dallas was a most conspicuous Republican, and Genêt may have felt that he could unbosom himself to him. At any rate, he went so far as to say that he would appeal from Washington to the people, and Dallas reported the statement. No promise was given that *The Little Sarah*, whose new name was *La Petite Démocrate*, should not go to sea, and the preparations for sending her out were not stopped. The cabinet was in deep apprehension. Should they allow the orders of the government to be violated before their very faces? Hamilton and Knox were for force, but Jefferson got all to agree that he should make an attempt to influence Genêt by persuasion. He sought out the Frenchman and urged him to promise that the ship should not sail till Washington, who was summoned, could arrive from Virginia. Genêt raged again, as was his custom; but he finally came to his right mind and said that the ship would not be ready to sail before the time named for the arrival of the president. He added that she would drop down the river at once to take on some stores, but

---

[1] See above, pp. 79–81.

would not go to sea. Jefferson concluded that this was a diplomatic way of saying that Genêt would do as was desired, and so reported to the cabinet. Ten days later, much to his astonishment, he learned that she was gone.[1]

Washington arrived on the 11th, full of chagrin. "Is the minister of the French republic," he said, "to set the acts of this government at defiance with impunity, and then threaten the executive with an appeal to the people?"[2] Various other small happenings tended to aggravate his impatience, and he decided to settle the matter once for all. As soon as the attorney-general could finish some business in court, a cabinet meeting was called to consider the state of affairs. After several days of deliberation it decided that Morris, our minister in Paris, should be instructed to ask the French republic to recall their representative. On the question of privateers and prizes it decided that we were responsible for failing to deny the use of our waters, and that we should pay for or restore all prizes taken by privateers fitted out in our ports and sent back to them after capture. The amounts thus expended were to be referred to France for future reimbursement.[3]

Genêt's whole course had an important political bearing. The Republicans received him with open

---

[1] Jefferson, *Writings* (Ford's ed.), I., 237–241.
[2] Washington, *Writings* (Ford's ed.), XII., 302.
[3] *Am. State Paps., Foreign*, I., 167.

arms. The great wave of enthusiasm for republican principles which his presence stimulated, coming as it did within six months of their success in
the last congressional elections, gave them much
encouragement. In Pennsylvania many Democratic
clubs were organized, after the model of the famous
French clubs of the day. Genêt probably was in
close association with them, although they had for
an immediate object the carrying of the elections
in that state. They were composed of enthusiasts
who roused the opposition of the steadiest men in
the community.

The Federalists watched the movement with anxiety. To them it seemed that it must culminate
in excesses which would produce a reaction. The
events connected with the sailing of *La Petite Démocrate* seemed to give them the opportunity which
they had awaited. Hamilton gave a hint to Jay,
who with King issued a statement charging the
French minister with having threatened to appeal
from Washington to the people. Genêt denied the
charge. He even wrote a letter to Washington in
which he demanded that King and Jay should be
indicted for slandering him. Dallas was the only
witness of his words, and he was assured that Dallas
would testify that they did not support the allegation of the two Federalists. The spectacle of a
foreign minister wrangling with everybody within
his reach had the expected effect. The American
people were disgusted, and even the Republicans

turned from him. He was on the point of being
dismissed incontinently when news came that he
was recalled.

His last follies were his worst. Although he
knew he was out of favor with the government of
the United States, and forsaken by that which sent
him out, he hoped to get Congress to do something
which would restore him to power, perhaps by making an investigation of his conduct. This step, he
said, "will give a great impetus to the necessary
revolution which is preparing here . . . America is
lost to France if the purging fire of our revolution
does not reach its midst." [1] When Congress met,
Washington submitted to it the full correspondence
with Genêt, saying that the tendency of the minister's conduct was "to involve us in war abroad,
and discord and anarchy at home." In the acqui-
escent reply of the two Houses, Genêt read his defeat. "Congress has met, Washington has unmasked
himself, America is befouled," [2] he wailed. He had
the madness to imagine that he could in the last
resort call Washington before the supreme court of
the land to answer for the wrongs which he imagined
the chief magistrate had done him.

Genêt's recall was accompanied with circumstances peculiarly unfortunate for him. The Robespierre faction, which was now supreme in France,
hated him because he was identified with the dis-
carded Girondins. His successor, Fauchet, brought

[1] Am. Hist. Assoc., *Report* 1903, II., 232, 248.   [2] *Ibid.*, 277.

orders to arrest him, and send him back to France to be tried for malversation in office. Washington, disliking to press him to this extremity, refused to allow him to be extradited, and thus probably saved his life. He remained in America and married a daughter of Governor Clinton of New York, where he lived to old age.

The ultimate result of the Genêt mission was to injure the Republican cause. Had he contented himself with a dignified protest against the attitude of the government when it ruled against him, the effects might have been otherwise. But his rancorous attacks had discredited all who had supported him. Jefferson at first tried to keep him within bounds, but without success. In disgust he relieved his feelings in a confidential letter to Madison: "Never in my opinion was so calamitous an appointment made, as that of the present minister of F. here. Hot headed, all imagination, no judgment, passionate, disrespectful, and even indecent towards the P. in his written as well as his verbal communications, talking of appeals from him to Congress, from them to the people, urging the most unreasonable and groundless propositions, & in the most dictatorial style." [1] Later, August 3, he wrote: "He will sink the Republican interest if they do not abandon him. Hamilton presses eagerly an appeal —i.e., to the people. Its consequence you may readily seize, but I hope we shall prevent it tho

[1] Jefferson, *Writings* (Ford's ed.), VI., 338.

the Pr. is inclined to it." [1]   And Madison replied:
"Your account of Genêt is dreadful. He must be
brought right if possible. His folly will otherwise
do mischief which no work can repair." [2]

Washington's attitude in the whole affair was
moderate. He had been up to this time sincerely
in favor of preserving friendship with France. He
was far more of a neutral than either Jefferson or
Hamilton. But this incident weakened his feeling
for the Republican party, and he felt a proportional
inclination towards the Federalists. From that time
till the close of his presidency he was more than ever
alienated from Jefferson and Madison, and the influence of Hamilton in political affairs was more marked.

Jefferson understood this and repeated his desire
to withdraw from the cabinet, first announced in
January, 1792, and since then frequently repeated.
He now announced his ultimate determination in
July, 1793. Washington urged the condition of
foreign affairs as a reason why the secretary should
not resign at that time. The force of this reasoning
appealed to Jefferson, and it was agreed between
them that he should hold office till the end of the
year. The two men then parted in good feeling,
Washington expressing his appreciation of his secretary's "integrity and talents." [3]   But the new

[1] Jefferson, *Writings* (Ford's ed.), VI., 361.
[2] Madison, *Writings* (Congress ed.), I., 586.
[3] Jefferson, *Writings* (Ford's ed.), I., 174, 214, 256; V., 435;
VI., 110, 132, 163, 360, 366.

French minister repeated the general opinion when he said, "He has retired prudently in order not to be forced to figure in spite of himself in scenes the secret of which will sooner or later be disclosed." [1] His position, indeed, had been a difficult one. He was a party man in a cabinet which was committed to a non-partisan policy. He saw the genius of Hamilton ride over his views in many measures the execution of which must come into his own hands. To get out of such a position and to assume the leadership of those who thought with him on political matters was natural and becoming. To his credit it must be said that in the course of his cabinet service he had always carried out the instructions given to him, regardless of his opinions about them. He differed from many of the decisions in regard to the Genêt affair, but he is not accused of having failed to execute them in good faith.

The mission of Genêt marks the beginning of the alliance between the Republican party and the French ministers, a relation which overshadowed for a long time the career of the followers of Jefferson. It affected unfavorably both the interests of the Republicans, and our friendship for France, and it lowered the national dignity. But for the good sense of Washington and the ultimate firmness of Adams it might have had serious consequences for the new government.

[1] Conway, *Randolph*, 211.

CHAPTER VII

THE WHISKEY INSURRECTION
(1793–1795)

WHILE transmontane affairs held the attention of the diplomatists, party discussion was assuming that violent tone which has ever since been one of its chief characteristics in America. Exaggeration, prejudice, denunciation, and angry personalities became the order of the day, as each side assailed the other in the process of educating politically the great American democracy. The Genêt incident had its political significance; but many less conspicuous matters served also as points around which the struggle centred. Finally there burst on the country a storm of insurrection which threatened to baptize the new government in the blood of its own citizens. How closely this movement was connected with the political agitation which was then at its height is a matter of controversy. That it was born out of an opposition to one of the cardinal features of Hamilton's system of government is without dispute. It is not too much to say that it was vitally encouraged by the violent denunciation of the Federalists by the Republicans.

The third Congress convened in its first session in November, 1793. A majority of the House were classed as Republicans, although their party allegiance was not as strong as it was later, when the party was better organized. Against Hamilton, as the most eminent Federalist, they concentrated their opposition. The financial policy of the government, although it had wrought brilliant results with the public credit, had its disadvantages: it leaned to extravagance; it was favorable to the interests of the bank; it facilitated the operations of the speculators; and the indifference with which it contemplated the management of the debt lent color to the idea that early payment was not intended. The Indian war and foreign difficulties made necessary increased expenses for defence. A large part of the debt had been so funded that it did not begin to bear interest till 1800, in which year the interest charge would increase by one million one hundred thousand dollars. In the face of such difficulties a policy of economy seemed to be best.

Out of these facts the Republicans got all the capital possible. They harped on the unnecessary assumption of state debts; they spoke contemptuously of Hamilton's purpose to saddle the country with a permanent debt like that of England; they charged him with mismanagement of the money borrowed abroad to pay off the foreign debt; they spoke darkly of collusion with the speculators; they ascribed to favoritism the anxiety with which he sought to launch the bank in safety; and they ever played on the string of monarchy and consolidation. To all he gave a quiet heed but turned not aside.

To pay for its two million dollars of United States bank stock, the government borrowed a like sum from the bank, agreeing to repay it in ten annual instalments. In December, 1792, Hamilton recommended that all this debt be paid at once by issuing bonds. The advantage to the government was that the new loan could be made at about four and one-half per cent. interest, whereas the present debt paid six per cent.; the disadvantage was that it fixed this debt on the public for an indefinite period, while as first arranged it would be paid in ten years. The Republicans attacked the proposition fiercely as but a veiled scheme to increase the national debt for the benefit of the stock speculators. One of them gave notice that if the bank must have the money he would move that it should be got by selling the government's stock. That was far out of Hamilton's calculations, and he was content to accept a compromise by which only enough money was borrowed to pay the instalment of the debt then due.[1]

This success encouraged the Republicans to a stronger attack. Giles of Virginia, a zealous and energetic, but clumsy, leader of his party, introduced into the house various resolutions calling for information about transactions in the treasury, the purpose of all of them being to prove that Hamilton

[1] *Annals of Cong.*, 2 Cong., 753, 897.

had been guilty of irregularities.   They were met in
the fairest spirit by the secretary.   Shutting himself
up with his assistants, he prepared report after report which showed that he was master of the situation, and the clearness of which left him entirely
justified.   But Giles would not be satisfied.[1]   In the
face of the reports before the House he introduced
resolutions of censure on Hamilton, and these the
republicans fought to a vote at the very close of
the session, the result being all that the Federalists
could desire.   Giles's resolutions were defeated by
majorities approaching two-thirds of the vote cast.[2]
His course had been nothing less than an attempt to
drive Hamilton from the cabinet, and its utter failure
left the secretary stronger than ever before.   He was
so confident of his position that, December 1, 1794,
when he at last wanted to retire, he was able to send
a challenge to his enemies to produce all that they
might want to charge against him before his retirement, so that he might refute it at once.[3]   In spite
of some fulminations by Giles, assisted by Gallatin,
no attack was made, and Hamilton was allowed to
go out of office in peace, January 31, 1795.[4]

Of all his financial measures, the most unpopular
with the people was the excise, which reminded them

[1] Tucker, *Jefferson*, I., 454; Madison, *Writings* (Congress
ed.), I., 575.

[2] *Annals of Cong.*, 2 Cong., 899–963; Hamilton, *Works* (Hamilton's ed.), IV., 495, 512, 516.

[3] Hamilton, *Works* (Hamilton's ed.), V., 56.

[4] See below, p. 116.

of the similar execrated system in England. Although the rate was very low, it was a prying tax, which had been resisted when set up a few years before by the state government of Pennsylvania; and how should they stand it in the untried federal government? This latent opposition was particularly strong in the south, where distilled spirits were generally produced and consumed. From the passing of the law in January, 1791, there appeared a marked dissatisfaction in the western parts of Pennsylvania, Maryland, Virginia, the Carolinas, and Georgia. The legislatures of North Carolina, Virginia, and Maryland passed resolutions against the law, and that of Pennsylvania manifested a strong spirit of opposition to it. As early as 1791, Washington was informed that throughout this whole region the people were ready for revolt. On his journey south in 1791 he was pleased to observe that the report was not true; but for all that there was much discontent, and the Republican politicians did not fail to make use of it.[1]

The whole region in question had been settled by a body of hardy farmers, the chief element of which was Scotch-Irish. These brought from Ireland the habit of making and using whiskey. Soon a still was established by every storekeeper and on every farm. Rum, which had been the common tipple of the country during the colonial period, was largely displaced by the new form of spirits. From fruit, rye,

[1] Washington, *Writings* (Ford's ed.), XII., 50.

and corn they made a cheaper article than could be furnished from the New England distilleries. To the farmers this was a matter of much importance, for whiskey offered a concentrated form in which their products could be carried to market, and a sure source of money for their simple needs. To tax their stills seemed to them a blow at the only thing which obdurate nature had given them—a lot hard, indeed, in comparison with that of the people of the seaboard.

The farther one penetrated into the interior, the more these conditions were accentuated, especially in the part of Pennsylvania which lay beyond the mountains. Here in the valley of the Monongahela were four settled counties—Washington, Alleghany, Fayette, and Westmoreland. In 1794 they held some thousands of people. The chief centre of the region was Pittsburg, where there was a weak garrison with supplies of military stores. By location and in sentiment these people were a part of the Ohio Valley settlements, and they were not entirely indifferent to that general feeling for separateness which was strong in Kentucky.

Among them the excise law soon aroused opposition. It is interesting to notice that this took a form like the protests by which opposition was expressed a generation earlier to the Stamp Act and the tea duty. In the summer of 1791 a meeting was held at which resolutions were passed calling on all good people to refuse to observe the law, and threatening punishment for those who should accept office under it. A year later another was held, this time at Pittsburg, in which appeared Gallatin and many other men who opposed violence. Nevertheless, the party of action, led by David Bradford and the less reckless Brackenridge, got control of the proceedings. They bore down the moderates under Gallatin and swept the timid ones along with them, and they adopted resolutions which went to the point of defiance of the national government. Hamilton, who welcomed an opportunity to try the power of the Union, thought that the meeting amounted to treason. At his suggestion, Washington issued a proclamation warning the malcontents that all lawful means would be taken to enforce the law. This strengthened the hands of the moderates in the west. In the next session of Congress the excise law was somewhat modified.

Throughout the years 1792 and 1793, matters remained much disturbed in the western counties, but violence did not occur. Many stills were licensed according to the law, and many were operated which were not licensed. Meetings continued to be held and numerous contemptuous placards were posted, signed by "Tom the Tinker," a name assumed by the protesting writers. Bands of disguised persons, known as "Whiskey Boys," visited those who were inclined to observe the law, smashing their stills and inflicting bodily injuries on the owners. The discontent was increased by the fact that all infractions of the law were punishable in the federal courts, the nearest one of which sat in Philadelphia. So great a hardship was this, that, early in 1794, a bill was introduced into Congress to allow the state courts to have jurisdiction over the execution of the excise law in regions more than fifty miles from a federal court.[1]

Before this law was passed, fifty warrants, returnable in Philadelphia, were issued against persons charged with breaking the law in the disaffected district.   The attempt to serve these writs produced an uprising in the region around Pittsburg.   When a band of the inhabitants came on July 16 to the house of an inspector named Neville, to force him to give up his commission, he fired upon them and they replied in a like manner. At the end of a few minutes they retreated with six of their number wounded and one killed.   Six hundred men now flew to arms, and Neville fled for his life.   The mob burned his house and stables in rage, and called a meeting to decide what should now be done.   The violent ones, led by Bradford, noisily wanted to commit all the people to the support of those who had attacked Neville.   Through his efforts a call was sent out for a general meeting of delegates from all the counties, to be held at Parkinson's Ferry on August 14, 1794. In the mean time he did all that he could to create a spirit of mischief.   Agitators took up the cry against the excise, the spirit of the west was invoked

[1] Adams, *Gallatin*, 88, 91, 123.

to protect the inhabitants, and all things possible
were done to stimulate the revolt to such a point
that retreat would be impossible. As a climax to
such efforts, Bradford got some of his agents to rob
the east-bound mail. Letters were found from the
moderates calling on the east for help, and these
were published as a means of arousing further the
resentment of the populace.

Pleased with his success, Bradford next issued a
flaming call for a meeting of the militia at Braddock's
Field on August 1. His purpose was thought to be
to overawe the garrison at Pittsburg, and to gain
possession of the supplies there. On the appointed
day a large body assembled, two thousand of whom
had arms in their hands. But the courage of the
leaders failed them; they dared not attack the federal soldiers, and contented themselves with marching through the streets of panic - stricken Pittsburg as a demonstration of their strength. The
inhabitants obligingly brought out quantities of
liquor, one of them asserting afterwards that he
contributed on that day four hundred gallons of
rare old whiskey to the cause of peace.[1]

Against the reign of the mob it was plainly the
duty of the governor of Pennsylvania to take action;
but Mifflin, who held that office, was timid. He
would not see the necessity of force, and he professed to fear that the militia would not serve against
the malcontents. Washington, however, was not

[1] Adams, *Gallatin*, 130.

timid. On August 7, 1794, he issued a proclamation against the rioters,[1] and called for fifteen thousand militia from the states of Virginia, Maryland, Pennsylvania, and New Jersey, to be ready to march by September 1. Meanwhile, he appointed three commissioners to go to the disaffected region to endeavor to bring the people to submission before the time set for the departure of the troops. To these Mifflin joined commissioners of his own. The militia responded to the call with alacrity, and on September 1 an army of more than twelve thousand men was gathering, ready for service.

The commissioners of peace reached the region over the mountains just as all that country was thinking about the great meeting at Parkinson's Ferry on August 14. On that occasion two hundred and twenty-six delegates were present, and Gallatin with much reluctance consented to serve as secretary. Bradford attempted to create a committee of safety with powers to rule the west in this crisis; but Gallatin opposed the motion, seeing that it would deliver power into the hands of the radicals. After a hot debate, a motion was passed to appoint a committee of twelve to treat with the peace commissioners, another committee with sixty members to have authority to call a future meeting if they thought it necessary. This was a defeat for Bradford, and the liberals took heart.

Between the commissioners and the committee

[1] Richardson, *Messages and Papers*, I., 124.

of twelve, negotiations were commenced immediately after the adjournment of the Parkinson's Ferry
meeting. At a conference held at Pittsburg the
committee showed a disposition to make peace,
whereupon they were denounced by the radicals as
having sold themselves for federal gold. A meeting
of the sixty was called, at which peace was offered
on condition that the leaders of the movement
should submit to the government. Bradford fought
hard to defeat acceptance of these terms, but Gallatin carried the majority on his own side. This
was promising, but the number who held out was
still strong. September passed in fruitless negotiations, the insurgents sending a committee of their
own across the mountains to meet Washington and
to ask for better terms. He was inspecting the
troops, but before an agreement could be had with
the insurgents he was called back to Philadelphia
to meet Congress at its approaching session.

Meantime the army was marching in two divisions
to the Monongahela, one by way of Carlisle and
Bedford and over the Alleghanies, the other by
Cumberland along the Braddock Road. Henry Lee,
governor of Virginia, was commander-in-chief, and
Hamilton had received permission to accompany the
expedition. Washington went as far as Bedford,
where he reviewed the forces. On November 8,
the two columns were united at Parkinson's Ferry,
and before the soldiery of the Union the last remnant
of resistance at once disappeared. Detachments

were sent to various sections to receive the submission of the people. Hamilton busied himself making arrests of the leaders, eighteen of whom were sent to Philadèlphia and marched through the streets with the word "Insurgent" on their hats. The secretary would have been glad to deal out a more severe penalty,[1] but more humane wills overruled him. Two thousand five hundred troops remained in the west during the winter to see that order was restored, and the rest of the army marched home as from a victorious campaign. In the following May a number of the insurgents were tried for treason in Philadelphia, and two of them, Mitchell and an ignorant German named Vigal, were convicted; but Washington pardoned both of them.

The outcome of the incident was of greater political than military significance. It was the first struggle of the nation against the internal forces which would have destroyed it. The unanimity of the response convinced the people that anarchy was further off than the excited political orators were wont to declare. With the insurrection suppressed, and with Wayne about to bring peace to the frontiers, American power gained considerable prestige with the two most lawless elements of our population.[2]

---

[1] Hamilton, *Works* (Hamilton's ed.), V., 50–55.

[2] See papers on Whiskey Rebellion, *Annals of Cong.*, 4 Cong., 2791–2868; Adams, *Gallatin*, 86–89, 91–93, 98, 123–141; Gallatin, *Works*, III., 3–67; Fisher, *Pennsylvania, Colony and Commonwealth*, 393. See also Brackenridge, *Western Insurrection*, and Brackenridge, *Incidents;* Findley, *History of the Insurrection*.

Far away from our own continent another incident added prestige to our flag. The freebooting dey of Algiers was, as usual, terrorizing the western Mediterranean, or forcing the nations to pay round sums for immunity from his attacks on their commerce. Since 1785 he had held thirteen American captives for whom he wanted an exorbitant ransom, and negotiations to secure their release except on his own terms were unavailing. The Portuguese, for a long time at war with the dey, kept up such a blockade at the Straits of Gibraltar that the Algerines could not get out; but in 1793 Portugal made a truce, through the instrumentality of Great Britain, and the straits were open once again, whereupon eight Algerine cruisers at once entered the Atlantic and began to seize American ships.[1]

Now, England had been able to make herself respected by these people, and her ships were in no danger. Her action, therefore, had the appearance of turning the scavengers of the sea loose upon the shipping of her enemies, and the Americans were disposed to think that they were the special objects of this policy. From all sides arose a cry for vengeance. The Federalists, who had long believed in defence, were glad of the opportunity to move the construction of six frigates, and the measure was carried, March 27, 1794.[2] Three of them were begun at once, although their completion was much de-

---

[1] *Am. State Paps., Foreign*, I., 413–423.
[2] *U. S. Statutes at Large*, I., 350.

layed by lack of funds. This was the beginning of the navy under the Constitution. Till the ships could be constructed, nothing better could be done than to purchase peace from Algiers, and to ransom the captives then held.

A further mark of national efficiency was the increased strength of the army. In 1789 it had consisted of a regiment of infantry and a battalion of artillery, in all 840 men, of whom only 672 were in actual service. In 1791, with the Indian troubles in mind, Congress voted another regiment, and in 1792 three others. This entire force was then organized into a legion, composed of four sub-legions. Each of the latter had 1280 men distributed as follows: dragoons, 80; artillerymen, 60; four rifle companies, 380; and eight infantry companies, 760; total, 5120. May 9, 1794, Congress added 800 artillerymen; and this nominal force of 6000 contained the strength of the army till the trouble with France brought about the augmentations of 1798. In reality the ranks were far from full: June 5, 1794, the non-commissioned officers and privates were only 3578.[1] Even this small force was denounced by the Republicans as a step towards military despotism.

From its political contentions Congress turned aside in 1794 long enough to adopt an eleventh amendment to the Constitution. The occasion was

[1] *Am. State Paps., Military*, I., 5, 40, 67, 109; *U. S. Statutes at Large*, I., 222, 241, 366, 430.

this: Chisholm, a citizen of South Carolina, brought suit in the supreme court against the state of Georgia for the payment of a debt. The state refused to answer the summons to trial, on the ground that the court had no jurisdiction over a sovereign state; but the court held, in February, 1793, that the Constitution gave a citizen the right to sue a state other than the one in which he lived. The decision involved such far - reaching consequences that both parties in Congress united in passing an amendment declaring the non-suability of a state by a citizen of another state. It was finally promulgated on January 8, 1798.

In 1794 the debates of the Senate were opened to the public, a step till then delayed by the Senate's idea of its superior dignity, and its sense of responsibility in regard to appointments and treaties. Washington expressed a common idea among senators when he said that he supposed that the Senate thought that there was too much speaking to the galleries in the other House.[1] If we may believe half the gossip of Maclay, it was well to keep secret the attitude of many senators towards government by the people. For example, Butler of South Carolina spoke disdainfully of the small salary of a senator. It ought, he said, to be enough to enable a member to live in proper style, and a member ought to spend it all in living. As for himself, he would give the excess to the poor before he would

[1] Washington, *Writings* (Ford's ed.), XI., 411.

take any of it back home.[1]   The secret sessions were undemocratic; and, as the sense of popular responsibility developed, they were doomed.   The Senate discontinued them as to legislative sessions, February 11, 1794.[2]

January 31, 1795, Hamilton retired from office. He had long wanted to re-enter his law office, and to build up the practice which his ability, his reputation with men of wealth, his knowledge of affairs, and his general popularity assured him.   Moreover, his personal affairs needed his attention, and he was tiring of politics.   Washington saw his departure with regret.   Between the two men there had been very cordial relations.   Jefferson was not wrong when he said that his rival had influenced Washington's action, although he exaggerated the extent of his power.   Even after Hamilton was out of the cabinet, his former chief wrote frequently to him to ask for advice on all points, from the manner in which he should receive Adet, the French minister, to the "re-dressing" of the Farewell Address.[3]

[1] Maclay, *Journal*, 135.
[2] Kerr, *Origin and Development of the U. S. Senate*, 40, 83, 99,
[3] See Washington, *Writings* (Ford's ed.), XIII., 97, 190, 217, 326, 329–331.

CHAPTER VIII

THE PERPLEXING PROBLEM OF BRITISH TRADE
(1793–1796)

THE rash conduct of Genêt in 1793 brought relations with France into a critical state; and
several causes, the chief of which was trade, brought
us to the verge of war with England in 1794. There
was the same necessity for neutrality in the latter
as in the former year: the true policy was one of
waiting, waiting for men to be born and to immi-
grate, for wealth to accumulate, for frontier problems
to be solved, for national spirit to spring up, for
national greatness to be recognized, and for a more
balanced public opinion to be created. Wise men
of the day realized this; but able Republicans like
Jefferson, Madison, and Gallatin, in the stress of
party opposition, used the unfair and arrogant conduct of England as a campaign weapon, and set in
motion a great popular movement for war which
could not be held back either by themselves or by
the faint-hearted Federalists, who could find but
scant approval for England. One man alone could
dare the popular indignation, and fortunately he
had the will to do it. Washington's immovable

spirit resisted the demand for war and accepted an unpopular treaty as a necessary act of humiliation, and his personal influence secured an approval of the deed. Out of the struggle he came covered with the mud which flew from the hands of those whom he ignored, but time quickly whitened the garments of his reputation.

The war between England and France had no sooner begun than the latter country threw open to neutrals the trade with her West India colonies.[1] Hitherto she had been as earnest as England in her contention that the trade of a colony should be directed for the benefit of the mother-country; but the supremacy of England at sea made it likely that communications between France and the islands would be much interrupted during the war, and the former proposed, by opening the trade of the latter, to prevent the complete isolation of those colonies. Of course, it was the United States which was expected to assume this trade.[2] It was not doubted by France that England would refuse to recognize such a trade, on the ground that it was a war measure, and if that should lead to a breach between England and America, so much the better would France be pleased with her policy of crafty generosity.

The spring of 1793 was not far advanced ere hundreds of American ships were unloading American products and loading French products in the French

[1] See above, p. 88.   [2] *Am. State Paps., Foreign*, I., 147.

islands.   It was a joyous opening for a trade which
had long been restricted to narrow channels; but
in June the British ministry issued orders to seize
for adjudication the vessels and cargoes engaged in
this trade.   This was a wide infringement of the
principle that neutral ships make neutral goods;
but that principle, though announced in 1780 by the
northern nations of Europe, had not been accepted
by Great Britain.[1]   Protest as we might against her
interpretation of international rights, we had no
recourse but war, and she well knew how poorly
prepared we were for that.

Now came from the West Indies the most dismal
news.   Hundreds of ships were seized under circumstances exceedingly irritating.   Seamen and
passengers on these craft were stripped of their
clothing, locked up in prisons, insulted by the rab-
ble, browbeaten by the corrupt and ignorant island
officials, and to their protests contemptuous an-
swers were made.   Full accounts of all were sent to
the American newspapers.   Even the British ministers were shocked by the manner in which their
licentious subordinates had executed the orders and
filled their own pockets in the mean time.[2]   While
the blood of Americans boiled at these indignities,
news of a still greater insult arrived.   November 6,
1793, England issued an order to seize for condemnation all ships carrying the property of French

---

[1] Lawrence, *Principles of International Law*, 566.
[2] McMaster, *United States*, II., 167.

subjects,[1] the effect of which was almost to paralyze the American trade; owners dared not send out their ships, prices fell, and labor was out of employment. Throughout the nation the war feeling ran high.

The situation which has been described gave the Republicans an opportunity which they sought to improve; but they were destined to be disappointed by the very violence of the feeling which was aroused against England. In 1791, Jefferson was asked by Congress to prepare a statement of our commerce with foreign peoples. He felt so little interest in the request that he did not comply till 1792, and then he did not send the document to Congress. The situation in France now gave him an opportunity, and in December, 1793, he accordingly sent in the report. It embodied the theory of equal trade privileges based upon the economic doctrine of free-trade; but if, said the report, a nation should find it necessary to put restrictions on our trade with her, we should equalize the matter by imposing a similar restriction on her trade with us. This policy would enable us to deal with other nations in a firm manner, and the probable result would be that we should bring them one by one to make advantageous treaties with us.[2] England, it is true, treated us substantially like other nations, but her colonial policy bore hardly on us, and Jefferson's report looked to its overthrow. It is doubtful,

---

[1] *Am. State Paps., Foreign*, I., 430.
[2] Jefferson, *Writings* (Ford's ed.), VI., 470–484, 491–494.

however, if we were then strong enough commercially for the task proposed.

January 3, 1794, Madison, in the House, offered seven resolutions, the purport of which was to put Jefferson's recommendations into effect. It was intended to be America's reply to the British navigation laws. If a nation restricted our trade by duties, tonnage, or positive prohibition of our ships, the president was to have authority to restrict her trade in the same way. France, who watched the developments of 1794 with extreme interest, would be drawn into a favorable commercial treaty, and England must either make concessions or lose the rich advantages of trade with us. In the long debate which followed, many able speeches were made. Smith, of South Carolina, opposed the resolutions in a speech the substance of which was furnished by Hamilton.[1] It was a protest in behalf of the trade with England, which furnished nearly seven-eighths of our total imports. This trade had sprung up in a natural way; no other nation in the world had such manufactures as England, no other offered such advantages in making up assorted cargoes, and no other could furnish the capital essential for American commerce. To break off all these relations and force our merchants to establish new ones which must be more or less artificial could not fail to produce great inconvenience in our business life. More-

[1] Hamilton, *Works* (Lodge's ed.), III., 423; *Annals of Cong.*, 3 Cong., 174–209.

over, the merchants, with rare exceptions, were
Federalists and in full sympathy with England.
They did not want war even for their own protection.
Far better, they thought, was a treaty which would
open West Indian ports. Before all these difficulties even our just resentment towards Britain hesitated, and the resolutions were postponed, till finally
the situation became so warlike that they were forgotten in the presence of more serious matters. It
was felt that the treatment we had received from
England, the arbitrary mistress of the sea, demanded
stronger action than trade retaliation.[1]

In March, 1794, news was received of the British
order of November 6, 1793.[2] At the same time
came accounts of Dorchester's remarkable speech
to the Indians of the northwest, which men thought
would produce war on the frontier.[3] Other causes of
irritation were the failure to execute the treaty, and
the impressment of American sailors. To the calm-
est men the situation seemed alarming.

The first action of the government was to recommend an embargo, which was adopted for one month
on March 26, and later extended for one month more.
It was a temporary measure, and its abandonment
was thought best, in view of the negotiations which
Jay was about to begin. But its repeal was very
unpopular with the non-mercantile classes, who disliked anything which seemed a yielding to England.

---

[1] *Annals of Cong.*, 3 Cong., 209–225, and passim.
[2] See above, p. 119.   [3] See above, p. 66.

Other measures of defence were taken. Congress
passed a bill to fortify the harbors, and all classes
of people volunteered to aid in the labor of erect-
ing forts and batteries. Military stores were voted,
eight hundred additional artillerymen were authorized, and a bill was passed to secure the calling out
of eighty thousand militia. Among the people
there was much drilling of volunteer companies. It
was at this time, also, that the frigates were ordered
to be built as a check on Algiers.[1]

In Congress the general indignation took a serious turn. Dayton, who had opposed Madison's resolutions, offered a measure of his own to sequestrate
British debts as an offset to the seizure of American
ships. Such a step could not fail to produce war.[2]
The approval which it received alarmed the ad-
vocates of peace. What new incident of wrong
should we next hear of, to push us over the edge of
the precipice of war?

Fortunately, the next news was conciliating.
April 4, Washington sent to Congress a copy of an
order of the British ministry of January 8, 1794, issued in response to the representations of Pinckney, our minister in England; it authorized the
seizure and adjudication of those ships only which
were carrying French property from the islands to
Europe.[3] Thus it released the trade between the

[1] *U. S. Statutes at Large*, I., 345, 350, 352, 366, 367, 372, 376.
[2] *Annals of Cong.*, 3 Cong., 535–556.
[3] *Am. State Paps., Foreign*, I., 430.

islands and the United States, which was more than half of our claim.

Before this occurred, the Federalists had decided that an envoy extraordinary ought to be sent to England to see if war could not be avoided through a treaty. A number of them had agreed that Hamilton ought to be the envoy, but Washington refused to appoint him, on the ground that he was not popular with the country.[1] He approved the plan of the mission, however, and seized the favorable relaxation after the notice of the British concession to place it before the Senate. He sent in the name of Jay for the proposed envoy, and by the middle of May that gentleman was commissioned and on his way to England. "If he succeeds, well; if he does not, why, knowing the worst, we must take measures accordingly," said Washington.[2]

In the mean time Congress was considering a non-importation bill, and sentiment for it was strong. There was a time, said men, when we knew how to bring England to her senses by refusing to buy her products. If in 1774, when we were a weak and disunited people, we could tame the British merchants, what might we not do now when we were a united and a vastly more numerous people? They forgot how greatly English sympathy for America had declined since we were an independent people, and how earnestly England in 1794 was committed to

[1] King, *Life and Corresp. of King*, I., 518.
[2] Washington, *Writings* (Ford's ed.), XII., 436.

the struggle against France, a struggle of which the restrictions on our trade were but an incident. Nevertheless, non-importation was popular in Congress: it passed the House by a good majority, and it was lost in the Senate only by the casting vote of the vice-president.[1]

In England, Jay was well received by Grenville, minister of foreign affairs. The king also received him with favor, saying, "Well, sir, I imagine you begin to see that your mission will probably be successful." To which Jay was fain to reply that recent circumstances seemed to point in that direction. Then his majesty smiled and nodded significantly.[2]

Jay's lengthy instructions embraced four large features: to secure the execution of the treaty; to get compensation for the seizure of American ships; to secure a treaty of commerce; and to procure, if England were not disposed to be accommodating, co-operation with the powers of north Europe in armed neutrality for the protection of neutral trade. His instructions as to the commercial treaty which he was to make were full and strict: he was to secure reciprocity of trade, particularly in regard to the West Indies, and to obtain the limitation of the right of search, recognition that free ships make free goods, assent to the American contention in regard to blockade, and, if possible, fishing privileges in the

---

[1] *Annals of Cong.*, 3 Cong., 561–603.
[2] Washington, *Writings* (Ford's ed.), XII., 477 *n.*

northeast. The life of the proposed treaty of commerce was not to exceed fifteen years. If England
would not agree to such a commercial treaty, he was
to communicate with his government and await
further instructions; and he was strictly charged to
do nothing which would infringe upon our treaty with
France.[1] Jay, Hamilton, King, and other Federalists consulted freely about Jay's instructions before
they were written;[2] and his departure from those
instructions in his treaty of commerce may have been
due to the support which he felt that these men
would give him when the treaty came up for ratification.

After four months of negotiation, a treaty was
signed on November 19, 1794. It contained ten permanent articles, which provided for the surrender
of the posts by June, 1796, and for the creation of
joint commissions to settle the claims arising from
the legal obstruction of British debts and the seizure
of American ships, as well as for settling the disputed boundary between Maine and Canada. Nothing was said about payment for the negroes which
had been carried away.

The rest of the document contained a treaty of
commerce widely at variance from that which had
been outlined in the instructions. Article xii. dealt
with the West Indian trade, by providing that Amer-

---

[1] *Am. State Paps., Foreign*, I., 472–474. For Jay's entire correspondence in regard to the treaty, see *ibid.*, 470–525.

[2] King, *Life and Corresp. of King*, I., 518.

ican ships of not more than seventy tons could carry American products to the islands and bring back island products without discrimination; that all British ships should trade with the United States without discrimination; that we should forbid our own ships to carry any molasses, sugar, coffee, cocoa, and cotton from the said islands or from our own ports to any part of the world except to the United States, and that this article xii. should be in force till two years after the end of the present war, when, if it could not be renewed on terms agreeable to both parties, all of the treaty but the first ten articles was to be suspended. Article xii. also contained a provision that the British trade in America was to be on the footing of the most favored nation, which precluded our passing in the future any resolutions like those proposed by Madison in January, 1794.

Other provisions were that England should have the free navigation of the Mississippi, that no enemy of England should fit out privateers in our waters (this with especial reference to the position taken by Genêt), and that Americans should not accept commissions to serve against England on penalty of being treated as pirates. About the right of search and the impressment of American seamen the treaty was silent.[1]

These were hard terms from an unforgiving mother. In return for complete freedom of trade we got the right to send our ships to the East Indies

[1] *U. S. Treaties and Conventions*, 379–395.

and our insignificant vessels to the West Indies; we might not carry the island products to Europe, and we bound ourselves not to carry cotton across the Atlantic. The invention of the cotton-gin in the same year in which this treaty was negotiated was probably not known to Jay. Had this feature of the agreement gone into force, it would have wrought a great injury to the southern states.

Jay's treaty was a home-thrust at our French alliance; for although it provided that nothing in it should violate any treaty we had with another nation, it was, nevertheless, true that certain of its provisions contradicted the interpretation which many Americans put on our treaty with France, an interpretation which the government had not always discountenanced. If left, as was probable, in Federalist hands for execution it would be a serious blow to French influence in the United States. The making of it, hard as its terms were, could not but be held as a triumph of English influence, and if ratified it was safe to say that the hopes of Jefferson and others for an advantageous commercial arrangement with France would be dissipated.

Two copies of the precious document were sent to America at once, while Jay delayed his departure for a spring voyage. One of them was thrown overboard to escape French capture, and the other came after many delays into the hands of Washington early in March, 1795. He immediately called the Senate in extra session for June 8. In the mean time the public knew that a treaty had been signed, but the nature of its contents was not revealed, though a few men got an inkling of what they might be.

When at last it came before the Senate there was a strong protest, and to get the necessary two-thirds majority seemed impossible. The twelfth article was especially objectionable. The best that the Federalists could do was to have the treaty accepted without this feature; and for that they had barely the necessary majority. Thus amended, it was recommended to the president for ratification on June 24.[1]

Washington was as little pleased with it as the Senate. Before he could make up his mind, he learned that England had renewed her order to seize provisions bound for France in a neutral ship. This unwarranted extension of the definition of contraband had been ignored in making the treaty, and it was feared that ratification under these circumstances would be taken as a tacit admission of the propriety of the order. Besides, it had brought up a storm of popular indignation. Washington, his mind already half made up, asked for advice from Hamilton as to what he should do. The reply was that he ought to ratify if England would repeal the provision order and accept the Senate amendment. There was good reason, it was said by friends of England, to believe that England would do both. In fact, there were those who thought that the provision

[1] Schouler, *United States*, I., 293.

order was issued at this time merely to hasten our action on the treaty.[1]

When the Senate ratified the treaty, they resolved that it should not be revealed till the president saw fit; but Mason, of Virginia, felt that he was not bound by this vote, and he gave a copy to Bache, the Republican editor, just as Washington was about to publish it himself.[2] The popular protest was now startling. Jay became in a day the most unpopular man of America. Party fury and national pride were united to cry down all that supported the treaty. The English minister was insulted, Jay was burned a hundred times in effigy, and Hamilton was stoned when trying to speak for Jay's handiwork.

Washington was no more moved by the popular storm now than in the days of Genêt. He knew how much of it was due to ignorance and how much to party. "While I feel," he said, "the most lively gratitude for the many instances of approbation from my country, I can no otherwise deserve it than by obeying the dictates of my conscience." To Randolph, the secretary of state, he announced that he would approve the treaty on the conditions just named.[3]

Randolph was opposed to the treaty, and his actions indicate that he wanted to delay ratification while public opinion was stimulated against it, in

[1] Washington, *Writings* (Ford's ed.), XIII., 69, 76, 96–98.
[2] Schouler, *United States*, I. 294.
[3] Washington, *Writings* (Ford's ed.), XIII., 61, 69, 75.

the hope that Washington would at length change
his mind.   He was the only man in the cabinet who
was not a Federalist.   In the belief that he was a
neutral he had toyed with each side till he lost the
confidence of both.   His colleagues would be glad to
get rid of him; and an opportunity now came to
defeat his plans with regard to the treaty, and perhaps to secure his complete overthrow.

In the preceding March a British ship had captured
one of Fauchet's despatches to his government in
which he referred to certain "precious confessions"
which Randolph had made to him at the time of the
Whiskey Rebellion.   The purport of the information was that an intrigue had existed between the
Frenchman and the secretary, and that it was
possibly a corrupt one.[1]   Grenville got possession
of the captured despatch and sent it at once to
Hammond, in Philadelphia.   This action recalls a
letter of his to Hammond the day after Jay's treaty
was signed.   Hammond was instructed "either to
convince Mr. Randolph of the necessity of his adopt-
ing a different language and conduct, or at least to
replace him in that situation where his personal
sentiments may not endanger the peace of two countries."[2]   Randolph's course had not been changed
and the alternate part of the instructions was now
carried out.   As to this British intermeddling, we
could censure it very severely if we did not know

[1] Am. Hist. Assoc., *Report* 1903, II., 411, 444.
[2] Conway, *Randolph*, 292.

that Randolph himself was engaged in as deep an intrigue for political effect with Fauchet.[1]

Hammond gave the captured despatch to Wolcott, who soon submitted it to his Federalist colleagues. They decided to summon Washington at once from his rest at Mount Vernon. When he saw the document he called a cabinet meeting on August 12. Here there was a long debate over the treaty, Randolph alone opposing ratification and the others urging that the necessary modifications would be made by England and that the interests of the country demanded immediate action. The arguments of a man charged with so great a crime as Randolph's did not weigh very heavily in the mind of the president, and the decision was to complete the treaty. August 14, Randolph submitted the ratified treaty to Hammond, observing that he had been overruled in the cabinet.

On August 19, Randolph was brought before his hostile colleagues and confronted with Fauchet's compromising despatch. He was asked to read it, and his opponents had been directed by Washington to watch his face as he read. He asked for time, and promised to explain all. In the evening he changed his mind, and sent his resignation to the president. He resented, he says, being called up for trial before those who were at best but his equals.[2] In truth,

---

[1] Am. Hist. Assoc., *Report* 1903, II., 376, 441, 444.
[2] Gibbs, *Adminis. of Washington and Adams*, I., 241-246; McMaster, *United States*, II., 233.

Washington's manner of dealing with him had been humiliating, and it is explained only on the ground that he was already convinced of Randolph's guilt.

Then followed a long delay in which the secretary's explanation was daily expected. Rumors flew thick and fast. Fauchet, who was about to sail from Newport for France, was chased down and induced to give at the last moment a lame explanation of his words. From the perusal of all his despatches, and from Randolph's own statements, we are able to acquit the latter of any corrupt dealings. But there can be no doubt that he had been indiscreet in his conversations with the French minister, and that he had been too free in lending himself to the French side of our national politics; and this was enough to show that he had violated his trust as head of the foreign office. His "Vindication" was delayed till it was thought that he was trying to identify his cause with the opposition to the treaty. It did not appear till December, 1795, and it was too shrewdly drawn to convince the impartial.

England modified the provision order, as was expected, and accepted the Senate amendment to the treaty; and on February 29, 1796, Washington promulgated the treaty as a part of the law of the land. The trading classes had come to accept it. Bad as it was, it was better than war. We were still a weak and defenceless people, and it was well that we should recognize the fact. But with the

great mass of the people the treaty was extremely
unpopular. "It thrust a sword into the body poli-
tic."[1] The controversy which raged did not spare
Washington; for the Republicans ceased to regard
him as a non-partisan.[2]

They had one more chance at the treaty; for an
appropriation by Congress was necessary to put it
into execution. As soon as they saw Washington's
proclamation of February 29, they opened their
campaign. Edward Livingston, a brilliant young
theoretical Republican, offered resolutions calling
for the papers used in Jay's negotiations. After a
long debate these were adopted by the House.
Washington took the advice of his cabinet, and of
Hamilton as well, and replied that he could not
furnish these papers, since it was solely the function
of the executive to negotiate, and of the Senate to
approve, a treaty. Hamilton agreed with this idea
and added that the instructions to Jay were crudely
prepared and contained things which ought not to
come to the public.[3] To the president the House
replied by a resolution which asserted its right to
consent to a treaty which involved the expenditure
of money, and which declared that otherwise the
executive and Senate might make any kind of
money appropriation under the guise of a treaty.

A bill was next taken up to put the treaty into

[1] Adams, *Gallatin*, 159.
[2] Madison, *Writings* (Congress ed.), II., 15.
[3] Hamilton, *Writings* (Lodge's ed.), VIII., 385-388.

execution, and the debate on this ran through the
latter half of April. It was marked by great earnest-
ness and ability. The previous action of the House
had shown a temper very hostile to the treaty, and
the Republicans, who conducted their debate with as
great ability as their opponents, believed that they
could hold their own on the final vote. Throughout
the country a changing of sentiment was going on,
and petitions came from various sections in favor of
adoption. To the surprise of all, some of these came
from Virginia.[1] To this was added the influence of
one great speech which came from Fisher Ames just
before the vote was taken. An invalid, he had remained silent by the advice of his physician; and
when he at last arose he appeared as but a shadow.
He did not try to conceal the faults of the treaty, but
showed that it was the only means of avoiding war.
His poetic imagination and surpassing eloquence
were given the widest play, and he carried the
House with him as he spoke. The members hung
breathless on his words, and when he ceased, the emotions of his hearers were wrought up to the highest
pitch. John Adams and Judge Iredell sat sobbing
together in the gallery. "My God, how great he is!"
said Adams. "Noble!" ejaculated the other.[2] The
next day, April 29, the bill was carried in the committee of the whole by the casting vote of the speaker.

---

[1] King, *Life and Corresp. of King*, II., 59.
[2] Schouler, *United States*, I., 314; see Hart, *Am. Hist. told by Contemporaries*, III., §§ 96-98.

CHAPTER IX

WASHINGTON AS A PARTY PRESIDENT
(1795-1797)

THE resignation of Randolph in 1795 marked the complete disappearance of Washington's non-partisan cabinet. He fought hard to prevent this event, not realizing how much his ideal was incompatible with representative government. Party lines were now strong, and the men of the Revolution, who, like Washington, had well-developed notions of the dignity of office, were not willing to enter a field in which personal abuse and popular passion held sway.[1] Five men of Revolutionary distinction refused the secretaryship of state in 1795 before a man was found to accept it—Timothy Pickering, of Massachusetts.

Pickering was a man of intellectual ability, industry, and energy, who had done good service in lower administrative positions; but his promotion to a cabinet position was too rapid for the best results. His worst points were a consuming ambition to take the leadership of the Federalist party; for he could see how popular feeling was removing

---

[1] Washington, *Writings* (Ford's ed.), XIII., 130 *n*.

Hamilton from party control. He counted on the
support of the financial classes and cared little for
the interests of those sections which were not in his
favor. For his political opponents his feeling and
conduct were brusque to the extent of narrowness.
He was personally vindictive and unscrupulous.
As the guiding spirit in the cabinet he kept closely
in touch with the policy of Hamilton, but he applied it with a hand that irritated more frequently
than it commanded the persons who ought to have
been his friends.

The other members of the cabinet were Oliver
Wolcott, secretary of the treasury; James McHenry,
secretary of war; and Charles Lee, attorney-general.
Wolcott was a kind of understudy of Hamilton. He
was a good accountant, an industrious adminis-
trator, and faithful to the interests of the treasury,
and he regretted the embarrassed condition into
which the unexpected expenses of the time brought
it. He lacked originality, and in distress was able
to do nothing better than appeal to Hamilton for
suggestions. McHenry had been anxiously hoping
for a lower office when suddenly fortune threw a
cabinet position into his lap. Washington pronounced him "Hobson's choice," and his career
confirmed the epithet. Lee was an insignificant
man, considered because he was connected with a
powerful family in Virginia, where eminent Federalists were few. Since Marshall and Carrington,
as well as the decrepit Henry, had already refused

to enter the cabinet, Lee was as good an appointment as the Federalists of the state afforded.[1]

The name of Washington was enough to preserve harmony and co-operation in this cabinet. He took advice freely from Hamilton, and his unsurpassed common-sense dominated the life of the entire government. Against him there was never, on the part of a man of influence, a question of obedience or difference of opinion. But when John Adams undertook to carry on the government with the same advisers the story was different. His weaker hand lost grasp on the situation, and dissensions marred all the policies that he tried to enforce.

While the growth of party transformed the cabinet into a Federalist group, it also intensified the life of the Republicans. The Jay treaty and the loud cry of aristocracy, monarchy, and plutocracy bred deep popular emotions, ever the basis of party life. Hatred of Federalists and hatred of Republicans characterized respectively two great groups of people. In the lurid struggle between the two, but little of calm reason appeared. It was the first step of our democracy along the road of national development. Happily, in a century of progress we have learned to march with a surer and a more decorous pace.

December, 1795, brought to the Republicans in Congress a great gain in the appearance of Albert Gallatin in the House. He was a Swiss who had

[1] Washington, *Writings* (Ford's ed.), 130.

received a good education, a man with a taste for
learning, a strong but not a brilliant debater, and a
devotee to the best ideas of Republicanism. Elected
to the Senate by the legislature of Pennsylvania in
1793, the Federalists refused to allow him to take
his seat, on the technical point that he had not been
a citizen of the United States for nine years. This
partisan action made him a national figure, and he
entered the House as a man of influence.[1]

Gallatin was, above all things, versed in finance.
Next to Hamilton he was the best-informed man in
fiscal matters then before the public. His appearance in Congress was opportune for his party, for
in this field they had always been weak. It meant
also that a strong fight would be opened against
the financial policy of the Federalists. The Republicans rallied around him with enthusiasm, in
the belief that they had at last found one who could
meet Hamilton on his own ground.

Gallatin had already mastered the financial situation, and on April 21, 1796, he delivered a speech
in which he declared that the debt of the nation
had increased since 1789 by five million dollars. It
was a distinct challenge to the enemy, and for six
weeks it remained unanswered. Finally, Smith, of
South Carolina, who was accustomed to draw his
financial data from Hamilton, arose to reply. He
exploited a long list of figures, and came to the
conclusion that the debt had not been increased,

[1] Adams, *Gallatin*, 119-121, 142, 154.

but reduced by two million dollars in the period mentioned.[1]

The difference between the two contentions was a matter of book-keeping. The sinking-fund, which had been relied upon to wipe out the debt, did not grow as had been expected. The interest on the whole debt for 1790 was funded along with the principal, and the money which had been collected to pay it was then turned into the sinking-fund to the amount of $434,855. Other sums went to that fund to the amount of $522,925, and bonds were purchased below par whose face value was $2,307,661.[2] This was an insignificant growth in a fund whose purpose was to wipe out a debt of seventy-seven million dollars. Besides this, there was a large floating debt, and it was owed to the bank, whose pressing for repayment gave its enemies an opportunity to descant on the tyranny of this monopoly. Smith's reply to Gallatin was made on the last day of the session; and he thus gave the latter an opportunity, which he improved, to publish a long "Sketch of the Finances of the United States."[3] It was an able but an intricate criticism of Hamilton's system from the beginning of the government to the day of publication, and it served the political purposes of the Republicans.

Against certain improper financial practices of Congress, Gallatin threw himself from the beginning

[1] *Annals of Cong.*, 4 Cong., 921, 1499.
[2] *Ibid.*, 1502.   [3] Gallatin, *Works*, III.

of his career in the House. He secured, without opposition, the creation of a committee of ways and means, which should consider all bills involving money votes. The effect was important. Before that time financial measures had been adopted chiefly through the suggestion of the secretary of the treasury; now the House itself became the guiding spirit in such matters, with the result that the power of the executive in financial legislation was materially decreased.[1] Another practice had been to make general appropriations for the use of the departments. Gallatin and his followers demanded specific appropriations, and the old custom was abandoned.[2]

The state of the treasury became alarming when in 1796 Wolcott tried to sell five million dollars' worth of six-per-cent. bonds which Congress had just authorized. Although they were offered at eighty-five per cent. of their par value, he could place no more than eighty thousand dollars' worth. War in Europe made it impossible to sell them there, and the greater profitableness of investments in America made people here unwilling to place their money at six-per-cent. interest. To get funds for immediate demands he was forced to sell a part of the government's stock in the bank. From Hamilton he received scant comfort when he unburdened his woes. "I received your letter of the 1st," wrote his mentor; "I deplore the picture it gives, and

[1] Adams, *Gallatin*, 172. [2] *Ibid.*, 157, 180, 299.

henceforth wish to forget that there is a bank or treasury in the United States."[1]

In this situation the campaign of 1796 opened. To the eminent satisfaction of the Republicans, Washington let it be known that he was not to be considered, and the withdrawal of his name opened the way for a clear party contest. Washington's action had been taken, not so much because he sought retirement in his old age as because he was disgusted with the abuse of the Republicans. He was charged with betraying the pledge given to France, and with taking more salary than was allotted to him. His mail was even tampered with, in the hope of finding political matters of advantage to his opponents, and a most shameful forgery of letters in 1777 was searched out and reprinted as genuine. He was sensitively devoted to official integrity, and all these attacks cut him to the quick.[2]

Most telling of all, perhaps, was the attack which Tom Paine delivered from across the water. This erratic American had been for some years in France. He had expatriated himself and become a member of the French Convention. Robespierre threw him into prison and our minister failed to get him out. Paine appealed to Washington, who refused to interfere in the internal policies of the French government; and he was not set free till the end of the

[1] Gibbs, *Adminis. of Washington and Adams*, I., 374, II., 164.
[2] See Ford, *Spurious Letters of Washington;* Washington, *Writings* (Ford's ed.), XIII., 266, 366, 378, 427 *n.*

Terror. Conceiving a deep hatred of Washington, he now, in his peculiarly direct and nervous style, launched against the president forty pages like the following: "Elevated to the chair of the presidency, you assumed the merit of everything to yourself, and the natural ingratitude of your constitution began to appear. You commenced your presidential career by encouraging and swallowing the grossest adulation, and you travelled America from one end to the other to put yourself in the way of receiving it. You have as many addresses in your chest as James I." And this: "As to you sir, treacherous to private friendship (for so you have been to me, and that in the day of danger), and a hypocrite in public life, the world will be puzzled to decide whether you are an apostate or an impostor; whether you have abandoned good principles, or whether you ever had any." This abuse was delivered in the belief that the author owed it to history to set forth the true character of Washington.[1]

The Republicans were at no loss for a candidate for the presidency. Jefferson had long been the head of the party, and to him they now turned, with Aaron Burr, of New York, as a second. But the Federalists were not so certain. Adams, through his present position and through his New England support, had a strong following; but he was not

---

[1] Tom Paine, *Writings* (Conway's ed.), III., 217; Washington, *Writings* (Ford's ed.), XIII., 360 *n*; Monroe, *Writings*, III., 20.

acceptable to Hamilton and the leaders who had controlled the party. He was a tactless, conscientious man, who did not lend himself to party co-operation. For some time he had not worked well with Hamilton, and the latter rightly felt that Adams's elevation would mean his own decline. His ingenuity conceived a plan, which was too shrewd by half, to bring out a southern man along with Adams, have them run side by side till the electoral college came to the voting, when a few of his own friends were to refuse to vote for Adams, which would bring in the other man as president. He first thought of Patrick Henry for his southern candidate, but Henry refused the honor.[1] Then he turned to Thomas Pinckney, of South Carolina, who had just negotiated the Spanish treaty and was popular on account of it. He was a man of the best character, but without important administrative experience, and it is probable that he would as president have been much under Hamilton's influence. It was impossible for Hamilton to keep his scheme from getting to the ears of the New England supporters of Adams, and this fact of itself would have killed it. The campaign received peculiar interest from the part that the French minister, Adet, took in it. Genêt, Fauchet, and Adet, who successively represented France in America after 1793, were all in close touch with the leaders of the Republican party,

[1] King, *Life and Corresp. of King*, II., 46–48; Henry, *Henry*, II., 572.

but only the last came out openly to influence an election.[1]

France was much disappointed by the Jay treaty. Her minister sought to prevent its ratification, and failing in that plan turned to the election in the hope that a party would come in which would favor French interests.   To secure Jefferson's election, Adet thought it wise to threaten Americans with a French war.   His plans were aided by the fact that France, in anger at the adoption of the Jay treaty, suspended the functions of her minister, although he was not recalled to his native land.   Continuing his policy of meddling, he wrote strong letters to the American government and gave copies of them to the newspapers.[2]   To his own government he avowed his purpose in explicit terms.   Of one of his letters he said, "I have had it published in order to catch the public attention when presidential electors were about to be chosen and in order to determine what effect it would produce upon the government and to see what I might expect from the next session of Congress."[3]   Such impudent conduct on the part of a foreign representative had the only possible effect of injuring the party in whose behalf it was performed.

When the electors had been chosen, the Federalists were seen to have carried most of those from the states north of Pennsylvania, and the Repub-

[1] Am. Hist. Assoc., *Report* 1903, II., 727, 836, 882.
[2] *Ibid.*, 1903, II., 727, 836, 882.   [3] *Ibid.*, 969–972.

licans the majority in all the others. When the presidential electors of each state met to cast their votes, as the Constitution required, Adams received 71, Jefferson 68, and Pinckney 59 votes. Several Adams electors in New England, probably fearing lest Hamilton's scheme might succeed, refused to vote for Pinckney, and the election went to Adams and Jefferson. It was our first great contest of a purely political nature, and the closeness of the vote gave courage to the Republicans and chagrin to the Federalists. To Adams's sensitive nature it was always a matter of reproach that he was a "President by three votes."

Amid the lurid scenes on the political stage, Washington was preparing to escape to private life. His parting was signalized by his Farewell Address, a document which the generation which came after him was accustomed to hold as one of their most sacred political treasures. He began to prepare it, with the help of Madison, in 1792, when he thought of retiring.[1] It was now finished with the large co-operation of Hamilton, and given to the public through the newspapers on September 19, 1796. Washington asked Hamilton when the document ought to appear, and the latter said that it ought to come about two months before the meeting of the electoral college.[2] It was issued three months before that event.

[1] Washington, *Writings* (Ford's ed.), XII., 123-131.
[2] *Ibid.*, XIII., 220, 221 *n*, 267, 277-325.

The address itself was filled with the best advice. It contained many truths of a general nature; but it was not possible to speak of the things which the people of that day needed to hear without entering the field of party discussion. This was particularly true of those parts, perhaps the strongest phrases in the long paper, which warned the people against being drawn into the meshes of alien factions, and which cautioned them against an "irregular opposition" to government and against the neglect of the public dignity. It was not unnatural that the highly excited Republican leaders gave such words as these something more than an academic interpretation, although an interference with the impending election was far from Washington's intention.

His last communication to Congress was also made to turn to the same purport. The Federalist committee of the House which had the duty of replying to it brought in a paper that went beyond personal compliment and gave approval to the policies of Washington's administration. At this the Republicans took exception. They made fruitless efforts to get the reply modified to suit them, and these failing, twelve of their number at last voted against its adoption. Among those who refused to give Washington the compliment of a last God-speed were Andrew Jackson, Edward Livingston, Nathaniel Macon, and W. B. Giles, men long afterwards noted for their unyielding Republicanism. Giles probably expressed the feeling of this group when he said in the debate on the reply: "I must acknowledge that I am one of those who do not think as much of the President as others do. When the President retires from his present station, I wish him to enjoy all possible happiness. I wish him to retire, and that this was the moment of his retirement." [1]

The near approach of the day on which he was to go out of office did not bring relenting to those who denounced Washington. March 4, 1797, Bache's *Aurora* sent after him this parting blast:

"If ever there was a period for rejoicing, this is the moment—every heart in unison with the freedom and happiness of the people, ought to beat high with exultation that the name of WASHINGTON from this day ceases to give a currency to political iniquity, and to legalize corruption. A new æra is now opening upon us, an æra which promises much to the people; for public measures must now stand on their own merits."

No doubt many well-intentioned people in America believed all that the editor asserted. But for Washington retirement meant release. He had long sought the quiet life of his estate, and the task of restoring his residence and repairing the waste on his lands was taken up with the zest of youth. For the storm of abuse which raged as he left office he had no complaint. The day before the *Aurora* made its rasping deliverance he wrote with his usual balance:

"In all free governments, contentions in elections

---

[1] *Annals of Cong.*, 4 Cong., 1616.

will take place, and, whilst it is confined to our own citizens, it is not to be regretted; but severely indeed ought it to be reprobated, when occasioned by foreign machinations. I trust, however, that the good sense of our countrymen will guard the public weal against this and every other innovation, and that, although we may have a little wrong now and then, we shall return to the right path with more avidity. I can never believe, that Providence, which has guided us so long, and through such a labyrinth, will withdraw its protection at this crisis."[1]

[1] Washington, *Writings* (Ford's ed.), XIII., 377.

CHAPTER X

THE REPUBLICAN COURT
(1789-1900)

THE first decade of the federal government witnessed as many contentions in social as in constitutional matters. In each colonial capital, as well as in New York and Philadelphia in the days of British occupation, and in the latter city in the days of the Continental Congresses, a well-formed colonial aristocracy had dominated social intercourse. When the new government was established, a similar ideal was set up; it was the old brought over into the new. The Federalists came readily to accept these forms; and some of them, notably Vice-President Adams, believed that it was essential to preserve ceremony in order to have the people respect the government. Those who believed in democratic equality found forms unnecessary, undemocratic, and intolerable. Class distinctions, when founded on nothing more than traditions of good society, seemed to them but the insignia of a hated despotism. They denounced fiercely every form which suggested the habits of European courts; although it is evident that if all that displeased them

had been omitted, society would have been most
promiscuous and stale.

Washington, both by training and instinct, was
devoted to the proprieties of life. He would do
nothing to cheapen the position to which he was
chosen, although he well understood that this involved a danger of running into superciliousness.
He insisted on living in his own house from the
first; for it did not seem dignified to him for the
head of the nation to be the permanent guest of any
one. He would not even accept the invitation of
Governor Clinton, of New York, to be his guest till
convenient quarters were prepared; and one of the
rules he made was to visit nobody.

He was no sooner president than he was overrun
with callers. "I could not get relieved from the
ceremony of one visit," he said, "before I had to
attend to another." [1] They came for business,
much of which could have been left to subordinates,
or from good-will or curiosity. To have the time
necessary for the discharge of official duties, certain
rules for receiving company were necessary. After
consulting with several of his friends he announced
that he would have one public levee a week to which
all might come, and that other persons who called
must make engagements in advance.[2] Tuesdays,
from three to four in the afternoon, became the
regular time of the levee. On such an occasion, at

[1] Washington, *Writings* (Ford's ed.), XI., 406; cf. also 390–393.
[2] *Ibid.*, XI., 405–408.

the appointed hour, the door of a great room would be thrown open, and at one end would be seen Washington standing erect, invariably clad in a plain black velvet coat and breeches, a white or pearl colored vest, yellow gloves, and silver buckles at the knees and on the shoes, his hair in a bag-wig and powdered. In his hand was a cocked hat, and at his side a steel-hilted sword with a white scabbard. As the visitors filed past they were introduced by name, and then they took their places at one side of the room. At a quarter-past three the doors were closed and the president would then go along the sides of the room speaking some words to every one. He had a good memory for names, and it was seldom that he was not able to say something to each which left the recipient of the favor well pleased with the speaker. When this was done he took his first position, and the guests approached, made their bows, and departed.[1]

On Friday evenings Mrs. Washington held receptions which were more informal than the levees, and the guests of both sexes lingered long in spirited conversation. At these receptions Washington always appeared, passing grave compliments with the ladies, and bowing and smiling with the gentlemen. He was not given to jests or brilliant conversation, but he did all things with good effect.

The dinners given by the president were strictly

[1] P. L. Ford, *True George Washington*, 173.

regulated also. The presidents of the old Congress
had received certain sums to enable them to entertain properly, and hence there was a feeling that the
president's table was a kind of a public affair. Washington was determined to make it an entirely private
entertainment. He invited as many as his table
would hold, and at frequent intervals, taking only
the chief officials of the government and distinguished foreigners. He made it a point to take members
of Congress in order.

Maclay, an intensely Republican senator from
Pennsylvania, gives us an account of one of these
ceremonies. At the middle of a long table sat
Washington, and on the opposite side Mrs. Washington; at one end one of his private secretaries,
and at the other end another. After the soup came
fish roasted and boiled; then meat, salmon, and
fowl. Dessert began with apple-pies and puddings,
and ended with ice - cream, jellies, watermelons,
muskmelons, apples, peaches, and nuts. The middle of the table was decorated with small images
and artificial flowers. "It was," says Maclay, "the
most solemn dinner I ever sat at. Not a health
drank, scarce a word said until the cloth was taken
away. Then the President filling his glass of wine,
with great formality, drank to the health of every
individual by name around the table. Everybody
imitating him charged glasses, and such a buzz of
'health, sir,' and 'health, madam,' and 'thank you,
sir,' and 'thank you, madam,' never had I heard

before." [1] Washington's dinners are pronounced good ones by all who have written about them. He was certain to have the best wines, especially Madeira and claret, the fashionable wines of the day, which he got from France. He was careful to have handsome plate, and that was necessary lest he be surpassed by the rich merchants of New York or Philadelphia.

The simple ceremony which he followed gave offence to ultra democrats. Colonel Bland, of Virginia, a congressman who had been accustomed to the ways of good society, took umbrage at what he called the "pomp" of the president On his return to his home he reported that Washington's bows were "more distant and stiff" than those of a king—and Bland had been at the court of St. James. Upon this complaint Washington thus commented: "That I have not been able to make bows to the taste of poor Colonel Bland (who, by-the-by, I believe never saw one of them), is to be regretted, especially too, as (upon these occasions), they were indiscriminately bestowed, and the best I was master of, would it not have been better to throw the veil of charity over them, ascribing their stiffness to the effect of age, or the unskilfulness of my teacher, than to pride and dignity of office, which God knows has no charms for me?" [2]

While Washington was settling the question of his

[1] Maclay, *Journal*, 137.
[2] Washington, *Writings* (Ford's ed.), XI., 488.

intercourse with the public, certain statesmen were deeply concerned about the title by which he should be addressed. The House in preparing their reply to his first speech called him merely "The President of the United States," which is what the Constitution denominates him. The Senate objected to this, and appointed a committee which reported in favor of "His Excellency." To the believers in extreme formality this seemed too plain. They ran through the lists of the titles of foreign rulers, and after much debate appointed another committee, which suggested "His Highness the President of the United States of America, and Protector of their Liberties." This was long enough to be ludicrous, and even such men as R. H. Lee, Izard, and John Adams were against its adoption. The Senate finally agreed to accept the idea of the House, and from that day to this the official title of the president is simply "Mr. President." [1]

Meanwhile the report that high titles were proposed had penetrated to every part of the country, and raised an outcry as unreasonable as the proposition itself. Patrick Henry, who was not yet reconciled to the new government, damned it with an epithet: the project "squinted towards monarchy." [2] The Senate, it must be remembered, had not yet found its true place in our government.

[1] *Annals of Cong.*, 1 Cong., 24, 33, 35; Madison, *Writings* (Congress ed.), I., 469, 471; John Adams, *Works*, VIII., 511–513; Maclay, *Journal*, 22–37.   [2] Henry, *Henry*, II., 447.

It was laboring under a notion that it was to have some of the privileges and dignity of the House of Lords in England, or of the old Upper Houses, which were usually councils, in the colonial legislatures. It was filled with inexperienced men, as is shown by the fact that by December, 1795, only eight of the original twenty-six Senators were still members. Their places were taken by men who knew what the people desired the Senate to be, and many of whom had served for a time in the House; and the result was that the Upper House became less arbitrary.

The salary of the president was fixed at twenty-five thousand dollars a year, and Washington was obliged to spend it all and more. His Philadelphia residence was a large double house which had been used by Robert Morris. It stood on Market Street near Sixth, in a fine old garden filled with trees. The first floor was given up to the public reception-rooms, the second to Mrs. Washington's drawing-rooms and her private apartments. On the third were the president's public offices and his private rooms. A housekeeper and his wife provided for the needs of the table, and the housekeeping was conducted with a force of white servants. Washington complained that another family could live in Philadelphia on twenty-five hundred dollars a year in as good style as he lived for twenty-five thousand dollars.

Social life was very gay in both New York and

Philadelphia, while they were the seats of government. Many members of Congress married into the prominent local families, and this gave a union of local and official society. In these cities, also, was a wealthy merchant class which liked to entertain company. By common consent Philadelphia surpassed its rival on the Hudson in social brilliancy. The most noted woman was Mrs. William Bingham, endowed with beauty, taste, immense wealth, a splendid house, and family prestige; and in 1795, when her husband became a United States senator, official position was added. An invitation to her balls was an admission into good society. Mrs. Washington's entertainments were dignified and simple according to Virginia usage; Mrs. Bingham's balls were splendid after the latest European fashion. French hair-dressers, French coats and gowns, powdered wigs, French bows, and cocked hats, which must be carried in the owner's hands as he bowed his way through the drawing-room, were to be seen everywhere.

Foreigners were struck by the signs of wealth at these receptions. They had expected to find rudeness in a new country, but they had forgotten that abundant opportunities in such a country resulted in great fortunes which naturally affected the manner of living. The Duke of Rochefoucauld-Liancourt gives his impression of society in these words: "The profusion and luxury of Philadelphia on great days, at the tables of the wealthy, in their equipages, and the dresses of their wives and daughters, are, as I have observed, extreme. I have seen balls on the President's birthday where the splendor of the rooms, and the variety and richness of the dresses did not suffer in comparison with Europe; and it must be acknowledged that the beauty of the American ladies has the advantage in the comparison. The young women of Philadelphia are accomplished in different degrees, but beauty is general with them. They want the ease and fashion of Frenchwomen; but the brilliancy of their complexion is infinitely superior. Even when they grow old they are still handsome; and it would be no exaggeration to say, in the numerous assemblies of Philadelphia it is impossible to meet with what is called a plain woman. As for the young men, they for the most part seem to belong to another species." [1]

A costume worn by a lady at one of the balls of the time is described as "a plain celestial-blue satin, with a white satin petticoat. On the neck was worn a very large Italian gauze handkerchief, with border stripes of satin. The head-dress was a pouf of gauze, in the form of a globe, the creneaux or head-piece of which was composed of white satin, having a double wing in large plaits, and trimmed with a wreath of artificial roses, falling from the left at the top to the right at the bottom, in front, and the reverse behind. The hair was dressed all over in detached curls, four of which, in two ranks, fell on

[1] Rochefoucauld-Liancourt, *Travels*, II., 385.

each side of the neck, and were relieved behind by a floating *chignon.*" [1]

The dress of the men was not so extremely fashionable as that of the women. To the foreigner it seemed plain but neat, probably because of the more serious occupations of the men. A dandy of the time describes his clothes at a certain entertainment as follows: " I was dressed in a light French blue coat, with a high collar, broad lappels, and large gilt buttons, a double-breasted Marseilles vest, Nankeen - colored cassimere breeches, with white silk stockings, shining pumps, and full ruffles on my breast and at my wrists, together with a ponderous white cravat, with a pudding in it, as we then called it ; and I was considered the best dressed gentleman in the room." [2]

One of the most interesting groups of men in the capital was the French refugees. They came seeking an asylum from the vengeance of the French republicans. Among them were the Duke of Noailles, brother-in-law of Lafayette and an old companion in arms of Washington; Talleyrand, destined to become foreign minister under the Directory and under Napoleon; the Duke of Rochefoucauld-Liancourt, who wrote a valuable description of American life of the day: and Louis Philippe himself, who was yet to be king of France. Their appearance aroused the jealousy of the French republican faction. When Washington gave Noailles a private interview as an

[1] Griswold, *Republican Court*, 155 *n.*   [2] *Ibid.*, 210 *n.*

old friend, it was charged that the duke had held a conference through a whole night in regard to securing American help for the French royalists, and the French minister gave open signs of his displeasure. Washington, to avoid grounds for further criticism, refused after this to give private audiences to the French refugees. Of Louis Philippe it is related that while he was in Philadelphia he desired to marry a daughter of the noted Mrs. Bingham, but that the father of the young lady objected, saying to the duke, "Should you ever be restored to your hereditary position, you will be too great a match for her; if not, she is too great a match for you."[1]

One of the most notable social events at the capital was the annual ball in celebration of Washington's birthday. As early as 1783 people began to observe February 22 as a holiday. But after 1789 the custom was looked upon by the Republicans as a servile imitation of the habit of Europeans to celebrate the birthdays of their kings. Members of that party denounced the custom with spirit; but the Federalists paid little attention to them, and the birthnight balls went on year after year. In 1798, when Washington was in retirement, both parties united to observe the day, the Federalists because they sincerely esteemed the custom, and the Republicans because they wished to show in so doing that they had great regard for Washington as a

[1] Griswold, *Republican Court*, 386.

private citizen but disliked the custom of observing the birthdays of rulers in office.

The transfer of the capital to Washington interrupted the social gayety of the people connected with it. In fact, "the republican court" may be said to have disappeared with the exit of Washington. Adams was not a man to arouse social enthusiasm, although he was sincerely liked by the few who were his intimates. When the congressmen and other officials first lifted their eyes in the autumn of 1800, over the bogs and hills on which it had been decided to plant the nation's capital, there was much sighing for the civilization of Philadelphia. It was a long time before the rudeness of nature could be brought into entire subjection to the wants of man.

The site of the city had been selected by Washington. Near the Eastern Branch was a beautiful plateau, one side of which fell down into a broad meadow. On this hill they placed the Capitol. More than a mile to the west was a level plain, and here they placed the president's house and the executive offices. Below "Capitol Hill," as it was called, was a sluggish stream called Goose Creek or the Tyber. Its alder-covered banks were suffiicently denuded to lay out across and along its course the great avenue which to-day is the most important in the capital. But in 1800 Pennsylvania Avenue was only a vista cleared through the forest and undergrowth. Neither the Capitol, the president's house, nor the two buildings for offices which arose on each side of the latter were completely finished.   Here and there were a few dwellings and boarding - houses.   The only thing which was plentiful was mud; it impeded the statesmen who went up to Capitol Hill, and the fine ladies who sought to call on the witty but much disgusted lady in the president's house. Prices for all things were very high, and service was very difficult to get.   Following this transfer into the wilderness came the democratic régime of Jefferson; and the two influences did much to destroy, at least for a time, that formality and social dignity with which life at the capital had hitherto been invested.

CHAPTER XI

THE STATE OF SOCIETY

(1789–1800)

THE independence of the United States caused the severance of many European bonds, and this reacted on American life. Government officials, ministers of religion, lawyers, physicians, managers of English investments in the colonies, and many other classes of leading men in colonial life had been largely drawn from England; and this influx now ceased, except for a number of influential English and Irish journalists. America was thrown more than ever before on itself for leaders and for ideals. There resulted an intensifying of distinctively American traits and a corresponding loss of cosmopolitanism.[1]

Three other notable influences ought to be mentioned. (1) Democracy had received a wonderful impetus. The influence of the "well born" was lessened and that of the "filthy democrats" was increased. Political life thus became cruder and more

[1] A variety of illustrative material on the conditions of the time may be found in Hart, *Am. Hist. told by Contemporaries*, III., §§ 10–36.

passionate, while inequalities began to disappear and the educative function of self-government was stimulated. (2) Our dependence on English constitutional liberty was modified. In the struggles of the colonists against their governors, and in the revolutionary debates as well, the appeal had always been to the chartered rights of Englishmen. Now the rights of man became the ideal, and precedent played a smaller rôle in public discussions. Americans were full of a notion that they were intrusted with ideals different from, and better than, those of other nations. They believed themselves pioneers in political philosophy. (3) American private law began to separate itself from English statute and precedent. The common law continued to be observed; but a body of American statutes and decisions could not but give the content of the law a strong tendency towards those distinctive forms which at the end of a century are easily recognized as American products.

Confidence in the future of his country was a supreme trait of an American in 1789. To immense physical resources there was added in his mind great human capacity to develop them. To utilize fertile lands, to build up manufactures, to construct means of transportation, to develop the organization of commerce, and to take care of public and private credit seemed to him the things first needed in our social progress. Next to these he placed what he would have called the ornaments of life—education, religion, art, literature, science, municipal comforts, and many other things which have become important in modern society. To the former group of forces, therefore, the men who saw Washington and Adams in the presidency, gave most of their attention. It was a day of material development.

In 1790, when the first census was taken, the population was 3,929,214, and in 1800 it was 5,308,483. About one-fifth of each number were negroes, and about half of the total was found on either side of the Potomac. The increase of population in this first census period was due chiefly to births; for immigration had been cut off by the Revolution, and although many efforts were made to attract it again with the return of peace, the estimated annual immigration was not more than four thousand persons, and it was not considerable till after the War of 1812. The outbreak of general war in Europe in 1793 was enough to account for this state of affairs.[1]

About ninety-five per cent. of the inhabitants lived in villages or the open country. The Atlantic coast region was one vast stretch of forests and farms. On the river-banks near the coast, and in the south in particular, much of the land had been cleared for cultivation; in the interior the cleared patches were smaller. Everywhere the inhabitants were looking for the best lands—for river "low-ground" for the great farmers, creek "low-ground" for the medium

[1] Blodget, *Economica* (ed. of 1806), 75.

farmers, and the meadows which lay between the upland hills for the small farmers.

The land which it did not pay to clear was left to the dominion of the forest. In the broad flat plains of Virginia and the Carolinas, where rivers and their tributaries are less abundant than in the narrow plain of the north, the forest had been but slightly subdued. Great stretches of pine land frowned on the traveller, where the cultivation of cotton was destined soon to work many changes. Through these great forests the roads were few and badly constructed. The people who lived in the clearings along them were too poor to build good roads, and the infrequent trips they made to the world beyond them did not justify the necessary outlay. Their lives were isolated, natural, and free. They were poorly educated, ignorant of the problems of the world, and fiercely democratic. These people far outnumbered the wealthy farmers along the rivers. They were the backbone of the democracy of the country.

The great planters of the south dominated the communities in which they lived; they were most numerous along the coasts where the lands were richest. They were people of education, and their ideals were broader than those of the men of the interior. Many of them were Republicans on philosophical grounds and because they favored France; but the majority were Federalists. All of them, whatever their politics, were aristocrats in their social ideals.

In the middle states the medium class and small farmers constituted the mass of the population. They were less isolated than the dwellers in the interior parts of the south, for the forest had yielded more of itself to the aggression of the settler. Distances from the large seaports were not so great, and roads were tolerable. Education was somewhat more advanced, churches were more numerous, ideals were less provincial.

In New England the forest had disappeared to a much larger extent, chiefly because of the lumber and ship-building industries. Villages were grouped along the edges of the bays, sounds, and various small streams; and around them lay the little farms upon which, with much labor, the food of the community was raised. The country was thickly settled compared with other sections, roads were better, houses were more attractively built, and the educational spirit was more generally developed than anywhere else in the country.

Towns were placed chiefly on the sea-coast and at the heads of navigation of the rivers. Commerce was their only support; for the days of the manufacturing towns had not yet come. The larger places attracted the foreign commerce. The smaller towns looked to the larger ones, sending thither the products which they had gathered from the surrounding communities and distributing the imported goods which they received from the seaports.

Most of the towns were north of the Potomac.

In 1790 Richmond, the largest town in Virginia, numbered 3761; and Norfolk, Petersburg, and Alexandria were the only other towns in the state with a population of two thousand or more. In North Carolina not a town of that size existed. In South Carolina, Charleston had a population of about fifteen thousand, and was the centre of a large trade in rice and slaves. It was a residence town for most of the wealthy eastern planters, and because of this and its large commercial interests it was strongly Federal. Savannah was still a small place. The interior of Georgia was undeveloped, but with the cultivation of cotton came a great impulse to progress, which soon gave the state's best seaport a flourishing trade.

The northern cities in 1790 were led by Philadelphia with a population of forty-two thousand. It was a wealthy centre of business, and drew its sustenance from the rich farming region of central and eastern Pennsylvania. The great demand for American grain while the European nations were struggling in war gave a remarkable stimulus to the commerce of Philadelphia. The fact that it was the home of the United States Bank made it a financial centre; and all combined to give it a rapid growth, so that in 1800 its population was seventy thousand. New York, next in size, rose from thirty-two thousand in 1790 to sixty thousand in 1800. This rapid progress indicates the state of development in the interior of New York state.

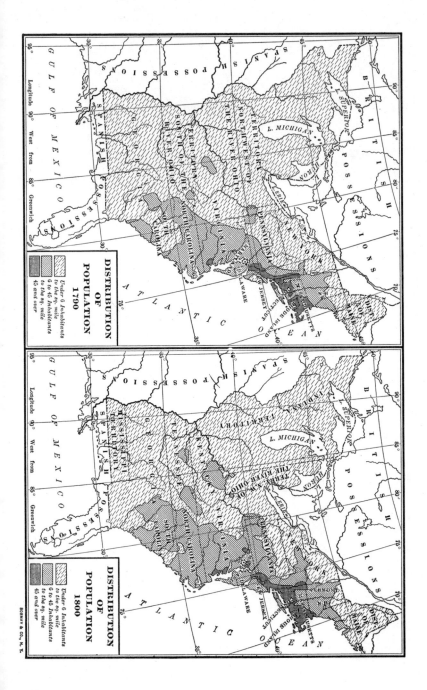

DISTRIBUTION
OF
POPULATION
1790

Under 6 Inhabitants
to the sq. mile
6 to 45 Inhabitants
to the sq. mile
45 and over

DISTRIBUTION
OF
POPULATION
1800

Under 6 Inhabitants
to the sq. mile
6 to 45 Inhabitants
to the sq. mile
45 and over

BUBAY & CO., N. Y.

For a long time this region was held back from the grasp of the settler through an unwillingness to dispossess the Iroquois; but that difficulty was now overcome. Great land companies acquired the central parts of the state, immigrants were turning thither, and their wants were supplied by the city, finely placed at the mouth of the Hudson. Boston, long one of the most remarkable of colonial cities, showed signs of lagging. Its population increased from eighteen thousand in 1790 to twenty-five thousand in 1800. This is accounted for partly because of the restrictions brought about by the Revolution, and partly because it had no such monopoly of trade in its neighborhood as Philadelphia and New York. Its opportunity came when it became the fiscal centre of New England manufacturing; but the day for that had not yet arrived. One of the remarkable features of town development in the period was the growth of Baltimore. Long a sleepy colonial community, it had suddenly awakened to great activity. Its population in 1790 was thirteen thousand; and in 1800, through the development of the Susquehannah Valley, it had reached twenty-six thousand five hundred. In size and in trade it then surpassed Boston.

The largest state of all was Virginia, with a population in 1790 of 747,000. After her came Pennsylvania with 434,000, North Carolina with 393,000, Massachusetts with 378,000, and New York with 340,000. Virginia's preponderating size had very much to do with her large influence in the Revolution and in the struggle for the adoption of the Constitution; she lacked only eighty thousand of having, in 1790, as many inhabitants as all the New England states which joined in the adoption of the Constitution. The financial policy of Hamilton combined the commercial states in behalf of their own interests. Virginia was left out of this movement, and it bore hard on her spirit to see the sceptre of power taken from her hand. Placed in opposition, she became the leader of a combination of agricultural states which at length managed to get control of the government and to rule it for many years with as little regard for the interests of commerce as their opponents had felt with regard to agriculture.

The transportation of heavy articles was confined chiefly to water-routes. At the head of navigation on each river a small town would be found, whence roads ran into the interior. A few of them stretched away to and beyond the Alleghanies into the western wilderness. The advantages of water-transportation turned the attention of the men of progress to building canals, of which few were fairly begun by the end of the century.

Travellers usually went by stage-coach. Where the country was thickly settled they might travel as rapidly as in the rural sections of Europe. From Bangor to Baltimore they could make four miles an hour. South of the latter point the roads were bad and conveyances were uncertain. The coaches were merely large wagons, with high sides and canopies supported by upright beams. If rain fell, heavy curtains of leather were hung up, much to the discomfort of the occupants who must steam within the coach till the rain ceased.

From a day's jolting in such a vehicle one came at length to an inn. If he were fastidious enough to ask for a room to himself he was received with astonishment. He soon learned to consider himself fortunate if he had a bed to himself. Many of the inns had large rooms with from six to ten beds in them. European travellers generally complained loudly of the fare at the inns, where fried bacon and corn - bread were served daily.[1] These conditions have survived till the present in the most isolated portions of the country. At long intervals good inns were encountered, and most of them were in New England, but in the larger towns accommodations were better. Here the tavern was giving way to the modern hotel, modelled after European establishments. Travellers from abroad found them convenient and comfortable, and to the Americans they seemed splendid.

The manner of life was hearty and natural. People of means lived in comfortable houses; poor people occupied the rude structures which had characterized frontier life in the seventeenth century. The plant-

---

[1] Brissot de Warville, *Travels* (ed. of 1792), 123; cf. McMaster, *United States*, II., 562–564; Weld, *Travels* (London ed.), 35, 84.

ers of the south sought to reproduce the life of English country gentlemen, and the wealthy merchants of the north imitated the manners they had seen or heard about in London and Paris. The old colonial usages were preserved by those who had the means; but the sudden accumulation of wealth in the towns brought many new families into prominence, and manners were a little less formal.

In New England, Puritan morals ruled social intercourse. Life was regular and recreation was simple. Sleighing, riding, dancing, shooting at a mark, draughts, and such innocent amusements were considered proper. The boys played football, quoits, and cricket, and everybody skated in season. The theatre was not allowed in Boston till 1793.

In the south, amusements were more unrestrained. Horse-racing had long been a favorite sport and cock-fighting was general. It was at this time that the famous stud "Diomed" was imported into Virginia; his offspring became famous on many a track in that and adjoining states. One of them was Andrew Jackson's famous "Truxton," long the king of the Tennessee turf. To own a champion race-horse was to give a man as much renown in his community as to win the Derby in England. Charleston was a famous centre for horse-racing. Its "Jockey Club" was a leading social organization. The habit of living away from their plantations brought many wealthy and refined people to the town. Nowhere else in the south was there so much wealth and good breeding.

The most universal phase of thought at this period was religion. In New England and among the
masses of the middle and southern states it was the
supreme authority in conduct; but many of the
planters of the south and some of the more intelligent
classes elsewhere had accepted the ideas of French
scepticism. In the villages of New England the
Congregational minister was still the most influential
person. He ruled the conduct of the town, censored
its manners, and did not hesitate to interfere in its
politics. Thomas Jefferson, whom the orthodox
freely denounced as an infidel, had much reason to
complain of the political activity of the New England ministry. Unitarianism, however, was beginning to undermine its domination, and the trend of
society towards wealthy classes was working for the
progress of the Episcopal church.

In the south the latter church, on the contrary, was
losing ground; it was disliked because it had been the
established church in several colonies, because many
of its ministers had proved themselves Tories in the
Revolution, and because it was in close alliance with
the aristocracy. It had but recently reorganized
itself on an American basis, it had lost much from
the defection of the planters to scepticism, and it
was in severe straits in many southern communities.
Other churches in the south were striving to adapt
themselves to new conditions and to recover from
the disorganization which followed the war.

At this favorable juncture there appeared in the

country a new church which was destined to have a powerful influence on religion there. The followers of Wesley had hardly got a foothold in the United States before the Revolution interrupted their progress. But in 1784 they organized a separate American body with authority from their founder. They appealed to the vast middle class of people; they caught the wasting fragments of other bodies; they gave a democratic fire to their preaching; they endured all manner of hardship in order to penetrate the vast upland forest region of the south and west; and thus they laid the foundations of a great movement which has exerted a powerful influence on the life of America. This success was largely due to the activity of Bishop Francis Asbury, a man whose perseverance, zeal, and devotion have suggested a comparison with another Francis who carried light to the dark places of the earth during the Middle Ages.[1]

The period from 1789 to 1801 was not characterized by intellectual progress. Education made little advance, and literature was all but dead. The after-effects of war and the tendency for all energies to run into physical recuperation were the chief causes. In 1800 the Harvard faculty consisted of the president, three professors, and four tutors. In 1797, Bishop Madison, whose vacant parishes had caused him to suspend his episcopal functions and become president of William and Mary College, was teaching a

[1] See Asbury, *Journal*, passim.

group of barefooted boys.[1]   In literature the group known as "the Hartford Wits" were most distinguished.   Perhaps the best poetry of the day was Freneau's.

The most significant social movement of the period was the extension of the frontier beyond the mountains, which began before the Revolution, but after 1789 it proceeded rapidly.   In 1790 the total population of Kentucky, Tennessee, and the northwest was 109,000; in 1800 it was 377,000.   Two roads led settlers from the east thither — one through western Pennsylvania by wagon to Pittsburg and thence by flat-boat down the Ohio, the other by wagon-road through southwestern Virginia to the Holston Valley and thence down the Tennessee River.

The Ohio was already bordered with towns.   From Pittsburg floating westward one came to Wheeling, Marietta, Belpré, Gallipolis, Limestone, Columbia, Newport, Cincinnati, and Louisville.   Farther down on the Mississippi were New Madrid and Natchez. Louisville had once been important because Fort Jefferson, which was placed here, afforded protection against the Indians; but the march of settlement had removed all danger from that source, and the chief significance of the place arose from the fact that it was placed at the rapids of the Ohio.   Cincinnati, on the north side of the river, looked out into hostile territory, till Wayne's victory in 1794 removed that

[1] Adams, *United States*, I., 77, 136.

danger.   In 1795 came the treaty with Spain, by
which the navigation of the Mississippi was secured.
Nothing now stood in the way of the dreams of the
westerners.   Whatever might trouble the east, they
had the simple task of developing the vast country
which was opened to them.   The confidence and
tumultuous joy with which they proceeded marked
the future character of the people.   Never did
American frontier shift more quickly and happily
into civilized communities than in the rich plains on
each side of the Ohio.   The creation of three states
and three territories between 1789 and 1800 marked
the future lines of national development.   In 1791,
Vermont was admitted into the Union, and in 1792,
Kentucky.   In 1796, Tennessee knocked at the door,
but the moment was inopportune for her ambition.
A close presidential election was about to be decided,
and it was pretty certain that she would vote with the
Republicans.   The Federalists, therefore, challenged
her right to become a state.   For several weeks they
kept her outside, but on the last day of the session
they relented and she was admitted.   In 1798 the
region between Tennessee and Florida was set apart
as a territory.   The lower part of it was still claimed
by Georgia, but negotiations were about to be begun
by which that matter was adjusted in 1802; and in
1800 a second act of Congress created a legislature
and otherwise completed the government of Mississippi territory.[1]   In 1800 the old Northwest Terri-

[1] *U. S. Statutes at Large*, II., 69; Riley, *Mississippi*, 94, 97.

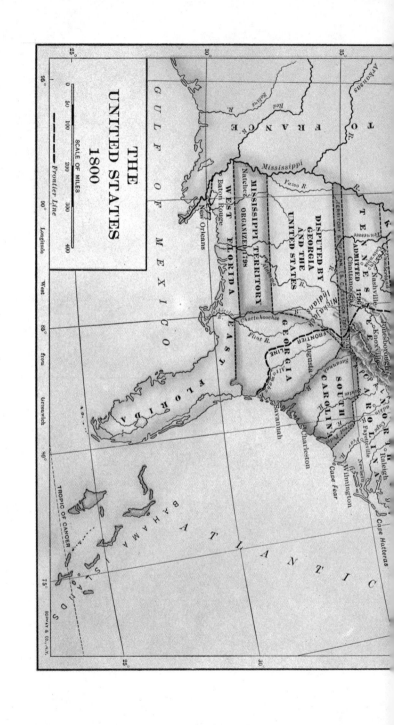

THE
UNITED STATES
1800

SCALE OF MILES

0   50   100   200   300   400

Frontier Line

GULF OF MEXICO

FRANCE

TO

Sabine R.
Red R.
Mississippi
Yazoo R.

WEST FLORIDA
Natchez
Baton Rouge
New Orleans

MISSISSIPPI
TERRITORY
ORGANIZED 1798

DISPUTED BY
GEORGIA
AND THE
UNITED STATES

TERRITORY S. OF THE TENN. S. CAROLINA'S CESSION 1787

T E N N E S S E E
ADMITTED 1796
Nashville
Chattanooga

Cumberland R.

EAST FLORIDA

Chattahoochee R.
Flint R.

Indian

Nickajack R.
FRONTIER LINE

G E O R G I A
Augusta
Milledge R.
Savannah

Jonesborough
Knoxville
Cumberland R.
Holston R.

N O R T H   C A R O L I N A
Raleigh
Cape Hatteras

SOUTH
CAROLINA
Charleston

Santee R.
Great Pedee R.
Cape Fear R.

Fayetteville
Newbern
Wilmington
Cape Fear

F L O R I D A

ATLANTIC

BAHAMA

TROPIC OF CANCER

KEYS

25°   30°   35°
95°   90°   85°   80°   75°

Longitude   West   from   Greenwich

BUFORD & CO., N.Y.

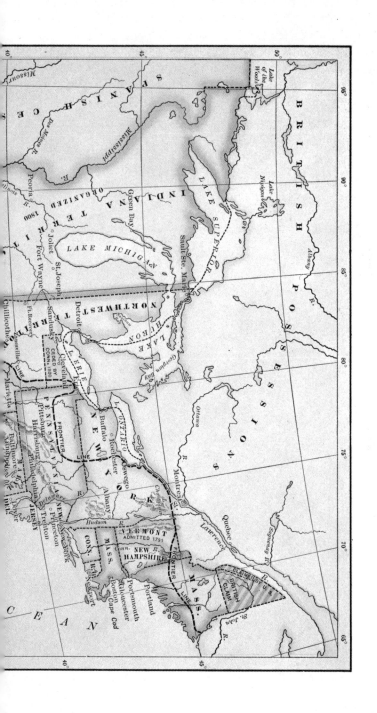

tory was divided preparatory to the admission of
Ohio, and the immense western portion was called
Indiana.[1]

[1] On the later history of the west, see Channing, *Jeffersonian
System*, chap. vii.; Babcock, *Am. Nationality*, chap. xv.; Turner,
New West, passim, (*Am. Nation*, XII., XIII., XIV.).

CHAPTER XII

THE FIRST VICTORIES OF ANTI-SLAVERY

(1777–1804)

TILL the extensive cultivation of cotton opened a vast field of rapid development in the lower south, there was in all the Union a steady progress in anti-slavery sentiment. This was due chiefly to the fact that slavery did not pay in the middle and eastern colonies, to the acceptance in the revolutionary period of the theories of the rights of man; to the continual fear of negro insurrections; and to the fact that most of the American slave-markets were overstocked.[1] This tendency manifested itself in two movements: one against the foreign slave-trade, by which that source of slavery was at length cut off from the whole country; and the other for the actual extinction of slavery, by which all the north and northwest except Delaware were made free territory.[2]

The attack on the slave-trade began with the

---

[1] Du Bois, *Suppression of the Slave-Trade*, 41.

[2] On earlier conditions of slavery, see Andrews, *Colonial Self-Government*, chap. xviii.; Greene, *Provincial America*, chap. xiv. (*Am. Nation*, V., VI.).

first Continental Congress. In the famous "Association," or non-importation resolutions of 1774, it was agreed that no slaves should be imported into any of the thirteen colonies after December 1, 1774, and that no colony vessels should engage, or be hired to others to engage, in that traffic.[1] In 1776 the Congress, now committed to resistance, reaffirmed their position in a special resolution. The war which followed throughout a period of seven years cut off importations so generally that it is impossible to estimate the precise effect of these restrictions; but it is certain that till 1783 slave importations almost entirely ceased.[2] No further restriction was placed on the traffic by the national government till the formation of the Constitution.

In the mean time individual states passed laws against the foreign slave-trade, and did much to rid the country of the evil. By 1778 all the north, and Virginia and Maryland as well, had by statute, or as a result of other action, made importations impossible. When the war was over there was a tendency for the far south to revive the trade; but in 1786 North Carolina laid a prohibitive duty on slaves brought into her borders, and in 1787 South Carolina declared for absolute prohibition. For a time Georgia held out for slaves; but the Haytian insurrection of 1791 created in the south a lively

---

[1] *Journals of Continental Congress* (Ford's ed.), I., 75–80; cf. Howard, *Preliminaries of the Revolution* (*Am. Nation*, VIII.), chap. xvii.   [2] Locke, *Anti-Slavery in America*, 73.

suspicion of all newly imported negroes. South Carolina passed a new prohibitory law in 1792; North Carolina, who had repealed her high duties in 1790, declared against all importations in 1794; and Georgia came reluctantly to the same position in 1798.[1] Thus by state action the country was rid of the slave-trade before the close of the eighteenth century.

Nevertheless, any of these states might, if left to themselves, repeal their prohibitions and restore the traffic, to prevent which result many people desired that the new national government be given control over the slave-trade. In the Constitutional Convention of 1787 such a proposition was made and supported by the northern states and by Virginia and Maryland; but the extreme south resisted it stoutly. It was well enough, they said, for the north, which had no slaves, and for Virginia and Maryland, which were overstocked with them, to desire to check importations, but for the lower south the matter was different. Georgia was still an unsettled region, and the same was true to a less extent in the Carolinas. So earnestly did these three states resist that the delegates were convinced that they would not ratify the Constitution if it contained the objectionable clause. The majority, therefore, did not dare force them, but adopted a compromise, the purport of which was to give the three states mentioned an opportunity to acquire

[1] Du Bois, *Suppression of the Slave-Trade*, 51, 71.

the desired stocks of negroes before the trade was
forbidden by national statute.[1] Congress, declared
the Constitution as finally framed, should not, before 1808, prohibit the introduction to the Union
of such persons as any state saw fit to admit, but
they might impose a tax of ten dollars on each imported person.[2] In 1807 a law was passed by which
Congress put into effect the powers granted to it.
Four years earlier the nation received an illustration
of how much the power was needed when South
Carolina repealed her law restricting the trade.
Various attempts were made to lay the ten-dollar
duty authorized in the Constitution, but for several
reasons they all failed.[3]

In another relation slavery proved a source of
dissension in the Constitutional Convention. When
the apportionment of members of the popular branch
of Congress was taken up, conflicting opinions quickly appeared over the counting of the slaves in the
south. Delegates from that section urged that the
whole population, black and white, ought to be the
basis of representation. The northern delegates generally opposed this claim. The south, they urged,
did not let the slaves vote and should not expect
to count them in fixing its share of representation. Much angry debate followed, till the amica-

[1] See McLaughlin, *Confederation and Constitution* (*Am. Nation*,
X.), 262–266.

[2] Du Bois, *Suppression of the Slave-Trade*, chap. vi.; cf. United
States Constitution, art. i., sec. 18.

[3] Locke, *Anti-Slavery in America*, 136–139, 145, 148–155.

ble conduct of the proceedings seemed in danger, when Madison and some of his intimate friends proposed a compromise. In 1777 a similar controversy had arisen over the apportionment of direct taxes, with the difference that at that time the north had desired and the south had opposed the counting of the slaves. The question, under the delicate adjustments of the old constitution, could not be settled; but it was now revived, and a compromise was made by which it was agreed that three-fifths of the slaves should be counted for the purpose of representation and three - fifths for apportioning direct taxes. The infrequency with which these taxes have been laid by the national government made the compromise result to the benefit of the south.[1]

While the slave-trade was being disposed of by state and national enactment an important movement was in progress against the very existence of slavery in a large part of the Union. One by one the northern states came to legislate against the legal basis of bondage, till by the time the traffic was forbidden every state but one lying north of Mason and Dixon's historic line had either established freedom or taken steps for its gradual accomplishment. It was not difficult for the north to do this, since slavery was not wide-spread or eco-

---

[1] Bancroft, *Formation of the Constitution* (ed. of 1885), 264–266; cf. McLaughlin, *Confederation and Constitution (Am. Nation*, X.), 255–260.

nomically profitable in that section. The non-slave-
holders in the south were always numerous, but they
were not people of influence. In the north they
were both numerous and influential; and when
those earnest men, like the Quakers, who believed
it a duty to rid the country of slavery, set out to
organize public opinion on the subject, they had
no great difficulty in succeeding. They sought to
destroy slavery by three methods — by constitutional enactment, by laws for immediate emancipation, and by laws for gradual liberation.

The first of the American states to declare for
freedom was Vermont, the state in which slavery was
weakest. In a bill of rights adopted in 1777, when
the people declared themselves a state, slavery was
forbidden.[1] New Hampshire in 1784 declared in
her organic law that "all men are born equally free
and .independent," and in the face of so plain a
declaration slavery, essentially weak in that state,
made no contest.[2] In Massachusetts it had a
stronger hold, but here the anti-slavery faction was
also strong and aggressive. Several attempts for
emancipation by legislative enactment having failed,
the friends of freedom now turned to a clause in
the Constitution of 1780 which declared that "all
men are born free and equal." A case was made up
for the courts, by which it was claimed that the
import of the clause was to establish freedom; and
these finally held, about 1783, that the contention

[1] Locke, *Anti-Slavery in America*, 80.   [2] *Ibid.*, 116.

was a good one. Thus Massachusetts became free
territory, and with it went Maine, then under its
jurisdiction.[1]

Immediate emancipation by state statute was
frequently attempted, but only successful in New
York, and then not till 1827, which was many years
after a law for gradual emancipation had been
passed. All the other northern states but Delaware
adopted this latter form of abolition. Pennsylvania,
urged to it by the activity of the Quakers, acted first,
passing her law in 1780. Connecticut and Rhode
Island followed in 1784, and New Jersey in 1804.[2]
Gradual emancipation is defined as "the extinction
of slavery by depriving it of its hereditary quality."[3]
In all those states in which slavery was forced out of
existence it was defended earnestly by the general
body of slave-holders and slave-traders; and when it
had been defeated it was necessary in some of the
states to pass laws to prevent these disappointed
ones from sending their slaves out of the states, pre-
sumably in order to sell them.

In the south there was considerable anti-slavery
feeling, especially in Virginia, where most of the leading public men were opposed to the institution. But
the mass of the people clung to their slaves, because
they were an important form of wealth, and the
wisest of the liberators could not suggest a practica-
ble method of disposing of the negroes after they

[1] Locke, *Anti-Slavery in America*, 80–82.
[2] *Ibid.*, 77–79, 123–125, 127, 128.   [3] *Ibid.*, 124.

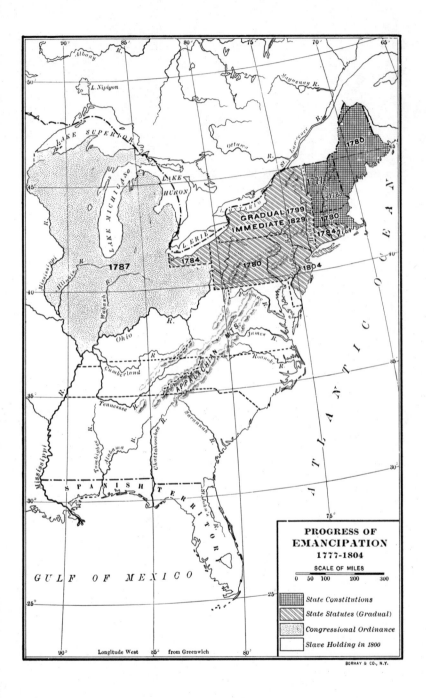

PROGRESS OF
EMANCIPATION
1777-1804

SCALE OF MILES

0 50 100   200   300

State Constitutions

State Statutes (Gradual)

Congressional Ordinance

Slave Holding in 1800

GRADUAL 1799
IMMEDIATE 1829

1787   1784   1780   1804

1780

1780   1784

1780

SPANISH   TERRITORY

GULF OF MEXICO

ATLANTIC OCEAN

Longitude West   85°   from Greenwich

BORMAY & CO., N.Y.

were freed; so the movement, although favored by
so influential a man as Jefferson, came to naught.
The failure here marked the point which peaceful
emancipation was to reach in its southward course.[1]
From the fading of hope in Virginia the country was
committed to a free and a slave section. In the
one was an aggressive element which proclaimed its
hostility to slavery and expressed freely its opinion
that it made the nation responsible for the crime of
denying liberty to human beings. In the other was
an increasing feeling that slavery was condemned,
and that all southerners must act together if it were
not overridden. Out of this grew a solidifying of the
sections, an opposition of north to south and south
to north, and a sensitiveness on the slave question
which, although for a time subservient to other
issues, was never quite forgotten, and which event-
ually became the cause of secession and civil war.

While the opponents of slavery contended against
it in the original thirteen states they did not fail to
try to forestall it in the west. In the part north and
west of the Ohio they won an easy victory, southerners and northerners uniting to dedicate it to freedom, and Jefferson led the movement. In 1784 he
and others supported a bill in the old Congress to
prohibit slavery after 1800 in all the west; but this
was defeated by one vote. In 1787 the demand was
limited to the prohibition of slavery in the north-

[1] Ballagh, *Slavery in Virginia*, 130–136; Locke, *Anti-Slavery
in America*, 129.

west, and this attempt was successful.[1]   Five states
were later hewn out of the region to which this Northwest Ordinance applied, and all of them were free
states.   Since nothing was done to prohibit slavery
in the territory south of the Ohio, slave-holders went
into it freely, and when it reached the stage of state-
hood it came into the Union as slave territory, thus
preserving the sectional character of the Union.
When Mississippi became a territory in 1798, an
attempt was made in Congress to have it declared
free territory, but so strong was the feeling that the
south was reserved for slavery and the north for
freedom that only twelve votes were given in support of the proposition.[2]   In another instance the
same determination was manifested in 1805, when a
bill was introduced in Congress to secure gradual
emancipation in the District of Columbia.   It was
rejected by a vote of 77 to 31.[3]

Soon after the organization of the new Congress
there began that series of petitions for the restriction
of slavery in one way or another which was not to
cease till 1865.   The petitioners knew that many of
the things asked for were impossible or politically im-
probable, but they continued their petitions, thinking that this would crystallize anti-slavery sentiment
and believing that in the long run constitutional re-

---

[1] McLaughlin, *Confederation and Constitution* (*Am. Nation*,
X.), 120–126.   [2] *Annals of Cong.*, 5 Cong., 1306–1312.
[3] Tremain, *Slavery in the District of Columbia*, 58; *Annals of
Cong.*, 8 Cong., 2 Sess., 995.

strictions and adverse public opinion would give way before their demands for what they felt was right. Many of the petitioners were Quakers, a people always active against slavery and at this time unpopular in sections where they had no political influence, because they would not fight in the Revolutionary armies.

In February, 1790, three petitions came to Congress for the prohibition or the restriction of the slave-trade. This was not unexpected by the southerners, who particularly desired that the first utterance of Congress on a question so dear to them should recognize the rights of the states over slavery. Cautious southerners, even those who like Madison were opposed to slavery, hoped that the southern congressmen would be reasonable and secure a clear statement of their rights.[1]   They were already caught in the great solidifying movement of the south on this question, and there could be no doubt that the petitions referred to were against the compromise of the Constitution on the prohibition of the slave-trade, an agreement to which Madison and the group of southern opponents of slavery had given their assent.   The south, therefore, stood together, but they did not show the temperateness which Madison had hoped for.   There were ever some southerners who would not be quiet when slavery was criticised, and these were soon on their feet demanding that the anti-slavery petitions should not

[1] Madison, *Works* (Congress ed.), I., 513.

be referred to a committee. Defeated on this point, they were thrown into a rage when the committee reported with a decided leaning towards emancipation in the abstract. A heated discussion followed in which the report of the committee was modified. Resolutions including the following important principles were adopted:

"1. That the migration or importation of such persons as any of the states now existing shall think proper to admit, cannot be prohibited by Congress prior to the year 1808.

"2. That Congress have no power to interfere in the emancipation of slaves, or in the treatment of them within any of the states, it remaining with the several states alone to provide any regulations therein which humanity and true policy may require.

"3. That Congress have authority to restrain the citizens of the United States from carrying on the African trade for the purpose of supplying foreigners with slaves, and of providing by proper regulations, for the humane treatment during their passage of slaves imported by the said citizens into the states admitting such importation.

"4. That Congress have also authority to prohibit foreigners from fitting out vessels in any port of the United States for transporting persons from Africa to any foreign port."[1]

The resolutions plainly declared that Congress would do all it could under the Constitution to re-

[1] *Annals of Cong.*, 1 Cong., 1182, 1197, 1413, 1414, 1450–1474.

strain the foreign slave-trade; and in 1794 it did pass a law in keeping with the third resolution.

The recovery of fugitive slaves was provided for in 1793 in a law concerning extradition,[1] and in this case the south got all that it could expect. It was provided that a master or his agent might recover a fugitive by taking him before a federal judge or local magistrate, who, without a jury and by oral testimony or by affidavits, was to determine the question of ownership. This law was made to meet a serious difficulty. A northern jury was not likely to be entirely unprejudiced, to carry before them ordinary witnesses from the south was practically impossible, and in the usual procedure the delays which the defendant could secure would be very trying to the claimant. All of this could make the recovery of a real fugitive slave so expensive that it would not pay the owner.

On the other hand, the law worked a hardship to the negroes. It made kidnapping of free negroes in the north easy and profitable. Even in the south a negro was treated as a freeman in a trial for his freedom; but as a fugitive in the north he was deprived of the rights of a freeman in anticipation of a verdict as to his freedom. The master's rights and the slave's conflicted, and the master was the law-maker. It was ever the habit of slavery to balance one wrong by another.

[1] *U. S. Statutes at Large*, I., 302; McDougall, *Fugitive Slaves* (*Radcliffe Monographs*, No. 6), chap. ii.; Hart, *Slavery and Abolition* (*Am. Nation*, XVI.), chap. ii.

CHAPTER XIII

ECONOMIC CONDITIONS
(1789–1800)

TO the average American in 1789 the most pressing national duty was to develop the vast resources which lay all around him. The national domain embraced about eight hundred and thirty thousand square miles, and the average density of population was less than five persons to each square mile. That the day would come when the country would be as well settled and as rich as the old countries of Europe was believed by all. A desire to anticipate such a development led to much speculation in land, and sometimes to rash public enterprises which could not be supported in the state of society then existing. In spite of such mishaps there went on from the beginning a rapid growth in all the forms of industry. The wars in Europe made a strong demand for provisions, wheat rose in price till it brought as much as two dollars a bushel, and in spite of the restrictions on neutral trade business conditions were good.

More than nine-tenths of the people were engaged in agriculture. Hamilton realized the disadvantage of this concentration of interests which

made the country dependent on foreign markets
for manufactured commodities, and preserved that
bucolic cast of thought which is ever the weakness
of an entirely rural people. In his report on manufactures he announced a plan for the artificial encouragement of town-building by protective duties
or bounties, the chief purpose of which was to bring
about a better distribution of rural and urban population. He was in advance of his day: the small
duties which Congress could be induced to lay gave
only incidental protection, and that did little towards developing manufactures.

Food products, tobacco, and lumber were the
chief articles marketed by the rural communities.
Wheat was raised everywhere except in the coast
plains of the far south. The farms of New England
were not rich enough to give the world much sur-
plus beyond home requirements, but the forests
were still abundant, and staves, masts, timber, and
boards were still exported. Fishing was also an
important industry, for the West India market was
always open, though not for American vessels. The
best wheat lands were in the middle states and in
the upper parts of Maryland and Virginia. The
tobacco industry of the latter suffered heavily from
the duties which as an independent people we now
had to encounter in England, and from the exhaus-
tion of lands where tobacco grew. The Virginians,
who saw the commerce of the north encouraged by
the national government, raised many complaints

that nothing was done to protect their ancient industry; but it is not clear that the government could have found a remedy for the evil.[1] Naval stores and pork were the chief exports from North Carolina, a rich agricultural region in which the lack of harbors was to retard its development till the days of railroads. South Carolina and Georgia raised rice and indigo with great profit. But the south stood at the beginning of its cotton cultivation, the most significant development in the history of American agriculture.

The raising of cotton in this region passed its experimental stage even before 1789. It was evident that the vast alluvial plains of the south, which produced neither wheat nor rice profitably, were peculiarly adapted to cotton. One difficulty only stood in the way, and that was the expense of removing the seed by hand. In response to this economic demand, Whitney invented the cotton-gin in 1793. He was a New England school-teacher then resident in the south. His ingenious mind fashioned a machine which he patented in 1794. He attempted to market his invention by a system of licenses approved and guaranteed by the state legislatures. This plan afforded abundant opportunity of fraud, and the inventor reaped but little advantage from his ingenuity.[2]

In the north, free hired labor was generally em-

---

[1] Tyler, *Tylers*, I., 164.
[2] See Olmsted, *Whitney; Corresp. of Eli Whitney* (*Am. Hist. Rev.*, III., 90–127).

ployed. The old system of indentured servants had not entirely disappeared, but it furnished an inconsiderable part of the labor supply. There is some reason to suppose that it was used frequently in bringing skilled labor into the country. Of such laborers the country had very few: the predominance of rural life was not calculated to develop artisans, and many such workmen who came to the country were drawn off into agriculture by the cheapness of land and the uncertain demand for their crafts.

In the south, slavery displaced all the lower forms of hired labor. The "new negroes" just from Africa tended to keep the standard of efficiency among the slaves at a point lower than that of fifty years later. The new arrivals were unaccustomed to the work they were expected to perform, and frequently intractable. Some of them pined away for their African homes, a few of them ran off to the forests, but the majority were absorbed into the mass of the black people among which they were distributed, took the habits of their associates, and their children became like other slaves. At its best, slave labor was rarely more than three-fourths as efficient as white labor. Among the small farmers of the interior of the south, slaves were at first found only in small numbers; but the extension of cotton cultivation into this region is marked by a rapid increase of the slave population there.[1]

[1] Bassett, *Slavery in North Carolina* (*Johns Hopkins University Studies*, XVII.), 394.

Commerce, of course, existed in every part of the country, but in the south it was small. Slavery precluded the existence of a wage-earning class, and thus mightily lessened the purchasing element. There was also a tendency for the plantation system to supply many of its wants from its own resources. The money of the planters was spent in large orders which could be filled most profitably through commission merchants in remote places. Local trade was thus reduced to trifling proportions.

The conditions of retail trade were, therefore, abnormal in the south. In the north trade proceeded in the usual manner. Local commerce looked to large commercial centres, sending thither its products and receiving from thence its manufactured goods. A commercial class was thus built up in a normal way, and in the large towns it was powerful and stood in close alliance with the financiers. In the rich opportunities of the day, trade became so prosperous, and so overtopped the modest exchanges of the rural regions, that deep-seated conviction spread in those parts that the merchants and ship-owners had not reached success by honest means.

The new status of American trade after the Revolution was the source of much distress; for although England made only trivial discriminations against it, it was a disappointment that she put it out of the pale of her navigation laws and steadily neglected to make the long-desired treaty of commerce through which American merchants hoped to get special concessions.[1] Hard feelings were more easily produced in America, because it was felt that we could not afford to break our trade relations with the only country which was prepared to give us the requisite credit and to furnish on short notice those assorted cargoes which our general trade demanded. The non-commercial classes in America talked bravely about breaking commercial bondage as easily as political bondage, but men who had embarked all their fortunes in the trade with England thought differently about it. To them it seemed that it would be possible to induce England to relent. They were not mercantile economists, and they were in a position to see the advantages of liberal intercourse between nations.

One British statesman, at least, did see these advantages, but he was impotent against the combined will of the English merchants. Pitt in 1783 offered a bill in Parliament to give trading concessions to the United States. He wisely saw that a conciliating spirit might preserve to his country the advantages of keeping one of her best customers. But he was in no position to encounter the opposition of the merchants, and the bill failed. In 1791 a slight concession was secured by which we were allowed to import into Great Britain on equal terms

[1] McLaughlin, *Confederation and Constitution* (*American Nation*, X.), chap. vi.

with other nations certain articles which her own colonies did not largely produce.[1]

The next step was the Jay treaty.[2] This instrument, after the omission of the twelfth article, left our trade in the following condition: each nation might freely trade with the other, subject to its ordinary customs duties and regulations; and the United States might trade freely with the British East Indies. Under this treaty our imports from Great Britain increased from $23,313,000 in 1795 to $39,519,000 in 1801; and our exports from $6,324,-000 to $30,931,000 in the same period.[3] Our trade with the French West Indies, which grew rapidly from 1793 to 1795, fell off to inconsiderable proportions by 1801,[4] no doubt because of the distressed condition of those islands by reason of internal commotions and the activity of English ships of war. In 1795 the total exports were $47,855,000, and in 1801 they were $93,020,000, the imports were $69,-756,000 in the former year, and $111,363,000 in the latter;[5] but of the exports nearly $25,000,000 in 1795, and over $46,000,000 in 1801, were foreign products re-exported.[6]

One of the greatest economic difficulties of this period was a lack of capital. A mint was established in 1793 and proceeded to coin into American mon-

---

[1] Pitkin, *Commerce of the United States*, 177.
[2] See above, pp. 124–135.
[3] Pitkin, *Commerce of the United States*, 179, 188.
[4] *Ibid.*, 218.   [5] *Ibid.*, 257–262.
[6] Seybert, *Statistical Annals*, 93.

ey the indiscriminate English, French, and Dutch coins which had up to that time been the money of the people. But at its best speed it could not make the transition quickly, and foreign coins were still in wide popular use. Credit also was freely employed, and by 1801 many banks of issue had been established. The following statistics are taken from the estimate of a contemporary and are probably nearly correct:[1]

Year	No. of banks	Metallic currency	Circulation	Capital
1790	4	$9,000,000	$2,500,000	$2,500,000
1801	31	$17,000,000	$11,000,000	$22,400,000

Although some of the bank-notes issued by these banks must have been poorly secured, the mass of bank money was not greatly discounted, and it did valuable service in aid of the business of the young nation. The extravagance of "wild-cat" banking was yet to come. In the abundance of business opportunities the rate of interest rose till ten per cent. or more was not unusual. The cheap rates in Holland tended to counteract this rise in America, but when the European war involved that country, money was no longer to be got there; and then the rate rose so high in the United States that the government itself at times paid eight per cent. on the funds actually realized from the sale of bonds.[2]

The collapse of the group of stock speculators

---

[1] Knox, *Banking in the U. S.*, 307; Blodgett, *Economica*, 216.
[2] Dewey, *Financial Hist. of the U. S.*, 112.

whom Duer led[1] did not put an end to over-specula-
tion: land companies embarked in extravagant enterprises; development companies of one kind and
another undertook tasks which could not be re-
munerative in a long time; and merchants went
deeply into debt in anticipation of enormous volumes of trade which did not materialize.   The seizure of American ships by both Britain and France
involved losses also.   In 1797 all these forces came
to a crisis.   Many a wealthy man was forced into
bankruptcy, among them Robert Morris, the patriotic banker of the Revolution.   He had bought
large holdings of western lands and had engaged
also in a real-estate venture in Washington.   From
neither could he realize the money necessary to
keep him out of a debtor's prison.[2]   The panic,
however, was only a temporary check to the business
of the country.   By the end of the century matters
assumed a normal condition, and the economic forces
of a new country carried industry forward with the
usual rapid stride.

Manufactures came slowly into a country where
the simpler forms of industry were so profitable.
English policy had thwarted their rise in colonial
times,[3] and the Revolutionary era was no time for
new developments of this kind.   Power machinery
and other inventions in England were effectively de-

---

[1] See above, p. 52.   [2] Oberholtzer, *Robert Morris*, 300–354.
[3] Cf. Greene, *Provincial America*, chap. xvi.; Howard, *Preliminaries of the Revolution*, chap. iii. (*Am. Nation*, VI., VIII.).

veloped by 1785, and it was impossible for the old
hand system, still used in America, to compete in
the production of manufactured commodities. Both
capital and governmental protection were necessary
to overcome the initial difficulties of such a step and
to enable the Americans to undersell England, and
the mild tariff policy of the period had not much
effect in this direction.

In the manufacture of cotton goods an early beginning was made which was to have an important
result in the history of manufactures in America.
In 1789, Samuel Slater landed in New York. He was
an ingenious and well-intentioned English lad who
had just completed an apprenticeship in one of the
newly established cotton factories of his country.
Slater expected to introduce the English machinery
into America, but strict regulations in England prevented any of the models or drawings of the new
machinery from getting out of the country. The lad,
however, relied on his memory for the designs. He
came at last to Moses Brown, of Rhode Island, who
had been making some unsuccessful attempts in the
same direction through persons who proved themselves incompetent to reproduce the coveted ma-
chines. Slater was able to do the things expected
of him, and became a partner with his employer.
In 1793, the same year in which Whitney invented
the cotton-gin, the firm of Almy, Brown & Slater
set up at Pawtucket the first successful New England cotton factory. By the end of the century

other factories were established;[1] and from that time
this industry has been exceedingly important in
American economic, social, and even political life.

In the period from 1789 to 1801 there was a thriving
hand industry in the homes of the people.   In New
England, for example, many families made nails in
the long winter evenings.   Furniture, hats, shoes,
simple iron implements, and a hundred other articles
which in later times have yielded to the advance of
machinery construction, were then made by village
artisans in the north or by plantation mechanics in
the south.

Dealing in frontier lands was ever a favorite way
of making money with the colonial capitalists.
Many a great fortune in the south and middle states
was made in this way.   The method was for men of
wealth to get large grants from the government in
advance of the tide of settlement, hold them till they
came into the market, and then sell at a profit.
There was a notion abroad that this was the best
way to settle the new lands, for men of means alone
were able to induce small farmers to emigrate
thither.

The beginning of national life turned men's attention to the west, where speculators began to buy
up the lands.   They secured in large quantities the
warrants of soldiers who had received land bounties
for their services in the army.   These warrants were
presented in great batches at the western land of-

[1] Bagnall, *Textile Industries of the United States*, I., 144–161.

fices, and expert judges of good land were employed to locate the best tracts for the owners. In this way much of the land of Tennessee and Kentucky was first taken up. From that region the movement went into the northwest and into the western portion of New York. These land speculators differed in their methods of procedure in no respect from the land-boomers of the more recent west. Voluble, overconfident, and not too truthful, they deluded the credulous in many cases, although it must be confessed that they planted the seed of American communities in many waste places. Sometimes they sold land to settlers the title to which they had not absolutely acquired, and this practice was called "dodging." They frequently sold to European peasants and shopkeepers, and in such transactions many instances of delusion occurred. In colonial times land speculations were usually conducted by individuals, and the tracts taken ran from twenty-five thousand to one hundred thousand acres. But after the Revolution, companies were organized which secured tracts ten times as great. In 1789 three great grants aggregating one million two hundred and fifty thousand acres in the northwest were secured from Congress.

The first regulations for the sale of lands provided that they should be sold at Philadelphia. Individual settlers were thus almost prevented from purchasing directly from the government, and the people of the west protested that it put them at the mercy of the speculators. It was more calculated, also, to draw settlers from abroad than from the east, and the people of the west believed that the east supported it in Congress from this design. From the beginning of our national existence easy sale of public lands has been a favorite policy of the frontiersmen.

Albert Gallatin, who was himself a westerner, in 1796 secured the passage of a new law which tended to satisfy the settlers. It applied to the lands of the Northwestern Territory, defined the township system which later became universal in the west, and authorized the sale of land in sections of six hundred and forty acres. Land offices were opened at Pittsburg and Cincinnati, and the price was fixed at not less than two dollars an acre. The sales of land went on so slowly under this act that in 1800 the principle of popular distribution was further extended. Four district land offices were now created, and purchasers were allowed to buy land on credit, complete payment not being required for four years.[1]

The land speculators were not exempt from the frauds which have so often existed in connection with government franchises. At one time a scheme was unearthed by which a company made extensive plans to secure a large part of the Michigan peninsula by means of a collusive grant from Congress. The most prominent scheme of this kind, however, was

[1] Adams, *Gallatin*, 167; Donaldson, *Public Domain*, 202.

that which grew out of the old Yazoo companies[1] which had first been prominent in connection with western filibustering.   These companies were revived under other names, and in 1795 the legislature of Georgia granted them for five hundred thousand dollars about thirty million acres on the Mississippi. It was soon discovered that every man but one of those who voted for the charters was concerned in the speculation.   The land was actually sold at about one and a half cents an acre.   Great indignation was aroused among the people of the state. James Jackson, noted for his peppery Republican speeches in Congress, resigned his seat in the federal Senate to lead the fight against the perpetrators of fraud, and the next legislature revoked the franchises.   Such action was later held by the supreme court to be contrary to the clause in the Constitution which forbids a state to violate a contract; but Georgia persisted in her position.   Congress was not prepared to coerce her, and in 1802 the dispute was compromised by a payment of money by the national government to the members of the fraudulent companies.[2]

[1] Haskins, *Yazoo Land Companies* (Am. Hist. Assoc., *Papers*, V.), 414–423.

[2] Donaldson, *Public Domain*, 83–85; see also Haskins, *Yazoo Land Companies* (Am. Hist. Assoc., *Papers*, V.), 414–437.

CHAPTER XIV

POLITICAL AFFAIRS EARLY IN ADAMS'S ADMINISTRATION

(1797–1798)

NO president of the United States ever desired a prosperous and peaceful administration more than John Adams, and none ever fell further short of his wishes. Franklin said of him that he was always honest, often great, and sometimes mad.[1] He himself, with that rare candor which ever characterized an Adams, described his own personality better than another could do it. "I have never," he said, "sacrificed my judgment to kings, ministers, not people, and I never will. When either shall see as I do, I shall rejoice in their protection, aid, and honor: but I see no prospect that either will ever think as I do, and therefore I shall never be a favorite with either."[2] He was tactless, immovable, honest, patriotic, and fearless. He was not a party leader, and knew not how to arouse the enthusiasm of his supporters. He probably saved the country from war, which the Pickering Federalists would

[1] Jefferson, *Writings* (Ford's ed.), V., 104.
[2] John Adams, *Works*, IX., 564.

have precipitated. He did not wreck his party, but
he contributed towards its destruction. His part
in that operation was a passive one. Had he been
another kind of a man he might have guided the
forces which destroyed him; but it was other hands
than his which set the wedge that rent Federalism.

Adams's inaugural address produced a good effect.
From the impression, long ago made on the public,
that he was a monarchist, people waited with interest to see what his ideas would now be. He disappointed those who thought most unfavorably of
him and went out of the way to laud the Constitution. "From an habitual attention to it," he said,
"satisfaction in its administration, and delight in
its effects upon the peace, order, prosperity, and
happiness of the nation, I have acquired an habitual
attachment to it and veneration for it." Dwelling
on the majesty of a people governing themselves, he
exclaimed, "Can anything essential, anything more
than mere ornament and decoration, be added to
this by robes and diamonds?" and this was meant
to meet the charge that he believed in ceremony.[1]

The Republicans received such sentiments as
these with satisfaction. Papers like the *Aurora*
openly commended them. The Hamiltonian Federalists, on the contrary, were alarmed. Their
opposition to Adams in the preceding election had
proceeded from the fact that he was not a good party
man: they never knew what he was going to do.

[1] Richardson, *Messages and Papers*, I., 228.

Could it be that now, in the beginning of his presidency, he was charmed by Jefferson's siren voice?

Jefferson had indeed made attempts in that direction. Knowing Hamilton's opposition to Adams, he hoped to draw the president nearer to the Republicans. December 28, 1796, he wrote Adams a letter and sent it to Madison. He expressed cordial friendship for Adams, and made some pointed references to "your arch friend of New York." In a letter to Madison he held out the idea with apparent honesty that the Republicans could be brought to support Adams's re-election in order to defeat Hamilton.[1] Madison exercised a discretion which was given him and did not present Jefferson's letter to Adams, but the substance of it reached him, and between the two men there sprang up in the weeks preceding the inauguration a good personal understanding. The public observed this development, and some of the Republicans boasted that the lion and the lamb were about to lie down together.[2]

But the Federalist politicians were not willing to return to Washington's non-partisan policy, and soon found means of checking Adams's enthusiasm in that direction. He came into office with a scheme of sending Jefferson or Madison to France as minister, in case Pinckney, who was already there,

---

[1] Jefferson, *Writings* (Ford's ed.), VII., 95, 98, 107, 108 *n;* Tucker, *Jefferson* (ed. of 1837), II., 7–10.

[2] King, *Life and Corresp. of King*, II., 148; Gibbs, *Adminis. of Washington and Adams*, I., 417.

should not be successful. Both of these men expressed themselves as opposed to the appointment.
Jefferson's excuse was his office of vice-president,
and it was a good one; Madison's is not so clear.
He and his party really were unwilling that he should
leave at this time when he would be much needed in the political conflict which was impending.
Adams might have taken some other Republican but
for the opposition of his own cabinet. When he
mentioned his idea to Wolcott a few days after the
inauguration, the latter expressed deep concern and
threatened to resign office.[1] Then the president
realized how deeply his supporters were committed
to a party administration, and he dropped the
matter. Soon afterwards the question of French
relations became decisive, party lines were sharply
drawn, and all hope of co-operation disappeared.

Adams retained Washington's cabinet in office, as
was natural, inasmuch as they really represented
the party better than he. They had been selected
under the influence of Hamilton, and by inclination
they were his supporters; indeed, Pickering and
Wolcott maintained a frequent correspondence with
him. It is singular how often ideas were communi-
cated by Hamilton to one of these men, then discussed in cabinet meeting, and with slight modifi-

---

[1] Jefferson, *Writings* (Ford's ed.), I., 272; John Adams,
Works, VIII., 536 ; Gibbs, *Adminis. of Washington and Adams*,
I., 465; Hamilton, *Works* (Hamilton's ed.), VI., 216–218, 221–
225.

cation included in some forthcoming message to Congress as Adams's policy.[1] John Adams, as the event showed, was not the man to act a nullity; but it took some time for him to realize how deeply he was betrayed in his own house, and when the explosion finally came it was too late to save Federalism from faction. Had Adams felt the inclination and been strong enough to take a new cabinet in the beginning, he would at least have had peace during his administration.

The presidency of Adams marks an increase in the virulence of party antagonism; for Washington was regarded with such popular veneration that the few vehement attacks upon him were deeply resented, and it was considered outrageous for the overcandid Bache to rejoice at his departure from office. For Adams, however, nobody felt reverence, and party abuse had full sway. The whole Republican pack, as soon as it was evident that he would stand by the Federalists, were in full cry after him. Jefferson did not restrain them: he has even been charged with secretly aiding them, but the allegation has not been proved to be true. He has also been criticised for not restraining them, but he was not party dictator. He merely rode at the front of the host, with an eye ever open to see the direction in which they wanted to go. Yet it will always be thought unseemly that the vice-president at this time gave his confidence and apparent approval to

[1] Gibbs, *Adminis. of Washington and Adams*, I., 483.

men who poured out fiercest calumnies on the official who sat next above him.

The most extreme of the Republican pamphleteers was Thomas Callender, a Scotchman who had fled from England to escape punishment for political writings. In Philadelphia he was first a reporter of the proceedings of Congress for the *Philadelphia Gazette*. Losing this position, in 1796 he became a teacher. In the same year he undertook, under the protection of Dallas and other Republicans, to publish the *American Annual Register*, an extravagant partisan history of events in that year. It was totally unreliable, so far as facts are concerned; and even Jefferson, who contributed money to the enterprise, was disappointed. In 1799 he went to Richmond, probably through the suggestion of Jefferson, to become a writer for the *Examiner*. Here he wrote his most scurrilous volume, *The Prospect before Us*. After Jefferson became president, Callender applied for, and was refused, the postmastership at Richmond. He then turned against the Republican president and published as fierce attacks on him as ever he had launched against Hamilton.[1]

An abler man than Callender, and a more moderate one, was William Duane, who became editor of the *Aurora* after the death of Bache in the autumn of 1798.[2] He was an active writer, an earnest believer

---

[1] W. C. Ford in Columbia Hist. Soc., *Records* (Washington, D. C.), VIII., 90–93.

[2] Ford, *Spurious Letters of Washington*, 158 *n*.

in Republican theories, and long one of the most important factors in supporting the cause which he proclaimed.

It was while party feeling was at the highest that the notable Mazzei letter was brought to light. In 1796 Jefferson wrote to Mazzei, an Italian friend, a free and personal account of what the writer thought was the true state of politics in America. It described the growth of aristocracy in the United States and said that Washington and other leaders were throwing themselves into the arms of England. It was translated into Italian and published, then into French and published in Paris, and thence came to New York, where it was turned back into English and published, in order to show that Jefferson was criticising Washington. In its various translations it had lost something of its original meaning; but Jefferson would not give out a correct copy, because he saw that Washington would take offence at certain allusions to the forms of government, and because in order to justify his position he would have to reveal state secrets. Much denunciation of his conduct appeared in the papers. It led to a permanent breach with Washington, but Jefferson did not lose his usual self-possession; he felt rightly that the storm would soon blow over. After all, the charges in the Mazzei letter were no worse than those daily uttered by most Republicans.[1]

Another matter which added flame to political

---

[1] Jefferson, *Writings* (Ford's ed.), VII., 72, 165.

excitement in the summer of 1797 was the recall of
Monroe from Paris. Our representation at Paris
had not been very fortunate under the federal
government. Gouverneur Morris, who was appointed in 1792, was a man of marked ability, but he was
so much out of sympathy with the republic that he
had not the confidence of the government to which
he was accredited. He could give no tone to the
French ideas in regard to America; hence the ministry was thrown entirely into the hands of its own
envoys in Philadelphia, and these took their notions
from the Republicans. Finally, the ministry asked
that Morris be recalled, desiring it as an offset to the
recall of Genêt. He had served through the period
of the Terror, and presented his successor a few
weeks after the fall of Robespierre.[1]

Monroe, who succeeded him, lacked diplomatic
skill. He was a heedless Republican, and he was as
little calculated to keep American interests on a
neutral tack as the aristocratic Morris. He arrived
in Paris in August, 1794, when Jay had just fairly
begun his negotiations in London. Desiring to give
the republic an evidence of American good-will, he
hit upon a singular mode of procedure. The Convention then ruled France and the executive functions were intrusted to a committee of safety, one
member of which was commissary for foreign
affairs. To him Monroe was introduced, but the

[1] Gouverneur Morris, *Diary* (Morris's ed.), I., 501–604; II.,
1–90.

American was told that no form for receiving a minister had been prepared and that some time must elapse before he could be regularly presented. After some days, Monroe decided to address the Convention itself. In a note to the president of the Convention he asked that body to designate how he should be received. In reply they declared that they would receive him themselves. On the following day, August 14, he was introduced to them, received from the president the fraternal embrace in behalf of his nation, and made a most cordial speech in praise of French republicanism. This exhibition of fervor caused some dissatisfaction in England, and the American cabinet disapproved of it in strong terms. At their direction, Randolph wrote a reproof to Monroe, the point of which he neutralized by a private communication written three days later;[1] but the minister changed not his course. If, he said, the American government expected him to reserve his assurances of friendship for private communication to the French executive they were mistaken in their man;[2] and this shows how little of a diplomat he was.

Throughout the following autumn and winter French curiosity was deeply aroused at the nature of the Jay negotiations, and Monroe was urged by his government to keep the French anxiety quiet. He was disingenuously informed by Randolph that Jay

[1] *Am. State Paps., Foreign*, I., 690.
[2] Monroe, *Writings*, II., 40.

was sent to negotiate about the execution of the treaty of 1783, and about indemnity for the seizures of American ships, and was instructed to do nothing "to weaken the engagements between this country and France." Monroe took this as ground for the opinion that Jay had no instructions to make a commercial treaty,[1] and to all the remonstrances of France he replied in the most confiding manner. When the treaty was revealed to France in the summer of 1795, Monroe was so dumfounded that he could only gasp. He did not try to set himself right, and thought himself lucky that the ministry did not call upon him to explain his position. In the autumn he received long instructions from Pickering, giving the grounds on which he ought to defend the treaty. So little had the republic attended to his predicament that he began to fancy that they had forgotten it; and averse to dwelling on his own humiliation he left the explanations undelivered. The French government determined to act without him. In February, 1796, he heard that they were about to send a special envoy to America to negotiate a new treaty, and he roused himself. By urging, he says, the consequences of a breach between the two nations, and by other arguments, he induced the minister to relinquish his purpose. What the other arguments were he does not say; but it is very probable that they had relation to the political situation in America. He was in close

[1] *Am. State Paps., Foreign*, I., 668.

correspondence with the Republicans at home, and he must have known that it had been agreed for some weeks that the treaty should be defeated in the House.[1]

Monroe could not keep his political activity from reaching the ears of the Federalists. It became known that he was furnishing information to the Republican press in America. At the same time France took an aggressive attitude towards our shipping. Hamilton and the cabinet brought to Washington's view the necessity of having a new minister in Paris, and in August, 1796, Monroe was recalled. C. C. Pinckney was appointed in his place, and in December he arrived in Paris.

Monroe welcomed his removal. He had felt for more than a year that Hamilton and the politicians behind the cabinet policies had used him as a pawn to keep France quiet while the Jay treaty was going through the formative processes. He declared that if he were recalled he would publish his instructions and show the whole affair to the public. The Republicans approved of the project. They received him with feasts and justifications. During the summer he busily worked out a statement which was duly submitted to the inspection of Jefferson. It was based on documents connected and explained by an abundance of that casuistry for which the author was noted. It was not completed without

[1] *Am. State Paps.*, *Foreign*, I., 737, 741; Monroe, *Writings*, II., 432, III., 52.

bringing Adams into the controversy. In his recall
he had been told that it was because he had failed to
obey Pickering's instructions in justifying the treaty
and for concurrent reasons. On his return he asked
Adams what the latter grounds might be. In reply
he was told that, as they concerned an administration which had gone out of office, the president did
not feel at liberty to reply. He would have been
glad to have had an avowal from the highest source
that his recall was partly due to political causes, for
it would have placed the controversy clearly in the
realm of politics. He adroitly used Adams's refusal to charge that he was removed for secret reasons. His "View," as he called his defence, makes
no strong impression upon the historian, but it was
well received by the Republican press. Monroe was
pronounced a martyr for his creed, and in 1799 he
was elected governor of Virginia, much to the grati-
fication of Jefferson.[1]

Soon after his arrival in America, Monroe gave
a savage blow to Hamilton, probably in retaliation
for the latter's influence on his recall. In 1792
one Reynolds had been suspected of frauds against
the government, and the affair had taken such a
turn as to suggest that Hamilton was compromised
with him. The evidence was embraced in certain
letters whose real import was far different from

---

[1] Washington, *Writings* (Ford's ed.), XIII., 214, 216 *n;* Monroe, *Writings*, II., 7; Jefferson, *Writings* (Ford's ed.), VII., 190,
322.

what appeared on the surface. The matter was referred to three members of Congress—Monroe, Venable, and Muhlenberg. To them Hamilton owned in confidence that the letters were written in connection with an illicit relation with Mrs. Reynolds, which had been carried on with her husband's knowledge, and by reason of which Hamilton had paid Reynolds about twelve hundred dollars for blackmail. The three men were satisfied, and assured the public that Hamilton was innocent. The papers were placed in Monroe's hands, all promising to keep them secret. To them Monroe added a statement by Reynolds, which was not submitted to Hamilton, the purport of which was to confirm the original charge of complicity in fraud. It was a piece of bad dealing on Monroe's part, and came near involving the two men in a duel at a later date. When Monroe went to France he left the papers in the hands of a friend in Virginia, whose name has never been revealed, but when Callender's *Annual Register* appeared in 1797 they were given to the public. Hamilton called on the three custodians for an explanation. Muhlenberg and Venable promptly and explicitly exonerated themselves, but Monroe halted and shifted his excuses in such a manner that it is evident that he was responsible for the revelation. It is assumed that he disclosed them in revenge for his own sufferings.

Hamilton now took the extraordinary step of publishing a full confession of the whole affair. He spared nothing, but laid bare the whole story of his adultery. Thus he protected his reputation as a public servant at the expense of his reputation as a man. It was wrung out of him with many pangs of anguish, which his opponents observed with delight. They reprinted the confession as a campaign document, and it undoubtedly injured him at the time, although posterity has come to esteem properly the courage which was necessary to make the confession.

While the two parties were thus fencing, political sentiment turned in favor of the Federalists. The congressmen of the day were not chosen on severe party lines, as later; but of those elected in 1796 a majority were conservative men who could be relied on by the Federalists. They came into their seats in May, 1797, being called by Adams in extra session in order to meet a crisis in the foreign relations. No Congress since the first had so much important business to transact as this one. A French war seemed imminent, and, in view of its difficulties, internal politics were cast aside by all but the more pronounced politicians on each side.

CHAPTER XV

THE QUARREL WITH FRANCE
(1796–1797)

ALTHOUGH the text of the Jay treaty contained a clause providing that the agreement should in no way violate our treaty obligations to France, its spirit was, nevertheless, hostile to our treaties of 1778. With England to interpret and a Federalist administration to revise their interpretation, it was not difficult to see that French interests would suffer. The extension of the definition of contraband so as to include materials for equipping ships, the allowance of the right of search, and the permission that British prizes might be brought into American ports, were all taken by France as infringements of her treaties. They were, no doubt, contrary to a spirit of alliance, which the treaties had bound us to observe, but which we had not been required by France strictly to execute.

But the Jay treaty aside, many people by 1797 had come to look upon the perpetual obligations which the French treaties imposed upon the United States as an inconvenience. A few men, and John Adams was one of them, took the same view in

1778;[1] but the needs of America were so great at that time that the French aid was accepted as it was offered, without attempts to modify the conditions. From the outbreak of the war between France and England in 1793 the extreme Federalists hoped that something would occur to justify the repeal of treaties on our part.

France did not leave us to annul the treaties. The Jay compact was published in the Parisian papers about August 15, 1795. For a time no complaint was made, but February 15, 1796, the foreign minister assumed a threatening tone and told Monroe that our English agreement annulled the old French treaties.[2] The clear purpose was to frighten the Americans into a relinquishment of the new connection with England. Monroe's indefinite course in Paris and the communications from Fauchet and Adet, French ministers in Philadelphia, tended to convince them that if France put on a threatening air Americans could be got to vote the Republican ticket in 1796 and reverse the policy of the country. They studiously withheld their intentions till the last hope that the Jay treaty would be defeated was gone, and then in the summer of 1796 they suspended the functions of their minister. He was not ordered home, but left in the country to watch the political situation.[3]

---

[1] *Secret Journals of Congress*, II., 7.

[2] *Am. State Paps., Foreign*, I., 720, 730.

[3] See above, p. 145.

In keeping with the same purpose, France began to punish us by seizing our ships. An order was issued to French privateers and national ships, authorizing them to treat neutral vessels in the manner in which they allowed other belligerents to treat them. If American ships allowed England to seize provisions and ship-supplies as contraband, French ships seized them on the same ground.[1] The indefinite manner in which the French order was stated opened the door to many abuses on the part of the French captains, who, in fact, needed no encouragement of that kind. From the beginning of Washington's second administration there had been complaints that the French were seizing our ships without sufficient grounds, but they were referred to the proper authorities for settlement and no difficulty was apprehended. As the American policy of neutrality was developed and the consequent French wrath at our conduct increased, the seizures became more frequent, and the restraint of the French government upon them seemed to become less vigorous. So far had they gone by January, 1796, that Hamilton thought that we ought to send to France an envoy extraordinary, as Jay had been sent to England, to come to a final settlement with that nation.[2] The order of 1796 was, therefore, not

[1] King, *Life and Corresp. of King*, II., 102, 109; *Annals of Cong.*, 4 Cong., 2769; *Am. State Paps., Foreign*, I., 741.
[2] Hamilton, *Works* (Hamilton's ed.), VI., 84; Washington, *Writings* (Ford's ed.), XIII., 370 *n*.

a sudden departure; it but authorized openly what had been practised covertly for a long time.

Something is to be said for the attitude of France at this time. By her treaty of 1778, contraband had been defined so as not to include provisions; but England never recognized that principle, and since by the Jay treaty we had agreed that provisions might be taken as contraband under certain conditions, she began to take our ships bound to the French ports, on the ground that they were necessary to France as materials of war. The French, therefore, felt that they were treated unequally. England might seize provisions bound to the French West Indies, but France might not seize them bound to the British West Indies. In this contention she was supported by the Republicans in the United States. Her other contention, that by failing to fight England because she impressed our seamen and seized our ships we became contributory to the war, was not so easily justified. She had no right to demand that we enforce our rights in order to safeguard the interests of France.[1]

Another grievance against France grew out of an embargo laid at Bordeaux in 1793, by which a large number of American ships were detained in French ports and their cargoes damaged or taken for the use of the French government. Bills for losses were presented to the authorities, and payment was offered in the depreciated currency of the French

---

[1] King, *Life and Corresp. of King*, II., 146.

republic; but it was refused by the American owners, and the matter remained unsettled and a source
of much annoyance.[1]

While affairs were thus becoming ever more grave,
in June, 1796, an American vessel, the *Mount
Vernon*, was sold in Philadelphia to an English
citizen. He could not register her in his own name,
and she sailed under the registry of her former
owner. She was watched by a French privateer,
The Flying-Fish, who followed her down the Delaware and seized her before she was well out of the
bay. The incident caused some excitement, till it
was understood that the American registry of the
ship was really a fiction.[2] It served to convince
Washington that our relations with France were
becoming critical. It was at this time, before he
knew that France would suspend the functions of
her minister to the United States, that he decided,
on the advice of the cabinet, to send to Paris a
more capable negotiator than Monroe.

Pinckney, Monroe's successor, arrived in Paris
early in December, 1796. Monroe was still exercis-
ing his functions, although he well knew on what
a basis Adet was remaining in Philadelphia. He
received his successor with kindness and put him
in communication with the French foreign office.
Pinckney's credentials were taken with the state-

---

[1] Monroe, *Writings*, II., 88; *Am. State Paps.*, *Foreign*, I.,
749, 753, 757.
[2] Hamilton, *Works* (Hamilton's ed.), VI., 132.

ment that they should be submitted to the Directory, then the French executive power.   A few days later Monroe was informed that France would not receive another American minister till her grievances were redressed.[1]

This left Pinckney in a delicate situation.   A law of the republic, made in the days when most strangers were considered spies, forbade foreigners to remain in France without written permission.   Such permission was promised him, but at the end of two weeks it had not been delivered.   Pinckney then asked if he would be allowed to remain till he could hear from his government.   The reply was noncommittal, and he continued in the country, although he received a broad intimation that he was rendering himself liable to arrest.   He knew full well that the government could not afford to imprison a man whose only offence was that he came in behalf of a sister republic which wanted to preserve peace. He preferred, also, to go, if go he must, with a clear utterance that it was the wish of the ministry.   Such an assurance he finally got on February 3, 1797, when he was officially informed that he had rendered himself liable to arrest by staying two months in the country without permission.   He got passports and left France at once.[2]

The general position of the Directory was at that time a confident one.   After many struggles, France

---

[1] *Am. State Paps., Foreign*, I., 746.
[2] McMaster, *United States*, II., 319–321.

seemed about to become under the new form of government a strong, victorious power in Europe. Napoleon was just winning glory for his country through his Italian victories. The Directory, ignorant of what his career would bring to them, felt able to ignore the rights of, and even the courtesies due to, the weak republic of the west. Their haughty indifference was stimulated by the fact that news from America indicated the election of a Federalist to succeed Washington in the presidency. To make their position clearer, they gave Monroe on his departure the most extravagant expressions of friendship. The world might take notice how little consideration they had for that Federalist agent who still waited at the gate for admission.[1]

When it was understood in America that Pinckney's mission was about to fail, the extreme Federalists became very angry. They would have severed all relations with France; and if this had resulted in universal seizures, which in turn would have brought war, they would have been glad of it. Pickering and the cabinet were disposed to accept this view, but Hamilton and Adams both thought otherwise. They realized that the United States were not ready for war, that they had no navy, and that such a step must have thrown them into close dependence on England, which in itself was a thing full of danger. They preferred to make another effort at negotiation, and while that was going on to

[1] *Am. State Paps., Foreign*, I., 747.

put the country in a better state of defence. They
were able to carry their point in this respect, although they did not get the cabinet to agree that a
Republican should be sent on the new mission.[1]

When full news from Pinckney was received,
Adams called Congress in extra session on May 15,
1797. His speech to it was full of force and of a
sense of national dignity. The Directory, he said,
in expelling Pinckney from French territory, had
treated us "neither as allies, nor as friends, nor as
a sovereign state." He called attention to the evident purpose of the Directory to distinguish between
the people of America and their government, and
declared that the time ought never to come when
the nation should fail to support its chosen agents.
He announced that he would make further efforts
to negotiate, and recommended the consideration of
measures of defence.[2]

On the question before it, Congress found itself
divided into three groups. The extreme Federalists,
led by William Smith and Harper and most of the
New England members, were ready for war. They
were supported also by the cabinet under the leadership of Pickering and Wolcott.[3] The Republicans insisted that the situation was not perilous,
that it had grown up by reason of Federalist mis-

[1] John Adams, *Works*, I., 510, VIII., 535–543; Hamilton,
Works (Hamilton's ed.), VI., 213–225, 229, 234, 238–243.

[2] Richardson, *Messages and Papers*, I., 233.

[3] Gibbs, *Adminis. of Washington and Adams*, I., 465, 502–517;
Hamilton, *Works* (Hamilton's ed.), VI., 216, 221–225.

management, and that proper negotiations would restore it to normal conditions. A third group was composed of moderate men who had usually acted with the Federalists. In the House they were led by Dayton. The Senate was in the hands of the first group, but the third controlled the balance of power in the House and gave direction to the policy of the government. Congress, therefore, was in a position to support Adams's recommendations. The extreme Federalists tempered their ardor while the president's policy was carried out.

It was determined to send three commissioners to France. By common consent one of them must be Pinckney, in view of his recent outrageous treatment there; the others were Marshall, of Virginia, and Dana, of Massachusetts. The Senate promptly confirmed the nominations, but Dana declined to serve. Then Adams seized the opportunity to return to his purpose to put a Republican on the commission. He realized, as Hamilton had realized, the advantage from such an appointment by quieting the clamors of his opponents at home and by lessening the resentment of the French ministry. He turned to Elbridge Gerry, of Massachusetts, who as a New England Republican was not entirely objectionable to the Federalists, and for whom he had a sincere personal esteem. The cabinet and many Federalists thought the appointment a bad one; but it was confirmed, although six of the extremists voted against it. Gerry hesitated about accepting, but Jefferson wrote urging him to take the offer, and he consented.   Adams joined his private persuasion; nothing, he assured Gerry, could ever destroy his confidence in his friend's integrity. The carping critics, however, dubbed Gerry the president's "own ambassador." [1]

In the mean time, Congress took up the situation. Steps were taken to keep the enthusiasm of the country from running into hostilities before the envoys could try to settle affairs.   An act was passed to prohibit the fitting out of privateers against a nation with which we were at peace, and Adams issued orders to prevent merchant-ships from going armed. Bills were also passed to prohibit the exportation of arms, to provide for calling out eighty thousand militia at a moment's notice, to strengthen the fortifications of harbors, and to complete and equip the three frigates which had been built out of the appropriations made for a navy in connection with the Algerine demands.   These ships — the *United States*, the *Constitution*, and the *Constellation*—were heavily armed for their size, the first two having forty-four and the third having thirty-six guns.[2] News of their construction caused much merriment among English and French naval officers, who had not yet acquired that respect for Yankee skill

[1] King, *Life and Corresp. of King*, II., 193; Gibbs, *Adminis. of Washington and Adams*, II., 32; John Adams, *Works*, VIII., 549.
[2] *U. S. Statutes at Large*, I., 350, 523.

which these frigates were destined to do much to establish.

Having thus taken steps to meet hostilities if they should come, and having put forth a last and most formal effort to settle the difficulty amicably, Adams was now in a position to await news from the envoys. The real interests of the country demanded peace: no one could tell what internal catastrophe a French war would bring. Some of the wisest men in the nation believed that in the existing state of feeling a large part of the people, especially those of the south, would refuse to fight our old ally, and possibly might secede from the Union and enter into an alliance with her. If this danger was not imminent, it was nevertheless evident that much of the feeling for an immediate declaration was pure braggadocio. The country was in no condition for war: it lacked material and organization, and public sentiment was not united. If Adams's course should not lead to peace, it would at least serve to unite the people in an active support of whatever decision might then be made, and it would give time to make necessary preparations. This was the idea of Hamilton, who at this time kept a firm grasp on the situation. "Real firmness," he wrote to Wolcott on June 6, "is good for everything. Strut is good for nothing." Whether his motives were patriotic, or prompted by a desire to organize that military establishment which a year later he is known to have so much at heart, his view of the situation in the summer of 1797 was a wise one.

He continually advocated moderation, supporting Adams and restraining the unreasoning zeal of the cabinet group.[1]

[1] Gibbs, *Adminis. of Washington and Adams*, I., 483 – 491; Hamilton, *Works* (Hamilton's ed.), VI., 216, 221, 239, 241, 247.

CHAPTER XVI

WAR OR PEACE

(1797–1798)

THE three American commissioners arrived in
Paris in October, 1797. The Directory ruled
the nation, but Talleyrand was the French foreign
minister. To him the envoys now brought their
affairs; but his stay in America had not given him
very pleasant notions of the people or of their government. He was closely associated with the rising
power of Napoleon, who had begun to undermine
the power of the Directory. An overbearing policy
towards the smaller states of Europe was already
adopted, and the Directory, corrupt to the core,
had established the practice of taking bribes from
whatever state or private interest could be benefited
by its action. Talleyrand, therefore, thought that
the arrival of the Americans would afford another
opportunity to fill his own coffers; and after that
was done he was prepared to open the game of
diplomatic fence which he knew so well how to
conduct.

His first move accorded with this purpose. He
delayed a formal reception of the commissioners, as

he might well do under the pretext that it was necessary to determine what policy should be employed.
In the mean time, three persons, designated later in
the despatches as X, Y, and Z, called on the envoys
as agents of the minister. They spoke of the difficulties to be overcome. The speech of Adams to
Congress in May, 1797, they said, must be explained,
and France would expect a large loan for public use.
Then they suggested that a gift of two hundred and
forty thousand dollars to the Directory would facili-
tate negotiations. The reply of the commissioners
was positive. They were not authorized or disposed to give a bribe. They put the proposition
aside as unworthy and went on to discuss the other
terms. The United States, they said, were determined to be neutral, and to lend France money at
this time would be to take part in the war. Then the
agents tried to play on the fears of the envoys—let
them remember the fate of Venice; let them consider
that French diplomacy could reach even to the internal affairs of America, where it could throw the
French party on the British party and change the
character of the government. To this the reply
was that France might possibly ravage our coasts,
but that she could not destroy our nation as she
had destroyed Venice. And thus with the bandy-
ing of words on each side the conversations were
carried on till one day the agents cried out: "Gentlemen, you do not speak to the point. It is money;
it is expected that you will offer money." To which

the envoys replied that they had already answered that. "No," said X, "you have not; what is your answer?" "It is," said the Americans, "No, no; not a sixpence." [1]

November 1 the envoys decided to deal no more with X, Y, and Z. They prepared a complete statement of our case against France and sent it to Talleyrand. The seizure of American ships, the embargo laid at Bordeaux, the operation of the Jay treaty on our treaties with France, and many more matters which we charged against that nation were all set down in the vigorous language of Marshall, who drew up the document. It made no impression on the Directory, but it served a good purpose when, a few months later, it was published in America.

Marshall's statement was submitted to Talleyrand about January 17, 1798. Two months later the minister replied. He summed up the French contentions and added some expressions of contempt. He said that we had purposely prolonged the misunderstanding and that we selected envoys known to be prejudiced against France. Why, he asked, did we not do as well by the republic as we did by England when we sent Jay, a known partisan, to make a treaty? He had the hardihood to add, in closing his letter, that he desired to treat through Gerry alone. It was a vulgar way to dismiss the conferences, worthy of the crude but strong spirit of a government which knew little of the courtesy

[1] *Am. State Paps., Foreign*, II., 158–160.

of that fine old French society which it had overwhelmed.[1]

The commissioners now realized that all hope of
success was gone.   They protested that no one of
them could take on himself to negotiate alone, and
prepared to leave the country.   Marshall's passports were given him grudgingly, and Pinckney, with
some difficulty, got permission to remain for a while
in southern France for the benefit of the health of his
daughter.

Gerry was invited by Talleyrand to remain and
continue communications; and disregarding the ob-
jections of his colleagues he accepted the invitation.
He announced to the minister, however, that he
would remain only as a private citizen.   He was
made to believe that France was about to declare
war, and that his influence might be useful to prevent such a step.   He was honest and patriotic,
but his decision was highly imprudent.   It gave the
French government ground to carry on its intrigue
with the Republican party for influence, and was
calculated to make them believe that America was
divided on the question before it.   Nothing but a
united stand was worthy of our representatives.
In the United States, Gerry's action was severely
condemned; even Adams lost patience with him
and ordered him to come home as quickly as possible.   He was able to convince the president that he
had acted innocently, and posterity has been in-

[1] *Am. State Paps., Foreign*, II., 188–191.

clined to make allowances for him; but his conduct discredits him as a man of judgment.[1]

Did the Directory desire war with America? All the evidence points to a negative answer; for war would merely deliver us into the arms of England, with our supplies of provisions and our active merchant marine. Talleyrand was not accustomed to muddle his diplomacy in order to gratify his prejudices. His real purpose was probably to frighten the Americans into a relinquishment of the newly formed connection with England, to help the Republicans get into power, and, by leaving the French privateers to continue their depredations on our commerce, to draw into his own hands a large supply of provisions. It did not displease him that the losses of Americans on this score would fall chiefly upon that part of the American people who were stanchly Federalist. For all her bluster, France took no step towards war.

In the mean time, public opinion in America awaited the results of the negotiations. Congress went languidly through the routine of the session. Measures of defence and money bills were contemplated, but nothing could be decided till news came from France. December passed without news, and then January came and went. With February men began to breathe more easily—no news, they said, was good news, for if the prospect were not favorable the envoys would have found some way of letting it

[1] Gordy, *Political Parties*, I., 311.

be known.[1] Then March came. On the 4th, Adams
received despatches covering events up to the first
of the year. A hasty examination showed that they
were unfavorable. Without waiting for a full trans-
lation, he sent, on the next day, a message to Congress giving an indication of what might be expected.[2]

Developments now strengthened in a striking
manner the hands of the war party. Pickering, at
the head of the cabinet circle, wanted an immediate
declaration, and was only restrained by the argument that such a step would endanger the lives of
our commissioners still in France.[3] But Adams
remained self-possessed. To ask for a bribe, and
otherwise to insult our representatives, was highly
humiliating, but it violated no interest in whose
behalf a weak nation would be warranted in beginning a burdensome war. It was for us, and so
Adams thought, to wait for France to declare the
war, and to accept it as a brave people, if she chose
to bring it on. In the mean time, we ought to be
preparing for hostilities. In these views Adams was
supported by Hamilton, who was in close touch
with Pickering and Wolcott, and his views tended
to moderate the spirit of the cabinet.[4]

Congress and the country were deeply impressed

[1] Jefferson, *Writings* (Ford's ed.), VII., 204, 213.
[2] Richardson, *Messages and Papers*, I., 263.
[3] Hamilton, *Works* (Hamilton's ed.), VI., 272–278.
[4] Richardson, *Messages and Papers*, I., 264; Hamilton, *Works*
(Hamilton's ed.), VI., 269–271.

by the turn affairs had taken. The Federalists pressed confidently for additions to the navy and army, and the Republicans were in terror lest in the excitement of the moment the Federalists should get all they wanted. Jefferson proposed to adjourn till passions were cooled, but his voice was not heard above the commotion. Adams's recommendations he called an "insane message."[1] Then the Republicans challenged the correctness of the message, and Congress asked to see the correspondence. Adams complied on April 3, withholding only the names of the agents who had dealt with the envoys, for which he substituted the letters X, Y, and Z. Even the Federalists, when all was revealed, were astonished at the insulting conduct of Talleyrand.[2] They voted to publish the whole correspondence, and soon the country was in a flame of indignation comparable only to that which had greeted the Jay treaty. Adams had managed the affair with ability and temper, and the people recognized it. In one of his messages to Congress he said, "I will never send another minister to France without assurances that he will be received, respected, and honored as the representative of a free, powerful, and independent nation."[3] This sentiment exactly expressed the feelings of the country. In Congress the moderates came to his support, and

[1] Jefferson, *Writings* (Ford's ed.), VII., 219, 221.
[2] *Annals of Cong.*, 5 Cong., 1374.
[3] Richardson, *Messages and Papers*, I., 266.

both Houses were safely committed to any policy of vigor which he would recommend. The Republicans became discouraged, and some of them went to their homes in order to do what they could to resist the tide of Federalism that was sweeping over the land.

Twenty acts were passed between March 27 and July 16, 1798, for strengthening the national defence. One of them established a navy department, at the head of which Benjamin Stoddert, of Maryland, was placed; others provided for equipping the three new frigates, and for purchasing or building twelve armed vessels and ten galleys. Adams had already removed the restriction on the arming of merchant vessels; and Congress now gave them the right to defend themselves, and empowered the president to allow the national ships to take French vessels which interfered with our commerce. Under these rules it was possible for United States ships to take French privateers and even vessels of war without a formal declaration of war. Congress also, to the great joy of many Federalists, on July 7, 1798, repealed the existing treaties with France. No longer were we bound by treaty in a defensive alliance with a European power.[1]

Among measures of defence were bills to enlarge the army. A new regiment of artillery was authorized, and the president was given authority to enlist for three years ten thousand volunteers. Ham-

[1] *U. S. Statutes at Large*, I., 5 Cong., Statute II.

ilton had hoped that the number would be twenty thousand; but the antipathy for a permanent army was so great that his plans could not be realized.[1]

The ships of the new navy were soon at sea. In December they numbered fourteen men-of-war properly armed, and eight converted merchant-men. Some of them were small, but most of them were fast and well manned. They were well able to deal with the French privateers; and the frigates, the pride of the fleet, showed that they could meet successfully ships of equal size from the French navy. Squadrons were stationed in the West Indies, where our commerce suffered most, with orders to seize privateers wherever found.

While on this service the *Constellation*, commanded by Captain Thomas Truxtun, fell in with the French frigate *L'Insurgente* on February 9, 1799. Truxtun gave chase boldly; the Frenchman tried to escape, but finding that impossible, came to, raised the tricolor, and offered battle. The *Constellation* outmanœuvred the *L'Insurgente*, kept her in an unfavorable position, and after a hot fight of an hour and a quarter forced her to surrender. The French captain was under orders not to fire on the American flag, and had avoided the fight as long as possible. When he came aboard the *Constellation* he cried: "Why have you fired on the national flag? Our two nations are at peace." But Trux-

[1] Hamilton, *Works* (Hamilton's ed.), VI., 269–271.

tun only replied, "You are my prisoner." [1]   The
American people received the news with great
satisfaction.   The *L'Insurgente* had made many
annoying seizures of American merchant-men, and
it was good to think that vengeance had been satisfied.

Other engagements followed this.   In February,
1800, the *Constellation* fought a drawn battle with
the French ship *La Vengeance*, of slightly superior
size; in October, 1800, the *Boston* captured the
Berceau, and in the same year Lieutenant Isaac
Hull daringly cut a handsome new privateer out of
a port in Santo Domingo.   This period of retaliation
lasted for two and a half years and cost France
eighty-four vessels, most of which were privateers.[2]
The part taken in it by our navy was very creditable.
It aroused enthusiasm at home and won respect
abroad.   The patience with which France bore our
sharp resistance shows how little she was inclined to
war.

While the navy was winning honors at sea, the
affairs of the new army were getting into a disgrace-
ful muddle.   Although it was voted for only three
years, the Federalists hoped to make it a permanent
thing, and Hamilton, who had persistently declined
to re-enter civil office, did all he could to get high
command in it.   He was eminently qualified for
the position; but if he held the views he was popu-
larly supposed to hold about the weakness of a re-

[1] Maclay, *Hist. of the Navy*, I., 177.   [2] *Ibid.*, 213.

public and the necessity for a strong government
in the United States, his ambition assumes a sinister
form.   For commander-in-chief all eyes turned to
Washington.   Adams was somewhat nettled because
his own position as head of the army seemed to
be ignored, but he made the nomination in good
spirit.

Washington was too old to take an active part in
campaigns; he accepted the command on condition
that he should not be called on for service till it was
absolutely necessary.   Hamilton's friends brought
many arguments to bear on him in behalf of their
plans.   Hamilton himself urged that the administration had no policy and could not carry on the
war of itself; McHenry, the secretary of war, and
Pickering urged that the whole country wanted
Hamilton for second place, and Washington, who
had supreme confidence in Hamilton, agreed with
them.   All these matters were gone over in a long
conversation with McHenry, the upshot of which
was that Washington insisted that he should have
the right to name his own staff.   The determination suited the purposes of the cabinet exactly, and
it was with satisfaction that they saw him send to
Adams the names of Hamilton, Pinckney, and Knox
for the three major-generalships which came next
to his own office.   Adams duly forwarded the
names to the Senate as he had received them,
though he resented the pressure in favor of Hamilton, and they were confirmed.   Immediately after-

wards the president went to his home in Massachusetts.[1]

Knox and Pinckney had both outranked Hamilton
in the old army, where the last-named was only a
lieutenant-colonel. Knox's friends, and there were
many of them in New England, began to say that
he would rank in the new army according to his old
standing. But the friends of Hamilton asserted in
reply that the rank would be according to the order
in which the names were sent to the Senate. The
newspapers discussed the matter warmly, and Knox
referred it to Adams, who decided that the old rank
should be followed, and sent orders to that effect to
Philadelphia, where they produced consternation.
Letters were immediately sent to Washington, who
wrote a strong protest to Adams. In the face of
this situation Adams relented, and Hamilton became the second man in the army and was named
inspector-general. Knox refused his commission;
and thus another section of the Federalist party
was arrayed in opposition to the brilliant New-
Yorker.[2] Adams was conscious of the intrigue
which had gone on, and wrote a sharp reprimand to
McHenry for his part in it.[3] It was already dividing
the Federalist party, and its effects were destined
to be more serious as the months went by.

[1] Washington, *Writings* (Ford's ed.), XIV., 8, 29, 33, 40, 92–
104; Hamilton, *Works* (Hamilton's ed.), VI., 290–294, 326, 327.
[2] Hamilton, *Works* (Hamilton's ed.), VI., 322, 325–346; Washington, *Writings* (Ford's ed.), XIV., 58, 65, 92.
[3] John Adams, *Works*, VIII., 587, 588 *n*, 593.

Hamilton's desire to get control of the army was but incident to a large plan of expansion which he had formed. "It is a pity, my dear sir," he wrote to McHenry, "and a reproach, that the administration has no general plan. Certainly there ought to be one formed without delay. If the chief is too desultory, his ministers ought to be more united and steady." His own policy, he added, would be to maintain a regular army and navy, then to get possession of Louisiana and Florida, and all the time "to squint at South America." [1] He was at that time deeply committed to the intrigues of Miranda in behalf of the freedom of the Spanish colonists. [2]

But the easy-going McHenry stood in the way of this policy of expansion. Left to himself, it was a question when the regiments would be ready for service. Hamilton, without the slightest hesitation, planned to supersede in part the functions of the secretary, and thus to secure administrative energy. "Scruples of delicacy," he wrote to McHenry, had long kept him from speaking, but he could delay no more. He saw that the work of the department was too heavy for one man. Part of it ought to be put upon the new major-generals, and he would take the recruiting of the new regiments. To Washington he wrote more plainly, and the commander-in-chief acknowledged McHenry's unfitness and prom-

[1] Hamilton, *Works* (Hamilton's ed.), V., 283.
[2] See below, p. 283.

ised to use his influence in behalf of Hamilton's
scheme.[1]   But the secretary was not so dull that he
was willing to admit a hand like Hamilton's to the
workings of the department, and nothing came of
the interference.

In November, 1798, the staff met Washington in
Philadelphia to select the officers for the new army.
He was much annoyed by political recommendations, for he had his own ideas about the selection
of his subordinates.   They ought to be, he said,
experienced Revolutionary officers of good present
conduct, or gentlemen of character, education, and
bravery; and all violent Republicans ought to be
avoided because they would produce dissensions.[2]
If only Federalists had been given commissions, the
war would have been a partisan affair from the beginning.

The indifference of the president to the raising of
an army became more and more manifest as the
weeks went by.   He felt no desire to aid Hamilton's
plans.   The state of the finances and the increasing
possibility that war could be avoided strengthened
this inclination.   When McHenry undertook to
press the recruiting of soldiers, Adams exclaimed:
"Regiments are costly articles everywhere, and
more so in this country than in any other under
the sun.   And if this country sees a great army

---

[1] Washington, *Writings* (Ford's ed.), XIV., 65; Hamilton,
Works (Hamilton' ed.), V., 138, VI., 333, 334, 337.
[2] Washington, *Writings* (Ford's ed.), XIV., 118 *n*.

to maintain, without an enemy to fight, there may arise an enthusiasm that seems to be little foreseen." [1]

After much delay, Hamilton got the recruiting under way in the spring of 1799, a full year after the reception of the X, Y, Z despatches. Enthusiasm was then gone and volunteers came so slowly that Troup could say, "The army is progressing like a wounded snake." The half-formed camps became the scenes of discontent, desertion was common, sometimes the soldiers did not receive their pay promptly, the officers got furloughs with ease, and the general condition of the force was such that Washington was disgusted.[2] All the time the Republicans let no opportunity escape to convince the country that no army was necessary, and in time many people became convinced that the great establishment was but a Federalist dream. "We are preparing for a war," said Monroe, "which does not exist, expending millions which will have no other effect than to bring it on us."[3]

Long before a regiment was enlisted, information was received in America that France would not make war. King sent such news to Hamilton and Pickering, but they heeded it not. Gerry arrived in the autumn of 1798, bringing assurances from

---

[1] Washington, *Writings* (Ford's ed.), XIV., 176 *n.*

[2] Hamilton, *Works* (Hamilton's ed.), V., 199–208, 239, 253, 263, 334; Washington, *Writings* (Ford's ed.), XIV., 208.

[3] Monroe, *Writings*, III., 120; King, *Life and Corresp. of King*, II., 597.

Talleyrand that war was not desired, but he was a discredited Republican and his words were lost. His report to Adams, which he counted on for his defence to the public, remained unpublished for months in the hands of Pickering, although the Republicans sarcastically called for its submission.[1]

Then came the "mission" of Dr. Logan. He was a Philadelphia Quaker, a man of social influence, and a Republican. He went to Paris, as it seems, to endeavor to get the government to do something which should show that it was inclined to peace. Federalist papers announced that he had gone to give treasonable information to the French to be used in the coming war. He succeeded in securing the release of some American prisoners taken by privateers, and he made earnest efforts to show Talleyrand how disastrous the recent French policy had been for the interest of France in the United States. The minister received him with marked respect, and he returned to America with the conviction that his journey had been successful. The affair caused much bitter comment. It was looked upon as a partisan interference in foreign affairs, and in that sense it was undoubtedly imprudent; but in a day when each party had its close foreign alignment it was not so much to be condemned as later. The Federalists carried a law in the follow-

[1] Jefferson, *Writings* (Ford's ed.), VII., 316; John Adams, *Works*, VIII., 616, 617; IX., 7.

ing session to forbid such interference in diplomacy by a citizen, and Washington gave Logan a plain evidence of his contempt, saying that it was singular that an unaccredited stranger could find out more of Talleyrand's intentions than three accredited ministers, and that if France really wanted peace, let her stop seizing our ships.   But Adams received Logan more considerately, and obtained from his report a definite impulse towards reconciliation with the French republic.[1]

In October, 1798, Adams received official assurances that Talleyrand was willing to resume regular intercourse.   That sagacious diplomat had already seen that he had gone too far.   Through the French representative in Holland he opened communications with William Vans Murray, minister at The Hague.   Murray reported that he was assured that a minister would be received if one were sent. Adams received this information in Massachusetts, forwarded it to Pickering, secretary of state, and asked him to sound the cabinet on two questions: ought we to declare war on France if she did not declare it on us? and should a new minister be sent? But the conclave budged not, and advised the president against sending a new minister.   When his annual message to Congress was delivered, Adams showed that he had not taken this advice.   Although he spoke in a firm tone of the situation with

[1] Jefferson, *Writings* (Ford's ed.), VII., 273, 325; Washington, *Writings* (Ford's ed.), XIV., 130.

regard to France, he said that we ought not to close all avenues of peace.[1]

The intriguers came to the Congress which met in December, 1798, with a good heart. The newly organized party caucus gave them a strong control over the party majority in Congress. They hoped to strengthen their plans by creating the office of general of the army, which would reduce the military power of the president to a shadow. When Sedgwick announced this to Adams the latter cried: "What! are you going to appoint him general over the president? I have not been so blind that I have not seen a combined effort among those who call themselves the friends of government, to annihilate the essential powers given to the president."[2]

For some months John Adams had been thrust into the background of his own administration. He now took matters into his own hands, and till the end of his presidency became the initiative force in its policies. On February 18, 1799, while measures of defence were being busily prepared and while the call for volunteers was being published to the country, he sent to the Senate the nomination of William Vans Murray to be minister to France. He announced that he had reasons to believe that a minister would be received, but that he would not allow him to go to Paris till he was assured from the

[1] Richardson, *Messages and Papers*, I., 271.
[2] Hamilton, *Works* (Hamilton's ed.), VI., 392–394.

French government that he would be received in a proper way.

This nomination fell on the Federalist leaders like a thunderbolt. "Surprise, indignation, grief, and disgust," said Cabot, "followed each other in quick succession in the breast of every true friend of our country."[1] Sedgwick said, "Had the foulest heart and the ablest head in the world been permitted to select the most embarrassing and ruinous measures, perhaps it would have been the one which has been adopted."[2] "We have all been shocked and grieved," said Pickering; and Hamilton said that the message would astonish him, if anything from Adams could produce that effect.[3] But the politicians were bagged; they must submit to the turn which affairs had now taken. They suggested that three commissioners be sent instead of one, and to this Adams consented. Ellsworth, Patrick Henry, and Murray were confirmed by the Senate for the proposed mission, but when the second refused to leave the country at his advanced age, W. R. Davie, of North Carolina, was appointed in his stead.

The abrupt method in which Adams announced his purpose to the world was justified by him on the ground that it was necessary in order to break the force of the intriguers. A calmer judgment, however, is that he would have done better to submit

[1] King, *Life and Corresp. of King*, II., 551.
[2] Washington, *Writings* (Ford's ed.), XIV., 156 *n.*
[3] Hamilton, *Works* (Hamilton's ed.), VI., 397, 398.

his plan to the cabinet in due course and then have
done as he chose.   That he shrank from such a plan is
indicative of his whole course in regard to his advisers: he knew not how to master men or to with-
stand their arguments.   Had he been otherwise, he
might have taken a ruling attitude in the beginning;
and this would have prevented much of the friction which the activity of outside influences was
making.   His action in February, 1799, was the
nervous up-flaring of courage on the part of one
who had retreated for a long time before dangers
which he was too timid to encounter with bold-
ness.

In May, 1799, word came that Talleyrand promised
to receive the commissioners, and Adams ordered
them to be despatched.   But the conclave had not
given up their purpose to delay, in the hope that war
might yet be brought on.   A change had just occurred in the French Directory, and Pickering affected to believe that this might alter their attitude towards the United States.   He postponed the
execution of the president's orders till Stoddert and
Charles Lee, two members of the cabinet who had
been gradually losing sympathy with Pickering,
wrote to Adams in Massachusetts saying that his
presence was needed.   The latter grasped the situation and wrote that nothing was to be done about the
French envoys till he arrived, and at once he started southward.   Pickering received this information
with satisfaction.   He interpreted it to mean some

change in the president's purpose to despatch the commissioners.[1]

When Adams arrived, on October 10, he observed the confident tone of the conclave. He noticed, also, that Hamilton and Ellsworth had come on as if to be where their presence might be of most service to their plans. Once more he determined to teach his opponents a lesson. In a long cabinet meeting he said nothing about postponing the mission; but he went over carefully and approved the instructions to be given the commissioners and ordered Pickering to despatch them at once.[2]

When the envoys met in Paris a change had occurred in the French government. The strong hand and wise head of Napoleon had replaced the corrupt and foolish Directory. The policy of nursing a French interest in America, which for seven years had been followed by Republican leaders in Paris, was now abandoned. The relations between the two nations were put upon the grounds of national dignity and national interests. No trouble was discovered in making such an agreement as secured neutrality and reasonable protection to commerce. When Davie returned late in 1800 with the completed treaty he was received with satisfaction. The Republicans were pleased because it brought assurances of peace with France. The Federalists found in it the consolation that the old treaties of 1778 were superseded. It was, in fact, a blessing that we had peace, and that

---

[1] John Adams, *Works*, IX., 25–29.   [2] *Ibid.*, I., 553–559.

we were no longer bound to another nation by so embarrassing an arrangement as our old French alliance; but the repeal of the old treaty cost us the spoliation claims, for Napoleon insisted that both should stand or fall together. The Senate hesitated: it ratified for eight years, and reserved our right to indemnity; but the matter was prolonged till the Federalists were out of office, and December 19, 1801, the treaty was ratified with indemnity left out. The claims have never been paid by France.[1]

As for Adams, he probably saved the country from war, and possibly from a train of internal dissensions through the machinations of Hamilton. He thought that this was his best public service, and long afterwards said that he desired no other epitaph than this: "Here lies John Adams, who took upon himself the responsibility of peace with France in the year 1800.".[2]

[1] McMaster, *United States*, II., 529, 606.
[2] John Adams, *Works*, X., 113.

CHAPTER XVII

ALIEN AND SEDITION ACTS
(1797–1798)

WHILE the attention of the public was so largely directed, in the years 1797 and 1798, to warlike measures, purely political affairs of much importance were happening. The predominance of the Federalists in Congress and in the country suggested to the leaders of the party that they might do what they pleased. It was a temptation of power to which the wisest of them yielded. Their idea that government should be in the hands of the capable classes might now for the first time in the history of the new government be put into operation. To those who held this theory it seemed, also, that never before had there been such a need for the operation of the theory. Never before had officials been so profanely denounced. To make matters worse, much of the abuse was uttered by foreigners; and since war with France was imminent it was concluded that these aliens were but agents of that nation. Most of the nations of the world had laws against seditious libels, and England in 1793 had made severe restriction in that respect.

It was arguments like these which induced the
Federalists to conclude that the government ought
to restrict the political activity of aliens and to punish the ranters who made false charges and who intended to degrade in public opinion the highest
officers in the land.   In this they did not go beyond
the government then existing in France, so much the
object of veneration to their opponents.   For even
Pinckney found that an alien could not dwell in
France without license, and one can easily imagine
what would have happened to a man in France who
undertook to organize a party opposed to the existing authority at any time from 1792 to 1814.   Of
course these things do not extenuate the repressive
measures of the party in power, measures out of
place in any government which had well-organized
parties and universal suffrage.   They merely account
for a course of action which on any other grounds
seems sheer madness.

The first notable political incident of the period
mentioned was turned to the advantage of the Federalists.   William Blount, a Republican senator
from Tennessee, was taken in 1797 in a conspiracy
to organize in connection with British assistance a
filibustering expedition against Florida.   The British
minister declared that his government had taken no
part in the plot; but it was clear that Blount was
guilty of scheming against the neutral rights of
Spain.   In the short extra session of 1797 he was
expelled from the Senate, impeached, and the trial

was set for the next session. Before that time he was elected to the Tennessee assembly, where he was made president of the Senate. As an official in the legislature of a sovereign state he denied the jurisdiction of the United States over him, refused to attend the summons to trial, and the case was dropped. He lived in undiminished popularity in his own state till 1810.[1] Blount could not be defended even by his own partisans, and the incident gave some basis for the Federalists to say that the Republicans were tainted with treason.

Less justifiable was the treatment of Matthew Lyon by the Federalists. This member of the House of Representatives from Vermont was an Irishman, a Republican of fierce temper, unconventional in appearances, but fearless and persistent in expressing his views. He attracted attention when he asked to be excused from the slavish custom of going in procession with the whole House to present the reply to the president's annual speech. He was made the butt of much contempt from the opposition. One of their gibes was to revive a story that he had been cashiered in the old army and compelled to carry a wooden sword. January 30, 1798, Griswold, of Connecticut, repeated this charge to Lyon's face under certain irritating circumstances while the House was assembled informally. The Vermonter, instantly in a passion, spat in the face of his opponent, who tried to strike him but was pre-

[1] Wharton, *State Trials*, 200–321.

vented by his opponents.   The Federalists now proposed to expel Lyon; but the Republicans, while
not condoning his offence, thought the penalty too
severe.   They were willing to vote for a reprimand,
although they insisted that the affair was not properly within their jurisdiction, because it was committed while the House was not in session.   The
Federalists declared for expulsion but on the final
vote failed to get the necessary two-thirds majority.

Griswold then undertook to right what he conceived his own wrongs.   February 15 he attacked
Lyon with a heavy stick as the speaker was about
to call to order.   The latter seized a pair of tongs
to defend himself; the two grappled and fell scram-
bling to the floor.   Quiet was restored only when
the speaker called the House to order.   There was
much excitement, and the Republicans moved that
both combatants be expelled; but the Federalists
rallied to the support of Griswold, who was a man
of influence among them.   They urged that as the
affair occurred before the House was in session no
notice could be taken of it; and here both sides were
content to let it rest.   This incident well illustrates
the air of contempt with which the Federalists were
accustomed at this time to treat their Democratic
opponents.[1]

To people who had been accustomed to the formal
dignity of colonial and Revolutionary government,
the crude campaigning of the day was very dis-

[1] *Annals of Cong.*, 5 Cong., 955–1058.

tasteful. It was an offence that a number of the most active pamphleteers were men who had recently come to America, some of them being Frenchmen, as Collot and Volney, while some others were Englishmen who had been forced to leave England on account of their republicanism. Of the latter were Dr. Priestly, Thomas Cooper, William Cobbett, and the elder Gales. That such men, aliens as they were, should be converted in the twinkling of an eye into champions of American liberty seemed a little too much for those who remembered the sacrifices of the Revolution.

A still more glaring offence was the great extravagance of partisan denunciation. About six weeks before the passage of the sedition act, Chief-Justice McKean, of Pennsylvania, an ardent Republican, described this abuse in his charge in the case against Cobbett as follows: "Every one who has in him the sentiments of either a Christian or gentleman, cannot but be highly offended at the envenomed scurrility that has raged in pamphlets and newspapers, printed in Philadelphia for several years past, insomuch that libelling has become a kind of national crime, and distinguishes us not only from all the states around us, but from the whole civilized world. Our satire has been nothing but ribaldry and Billingsgate: the contest has been, who could call names in the greatest variety of phrases, who could mangle the greatest number of characters; or who could excel in the magnitude and virulence of their lies. Hence the honor of families has been stained; the highest posts rendered cheap and vile in the sight of the people, and the greatest services and virtue blasted." [1]

It was the Federalists who undertook to right matters by law; and in doing so they carried injustice far beyond the limits reached by the scribblers. They decided to deal with the political aliens and to stop the publication of seditious libels. Three principal measures grew out of this determination.

First they took up the question of naturalization. A law of 1795 had given this privilege to aliens resident in the country for five years. Some of the Federalists would have withdrawn the process altogether; but the Constitution used such words in giving Congress the power that it was doubtful if such a position could be maintained. The best they could do, therefore, was to fix the requirement at a long term. It was enacted on June 18, 1798, that fourteen years of residence and a declaration of intention five years before the application should be necessary to naturalization; but the law was not to apply to those who had already arrived in the country. This drastic law was repealed in 1802, when the old law of 1795 was essentially re-enacted. [2]

The law was passed while the country was in a ferment of excitement over the publication of the X, Y, Z papers. Just as it was finally approved,

[1] Wharton, *State Trials*, 322.
[2] *U. S. Statutes at Large*, I., 103, 414.

Marshall arrived from France with his hands filled with the fuel for a great popular conflagration, and declaring that France would soon announce war. The Federalists felt strong enough for anything, and they proceeded to devise a means of dealing with the objectionable aliens already in the country. Two laws were passed, one applying to aliens in time of peace, and one to enemy aliens in time of war. By the former the president was given the power to order out of the country any alien whom he thought dangerous to the public peace or whom he had reasonable grounds to suspect of plotting against the government. If an alien did not obey the law he might be imprisoned for three years, and if he returned after leaving he was to be imprisoned at the will of the president. The enemy alien act gave the president the power in a state of war to arrest, imprison, and banish all enemy aliens whom he might think dangerous. The worst feature of these laws was the extent of the power that they left to the president. "The poor aliens," as the Republicans called them, were placed at his mercy; but since they could have no standing in the courts, it was necessary to create some authority for the enforcement of the law, and Congress considered that the president, through his marshalls, could best execute it.[1] Like the sedition law, it was a temporary measure, passed in view of the expected war, and in its own terms was limited to two years

[1] *U. S. Statutes at Large*, I., 570, 577.

duration. Many Frenchmen left the country in anticipation of the law; and we may believe that it was chiefly planned *in terrorem*, for in not a single case was it applied.

The sedition act, which was carried through Congress a little behind the alien acts, was intended to deal with citizens or aliens who too severely criticised the government. Like the alien acts, it originated in the Senate, where Federalism was most rampant. In its original form it was made illegal to justify the present attitude of France, or to imply that the administration acted contrary to the Constitution or to the liberties and happiness of the people. Twelve out of a possible thirty-two senators voted for this feature of the bill. In its final shape it was made a high misdemeanor "unlawfully to combine and conspire" in order to oppose the legal measures of the government, or in order to prevent a federal officer from executing his office, or with such purpose "to commit, advise, or attempt to procure any insurrection, riot, or unlawful assembly, or combination." The penalty was to be a fine not exceeding five thousand dollars and imprisonment not exceeding five years. To publish a false or malicious writing against the government of the United States, the president, or Congress, with the purpose of stirring up hatred or resistance against them, or to incite any foreign nation to war against the United States, was made a misdemeanor punishable by fine of not more than two thousand dollars and imprisonment not longer than two years. The accused was allowed the benefit of trial, and the majority consented with reluctance to allow him to prove the truth of the words charged as seditious. The latter concession, however, was largely nullified by the fact that he could not prove his charges without going into an elaborate investigation of the conduct of the officials, and also by the fact that he could not summon the high officers of the government for witnesses or demand public documents.[1]

Of all the Federalist leaders, only Marshall opposed these bills openly. His legal mind could not approve this violation of natural rights, an attitude for which he was soundly denounced by the New England Federalists. Cabot thought he had much to learn about practical government,[2] and Goodhue said that he had degraded himself. Marshall had already begun to separate from this extreme wing of his party.

The Republicans held that the sedition law was unconstitutional because the federal courts had jurisdiction over those crimes only which were mentioned in the Constitution; they declared that these courts had by the Constitution no common-law jurisdiction, and they thought that this attempt to assume one was a dangerous advance in consolidating the federal government. The point was not settled at the time, but in 1882, after much uncer-

---

[1] *U. S. Statutes at Large*, I., 596.   [2] Lodge, *Cabot*, 176, 179.

tainty had existed for some time, the supreme court held that the federal courts have no common-law jurisdiction in criminal cases.[1]

Another law of this session which aroused the op-position of the Republicans was the act to prevent frauds on the Bank of the United States. It was aimed at the counterfeiting of the bills of the bank. To the Republicans it seemed to be an extension of the powers of the federal government; and it sug-gested the principle that the federal courts should replace the states in the care of the interest of the bank, which was a federal institution.[2]

Nothing better illustrates the extent to which the sedition law imperilled personal liberty than the at-tempts to put it into operation. A typical case is that of Dr. Thomas Cooper. He was not as extreme a partisan as Callender; and Justice Chase, who pre-sided at his trial, was not then in his most savage frame of mind. The incident, therefore, will enable one to form a fair judgment of the practical side of the law.

Cooper was a prominent Republican of Pennsyl-vania, who in 1797 had applied through his friend Dr. Priestly for a federal office; but Adams had not noticed the request. In 1799 he was openly in opposition to the administration, and one of his opponents brought up his former willingness to ac-cept office under the administration. He justified

[1] 108 U. S. Supreme Court Reports, 119; 7 Cranch, 32.
[2] U. S. Statutes at Large, I., 573.

himself by saying that in 1797 Adams was "hardly in the infancy of political mistake: even those who doubted his capacity thought well of his intentions; . . . nor had he yet interfered, as president of the United States, to influence the decision of a court of justice." The last fling had reference to the Robbins case.

There is hardly an election in the country to-day in which more violent charges are not made daily and without comment; but in 1799 they were considered highly dangerous, and Cooper was arrested, indicted for sedition, and tried in Chase's famous spring circuit of 1800. Cooper offered to summon Adams and certain congressmen in order to prove the correctness of his assertion, but this was denied as unseemly. Perhaps it had dawned on the Federalists by this time that any attempts to discuss the truthfulness of one of the seditious utterances at which they were aiming must degenerate into a political wrangle which would prove nothing, convince nobody, and degrade the courts of justice.

Chase interpreted the law in such a way that the jury must convict; and when a verdict to that effect had been given, he asked if the Republicans would pay the fine he would impose. In that case he would make it heavy, otherwise he would regard the circumstances of the prisoner. At this the circuit judge who sat with him interposed, saying, "I think we have nothing to do with parties"; and Chase relented. Cooper was sentenced to pay a fine of four hundred dollars, and to be imprisoned for six months. Adams caused it to be known that he would pardon the prisoner, but Cooper charged the president with improper conduct in giving to the public the letter in which his original application for office had been contained, and he refused to accept clemency unless it should be accompanied with an acknowledgment of the president's error. This Adams would not agree to, and no pardon was issued.[1]

Judge Chase's charge to the jury stated with clearness the view of those who believed in the sedition law. "All governments which I have ever heard or read of," he said, "punish libels against themselves. If a man attempts to destroy the confidence of the people in their officers, their supreme magistrate, and their legislature, he effectually saps the foundation of the government."

The enforcement of the sedition law quickly became a partisan affair, for under it the juries were to be selected by the same method as the juries in the state in which the case was called. Hence, wherever the local juries were selected by the sheriffs, the federal juries were summoned by the marshals. This threw the jury into the hands of the Federalists, and it was charged with much apparent truth that nobody but Federalists were selected. Where political lines were sharply drawn, it must have been difficult to get impartial jurymen.

[1] Wharton, *State Trials*, 659.

Ten persons, all Republican editors and printers, were tried and convicted under the sedition act. Many others were indicted but not tried. The great political effect of those cases which were tried soon opened the eyes of the government, and the execution of the law was abandoned. Matthew Lyon, Duane, and Callender all were made to feel its rigors. But they became popular martyrs by reason of it, and in 1840 Congress refunded the fines which had been collected from the first of these, together with that collected from Cooper.

The alien and sedition laws grew out of a momentary hysteria, not incomparable to that which produced the Salem persecutions for witchcraft. They were passed by men of strictly honest convictions, in the belief that they would redress an evident evil; but they rested on an outworn ideal. Their failure left a deep impression on the public consciousness. Never since that day has our government attempted to regulate what citizens should think or say about public officials.

CHAPTER XVIII

KENTUCKY AND VIRGINIA RESOLUTIONS
(1798–1800)

THE year 1798 was a gloomy one for the Republicans. Believing that Hamilton and his followers were bent on making the government into a centralized authority, they now thought that their worst anticipations were about to be realized. They had seen a standing army created, with the much-dreaded Hamilton in a position to control it. They had seen three laws enacted which they did not believe warranted by any grant of power to the national government, and which gave that government wide power over the rights of individuals. They saw the Federalists drunk with power and prepared to go still further in the direction of consolidation. They saw the people greatly excited at the conduct of France and ready to give the war party all that it should ask, without thinking to what abuses their confidence might lead.

In their discouragement, some Republicans had thoughts of dissolving the Union. One of them, John Taylor, of Caroline County, Virginia, wrote to Jefferson to that end. He suggested that his own state and North Carolina might be withdrawn from the Union and united in a government which should preserve the ideals that he loved most. But Jefferson had not lost his head. To Taylor he wrote in a temperate tone. Party divisions, he said, would always exist in a representative government, and no Union could continue if the minority should resort to secession whenever it did not have its way. He asserted that the people were only temporarily misled, and that he believed they would soon come to their normal ways of thinking.[1]

Jefferson was willing, however, to have the states make a protest against the tendency of the Federalists. He expected that such a course would be a means of calling attention to the evils which he saw and at the same time furnish an authentic statement of party principles. In the autumn of 1798 he decided, after consulting with his friends, to introduce such resolutions into the legislatures of Virginia and North Carolina. The latter state had been reliably Republican, but the Federalist movement of 1798 reached it in the autumn election, and he changed his plan, choosing the state of Kentucky instead.[2] Thus were planned the famous Kentucky and Virginia resolutions. The former were written by Jefferson himself, although under strict injunctions that his authorship should not be revealed, and were adopted in November of the same year by a

---

[1] Jefferson, *Writings* (Ford's ed.), VII., 263.
[2] *Ibid.*, 281, 290 *n*.

vote practically unanimous. The latter were written by Madison, and were carried through the Virginia assembly in December, 1798, by a vote of 100 to 63 in the House of Delegates, and 14 to 3 in the Senate.

The Kentucky resolutions were nine in number. The first asserted that the Constitution was a compact of states, and "that as in all other cases of compact among parties having no common judge, each party has an equal right to judge for itself, as well of infractions as of the mode and measures of redress." Other resolutions arraigned the alien and sedition laws, and pronounced them "void and of no force." The seventh declared that the whole system of broad construction was unconstitutional; the eighth ordered the transmission of copies of the resolutions to Congress; and the ninth called on all the "co-states" to unite with Kentucky in suppressing the unconstitutional action of the general government. It declared, also, that Kentucky would "submit to undelegated and consequently unlimited powers in no man, or body of men, on earth." [1]

The Virginia resolutions were more moderate than those of Kentucky. "In case," they ran, "of a deliberate, palpable, and dangerous exercise of other powers not granted by the said compact, the states who are parties thereto have the right and are in duty bound to interpose for arresting the progress of

---

[1] Warfield, *Kentucky Resolutions of 1798*, 75; Jefferson, *Writings* (Ford's ed.), VII., 288, 289–309.

the evil." They regretted that Congress by forced construction showed a disposition "to consolidate the states by degrees into one sovereignty"; they denounced the alien and sedition laws; and they called on the other states for aid in maintaining the liberties reserved to the states.

These two sets of resolutions differed as the men who wrote them differed. The former were the words of a man whose function was to arouse and fix public opinion. He was not judicially minded; he was an imaginative philosopher. He believed in the compact theory of the Union and he followed it to its logical conclusion. In a clause of his original draught of these resolutions, but whether eliminated by his hand or not is not known, there is an expression which goes to the limit of state nullification. It declares "that every state has a natural right in cases not within the compact to nullify of their own authority all assumptions of powers by others within its limits." [1] In this clause "every atom of Calhoun's perfected theory finds a perfect ante-type." [2]

Jefferson was intent on the present. He wanted to arrest the tendency of Federalism, and looking intently at that end saw not the remote effects, and perhaps cared not for them. Speaking of his own resolutions, he said at the time they were announced, "I think we should distinctly affirm all the impor-

[1] Jefferson, *Writings* (Ford's ed.), VII., 301.
[2] Alexander Johnston, in Lalor, *Cyclop. of Polit. Science*, II., 676.

tant principles they contain, so as to hold to that
ground in the future, and leave the matter in such a
train as that we may not be committed absolutely
to push the matter to extremities, & yet may be
free to push as far as events will render prudent." [1]
A cautious and practical leader of men, he had the
spirit of wise expediency.   He was prepared to claim
much and to take what seemed best.

Madison's resolutions were drawn in a judicial
spirit.   Where Jefferson had declared that the states
might judge infractions of the compact for themselves, Madison was content to say that they might
"interpose" to obtain redress.   What form interpo-
sition might take was not indicated.   This was a
temperate way of announcing his views, and was
better adapted to campaign purposes in a state
like Virginia than the more extreme utterances of
Jefferson.   In 1831, Madison declared that his own
resolutions, and those of his colleague as well, were
prepared merely for political effect, and that they
were not to be taken as an exposition of constitutional doctrine.[2]

The Kentucky and Virginia resolutions were sent
to the other states for consideration.   In the north
the Federalists controlled the legislatures, and all of
the states north of the Potomac made replies unfavorable to the resolutions.   All defended the alien

---

[1] Jefferson, *Writings* (Ford's ed.), VII., 288.
[2] Hunt, *Madison*, 252–258; Madison, *Writings* (Congress ed.),
IV., 204 et seq., 357, 358.

and sedition laws as proper and legal, and all declared that the federal courts were the legal interpreters of the Constitution. In their replies only one, the small state of Vermont, undertook to deny in a clear manner the compact theory of the Union; and this seems to indicate that the theory was so generally accepted by the people that the makers of the replies were unwilling to commit themselves in specific antagonism to it. Federal consolidation was unpopular, and the nearest they would go to it was to express confidence, as most of them did, in the power of the United States supreme court to pass on the constitutionality of an act of Congress. In the great Revolutionary struggle the idea that government is a compact had taken a firm hold on people. It was an idea better suited to a simply organized society than to one highly complex in its distribution of power. It was still a popular idea, as the Republicans well knew; and it lingered long in the consciousness of certain parts of the nation.[1]

The southern states made no replies. Federalism had made considerable gains in the Carolinas and Georgia in the elections of 1798, and it was probably not thought advisable to bring on strife on such a question as the resolutions. Quiet and good management would without doubt restore these states to

[1] Cf. A. C. McLaughlin, *Social Compact and Constitutional Construction* (*Am. Hist. Rev.*, V., 482–484); Anderson, *Contemp. Opinion of the Va. and Ky. Resolutions* (*ibid.*, V., 45, 225); Elliot, *Debates*, IV., 532–580.

Republicanism as soon as the excitement had subsided, and for that event it would be better to wait than to bring on a doubtful struggle.

In November, 1799, Kentucky considered the replies of the states, and her legislature enacted an additional set of resolutions. It reaffirmed the declarations in the former resolutions, saying that for the federal officials to interpret the federal Constitution was nothing short of despotism. It reserved the right of interpretation to the states, and said, "A nullification, by those sovereignties, of all unauthorized acts done under color of that instrument, is the rightful remedy." This clause is the only place in which the word "nullification" is used in either set of resolutions.[1]

In the Virginia assembly the replies of the states were referred to a committee the report of which was submitted by Madison. It contained a long preamble and a short resolution. The former was an exhaustive defence of the compact theory of the Constitution, and the latter reasserted the faith of the assembly in the principles of their first set of resolutions.[2]

The Kentucky and Virginia resolutions made a commotion in public life. The Federalists attacked them vigorously. They had no concept of the effects which the resolutions might have on public opinion. They turned to the theory of a French plot, an ex

---

[1] Warfield, *Kentucky Resolutions*, chap. v.
[2] Elliot, *Debates*, IV., 532–580.

pedient which they could employ on any occasion. France, they said, was seeking to detach Kentucky from the Union, in order to unite it to Louisiana, which she was trying to get ceded by Spain; and the resolutions of that state were regarded as the first step in that direction. They considered dissolution of the Union as a probability, both from Virginia's evident desire for it and because New England wanted to break away from the bonds which bound it to the south. Fenno said that the federal government was "a jangling and chaotic confusion," comparable to "a farrow of pigs" which had so thriven on the nourishment of their mother that they were "able to insult her authority and resist her controul." [1]

The imputation of a French plot could not be sustained by the Federalists. The public realized that the issue was the alien and sedition laws, and back of that was the consolidating tendency of Federalism. In this respect the Republicans were fortunate, for they had at last a predominating issue which was free from the miserable French entanglement. It concerned internal politics, it was democratic in tendency, and it appealed to the consciousness of every man. By discussing it in so many of the state legislatures, they had put it before the people in a most extensive sense. Their local leaders followed this success by earnest work. Grand juries and local committees everywhere made

[1] F. M. Anderson, in *Am. Hist. Rev.*, V., 48.

addresses, public discussions were held, and newspapers scattered the arguments. It was the most
intense purely political appeal the country had up to
that time witnessed. The effects were seen in the
outcome of the election of 1800.

The Kentucky and Virginia resolutions produced
a singular scheme in the brain of Hamilton. He
seems to have thought them the rash scheming of
irresponsible men, and to have believed that the
best way of meeting them was by aggressive action.
Catching at a report that Virginia was preparing to
support her position by arms, he suggested that the
United States enlarge its own functions by extend-
ing the judiciary so as to carry its power more completely to the every - day life of the citizens, by a
large system of public roads and canals, by national
patronage of agriculture and the arts, by enlarging
the navy to six ships of the line, twelve frigates, and
twenty-four sloops of war, by keeping up the army
on a basis like the present even if war with France
should be avoided, by establishing a military acad-
emy, by strict laws to punish in federal courts seditious libels and to send away aliens, and by giving
Congress, if possible, the right to divide the large
states.[1] Hamilton's friends were wiser than he,
and made no attempt to put this scheme into execution: when they received it they had already
realized that public opinion was moving against
them. The avowal of his plan, however, goes far

[1] Hamilton, *Writings* (Lodge's ed.), VIII., 517.

to support Jefferson's contention, often announced, that the Federalists would follow the alien and sedition laws by further advances towards a strongly centralized government.

The nullification movement in South Carolina, which occurred in 1828 to 1832, aroused renewed interest in the resolutions of 1798, and the promoters of nullification drew many of their principles from that source.[1] They sought out the old theory and carried it somewhat further than it had gone in 1798. No resolution passed by Kentucky or Virginia asserted the right of nullification by a state, but by the states. Under the older theory, therefore, it is possible to claim that the intention was to secure redress by a convention of the states; but the South Carolinians declared openly for the right of a state to nullify a law of Congress of its own action, and to go on defying it as a member of the Union.

The nullifiers of 1828–1833 were very anxious to have the support of Virginia, then the long-honored leader of the south, and they made strenuous efforts to show that the doctrines for which they contended were identical with the theories of Jefferson and Madison. They were mistaken. Madison, who was still alive and long past that buoyant period of life in which the nullifiers still flourished, wrote earnestly against the contention.[2]

[1] Cf. MacDonald, *Jacksonian Democracy* (*Am. Nation*, **XV.**), chap. ix.
[2] Madison, *Writings* (Congress ed.), IV., 204, 357, 358.

The older resolutions were an important step in the development of secession. They summed up in tangible form a strong feeling for disunion at the time when they were passed, and the leaders of government did not dare resist it. The yielding of the government to the Republicans in 1800 produced the recession of disunion; it was a triumph for the protesting party. In 1833 neither side could be said to have triumphed, but there came a time when the protesting party was in a clear minority. Then there was no yielding to them; the movement ran on into open secession, and the result was its final extinction.

CHAPTER XIX

DOWNFALL OF THE FEDERALISTS
(1798–1801)

THE congressional elections of 1798 were hotly contested by the Federalists. That party felt a supreme necessity for success, and attained it in a quarter in which the Republicans had hitherto been the stronger. Out of the thirty-seven southern congressmen, they secured twenty-two, among them John Marshall, whose candidacy was due to the urgent appeal of Washington himself. He became the leader of a tolerant group of southern Federalists, who were not committed to the leadership of Hamilton and Pickering, and who did not think that the Republicans were traitors and infidels. They were consistent supporters of Adams and party integrity, and had they controlled the policy of Federalism its history would not have been so brief.[1]

Besides the alien and sedition laws several forces and events worked for the destruction of the Federalists. Among these the condition of the finances

---

[1] Illustrative extracts on the subject of this chapter in Hart, *Am. Hist. told by Contemporaries*, III., §§ 99–105.

was important. The warlike demonstrations cost money, and imports were so reduced that the revenues fell off one million dollars; and when Congress met in 1799, it was forced, after making all possible reductions, to borrow three million five hundred thousand dollars at eight per cent.

Another factor was the natural reaction from a high state of public excitement. Men had lived for a year in constant expectation of war; business was deranged, and officers of the new regiments and volunteers had waited at some personal sacrifices to be called into active service. The Republicans insisted that the commotion had been for political effect, and there were people who believed them. They also pointed out that Hamilton had taken advantage of the situation to advance a system of military government which, up to that time, had been steadily resisted. ʳJefferson declared that the government by this means had become "what the French call, a *monarchie masquée.*" [1]

The Congress elected in 1798 met in December, 1799. Cabot had predicted that, if his party controlled it, "the hands of the country need be bound no longer, and in that case, I think," he added, "the Executive can do everything." [2] The Federalists did, indeed, have a majority of twenty in the House, but it was composed of conservative men who would not go to extremes. As the policy of the

---

[1] Jefferson, *Writings* (Ford's ed.), VII., 464.
[2] Gibbs, *Adminis. of Washington and Adams*, II., 110.

northern faction developed, the support fell away, till the radicals found themselves in a minority.[1]

The contempt with which the Federalists overwhelmed the Republicans disgusted fair-minded men, and taught them to despise that superior wisdom on which rested the claim of what Hamilton called the right of "men of information and property" to govern. It also welded together the Republicans. In viewing their solidarity, Washington exclaimed in despair, "Let that party set up a broomstick, and call it a true son of liberty—a democrat—or give it any other epithet that will suit their purpose, and it will command their votes *in toto*."[2]

In their own minds the Republicans stood for large powers of the states, religious liberty, freedom of speech, trial by jury, economy by the government, opposition to standing armies, to paper currency, and to war, and for non-intercourse—except as to commerce—with foreign countries.[3] Between these measures, which were loudly proclaimed, and the strong policies of the Federalists it was natural for a rural people to turn to the former.

Adams, forced into reserve by the cabals against him, was less tactful than ever. In the very culmination of the campaign, McHenry described him as one "who, whether sportful, playful, witty, kind,

---

[1] Jefferson, *Writings* (Ford's ed.), VII., 446.
[2] Washington, *Writings* (Ford's ed.), XIV., 191.
[3] Jefferson, *Writings* (Ford's ed.), VII., 327–329, 450.

cold, drunk, sober, angry, easy, stiff, jealous, careless, cautious, confident, close, or open, is so, almost
always in the *wrong place, and to the wrong person.*" [1]
Adams made the mistake of naming Smith, an incompetent son-in-law who had been charged with
frauds, for a brigadier - generalship; and Pickering
took advantage of the opportunity to annoy him,
going beyond the strict letter of his duty in prevent-
ing confirmation. The rejection of Smith reached
Adams in a tender spot. It gave his enemies a
chance to charge him with nepotism; and he never
forgave his secretary for meddling in the affair. [2]

While the war of faction was at its highest, came
news of the death of Washington, the one man in the
country who was universally loved. He died on
December 14, 1799, and his short preceding illness
had given the country no opportunity to prepare
itself for the event. He had been worth much to
the Federalists: whatever charges might be made,
there were men who believed that Washington would
not let the party go wrong. Realizing the value of
his name, the Hamilton faction tried not long before
his death to get him to stand again for the presidency,
but their overtures met with a firm refusal. [3] In his
later life he was, in fact, largely under the influence of his old secretary of the treasury, probably

[1] Hamilton, *Works* (Hamilton's ed.), VI., 479.
[2] John Adams, *Works*, VIII., 566; Hamilton, *Works* (Hamilton's ed.), VI., 327, 328, 330.
[3] Washington, *Writings* (Ford's ed.), XIV., 191, 199.

because his faculty of independent judgment, formerly strong with him, was weakening with the advance of age and from long and anxious service.[1]

Other events made for Republican success. In March, 1799, came in eastern Pennsylvania a protest against the direct taxes which the preceding Congress had levied on houses. The indignant people, under the leadership of John Fries, beat the officers, liberated prisoners, and held the country in terror till soldiers came and arrested the ringleaders. Fries was convicted of treason, and was only saved from the gallows by a pardon from the president. The riot occurred in a Republican stronghold, and the Federalists declared that it was the beginning of that anarchy which they long ago pronounced imminent.[2] The officers in the army bore themselves with unnecessary harshness towards the prisoners. Stories of ill-treatment were widely circulated by the Republicans, and it is probable that the incident in this way had considerable influence on the Pennsylvania vote.

Another memorable incident of the same period was the case of Jonathan Robbins, a sailor arrested in 1799 on the charge of mutiny and murder on a British ship in 1797. He swore that he was a Connecticut-born American citizen; but the court decided otherwise, and he was surrendered to the

---

[1] Jefferson, *Writings* (Ford's ed.), I., 168, 175.
[2] Wharton, *State Trials*, 458–648.

British under the extradition clause of the treaty of
1794, and executed. The case attracted much attention because of the feeling against England. The
Republicans promptly took the side of Robbins, declared that he was a martyr, and charged Adams
with his murder.[1] The matter came up in Congress,
and served to call forth a remarkable speech from
John Marshall in defence of the administration. It
has been pronounced the best ever made in Congress,
and Marshall's opponents avowed that it was in
recognition of this defence that Adams later made
him secretary of state.[2]

Meanwhile, there was a general revival of feeling
against England, largely due to her continued impressments. She was in great need of sailors for her
navy, and stood not on our rights. A particularly
annoying incident was that of the *Baltimore*, a
twenty-gun American ship under the command of
Captain Phillips. In November, 1798, he ran into a
fleet of five English men-of-war, the commander of
which boarded him, took off fifty-five of his crew,
and utterly disregarded his protest that a national
ship was exempt from search. Fifty of the men who
had been taken were, on consideration, sent back,
but the rest were retained. The incident caused
great excitement in America, and Phillips was dismissed the service because he had not resisted. The

[1] Jefferson, *Writings* (Ford's ed.), VII., 397; Wharton, *State
Trials*, 392.
[2] Adams, *Gallatin*, 232; *Annals of Cong.*, 6 Cong., 596.

British ministry disavowed the action of their captain and gave orders that American ships of war should be respected; but it was hard to restrain their commanders, who felt generally a contempt for the American navy. An argument which they understood better was employed by Captain Tengey of the American ship *Ganges*, who when asked in 1799 for a sight of his "protection" papers, replied to the inquisitive Englishman, "A public ship carries no protection for her men but her flag." Then he manned his guns to the tune of "Yankee Doodle"; but the British captain did not press the inquiry.[1]

Impressment was a difficult subject. It was likely to continue to give trouble as long as the American navy was weak and the British navy was in need of sailors. The fact that British seamen did desert and join the American navy under false papers, and the conflicting views of the two nations as to inalienable citizenship, went far to enable Americans to endure the existing situation. England was, moreover, wedded to the practice; and though she listened to King, our minister in London, when he pressed, according to his instructions, for a relinquishment of impressments, she finally refused to abandon her position.

The feeling against Britain was further stimulated in 1799 by the sudden suspension of the commission

---

[1] Maclay, *Hist. of the Navy*, I., 170, 177; King, *Life and Corresp. of King*, II., 553, 560.

appointed under the Jay treaty to settle the British debts. The committee on spoliations had allowed Americans about half a million of dollars, and this seemed small enough; but the commission on debts included every variety of American indebtedness they could gather up, and when about to make report the total reached nearly nineteen million dollars,[1] enough to swamp the United States treasury. Adams learned of it and ordered the American commissioners to withdraw, and the negotiation was suspended. It was afterwards taken up, and an agreement made on January 8, 1802, by which the claims were settled for $2,664,000.[2]

Meanwhile, Hamilton was watching the Miranda filibustering movement with much interest. England held this South American agitator in leash, with the evident purpose of loosing him against the Spanish colonies should France gain Spain to her side, as was generally expected in 1798. Hamilton had a good understanding with King, our minister in London; and the plan which they had formed, with the apparent approval of England, was that the United States should co-operate in the movement against the colonies. Hamilton saw here a field for the employment of the army which he had almost got into his hands; but Adams was not an expansionist, and he would have nothing to do with the

[1] King, *Life and Corresp. of King*, II., 534.

[2] *U. S. Treaties and Conventions*, 398; *U. S. Statutes at Large*, II., 192.

scheme. Thus fell this last and most fanciful of Hamilton's military projects.[1]

In Congress the spirit of peace was running strong. Vote after vote fell away from the war faction; and the Republicans took courage, and joined with the moderate Federalists to pass a law in February, 1800, authorizing the president to suspend enlistments. As news from the new commissioners became more pacific, Congress, in March, 1800, passed a law for the discharge of the new army. The navy was kept intact, but the construction of the large twenty-fours, which had been authorized, was abandoned. Thus the campaign of 1800 was robbed of that warlike front, behind which the Federalists for two years had found it so profitable to hide.

If men fancied war, they might see an exhibition of its passion in a small way in the conduct of Justice Chase of the supreme court, who in his spring circuit, in 1800, was taking up cases under the sedition law. In the case of Dr. Cooper[2] he was in his milder humor. In the second trial of Fries he so browbeat the counsel for the defence that they withdrew from the case. Chase's rulings were so evidently unfair that public sympathy was created for the prisoner, and that had much to do with Adams's action in pardoning him. In the trial of Callender, in Richmond, Chase ruled so partially that the law-

---

[1] King, *Life and Corresp. of King*, II., 281, 283, 300, 306, 649–666; John Adams, *Works*, VIII., 581, 585, 600; Hamilton, *Works* (Hamilton's ed.), VI., 347, 348.   [2] See above, 261.

yers for the defence, one of whom was the young
William Wirt, gave up their case, protesting that
their client could not get justice.   These trials, in the
opening of the presidential campaign and connected
with matters which so nearly concerned the issues
of the day, were most untimely for the Federalists.[1]

The campaign was not fairly begun when Adams
came to a determination to reorganize his cabinet.
The first to go was McHenry, recognized by all as
most incompetent and completely the tool of Hamilton and Pickering.   In conversation with the secretary, Adams fell into some violent expressions,
which he afterwards regretted; and McHenry offered
his resignation.   To the secretary's surprise it was
accepted.   This was on May 6, and Adams then
turned on Pickering.[2]   He wrote him a note saying
that he wanted to change his advisers and asking
him to withdraw.   Pickering's Puritan courage stif-
fened him and he refused, making a cool and half-
contemptuous allusion to the expected election of
Jefferson.   In four lines, and with scant courtesy,
Adams sent him a dismissal.[3]   The unctuous Wolcott, who had been as deep in intrigues as either
of the others, was not suspected by the president.
He remained in office till he retired of his own will
at the end of the year; and one of Adams's last ap-

[1] For impeachment of Chase, see Channing, *Jeffersonian System* (*Am. Nation*, XII.), chap. xii.

[2] John Adams, *Works*, IX., 53–55; Hamilton, *Works* (Hamilton's ed.), VI., 442.

[3] Pickering and Upham, *Pickering*, III., 480–488.

pointments was to make him a circuit judge with life tenure.[1]

The place of Pickering was taken by Marshall, and the secretaryship of war by Samuel Dexter, of Massachusetts. Both selections were admirable. Stoddert and Charles Lee remained secretary of the navy and attorney-general respectively. Wolcott made no trouble, and there were no more dissensions in Adams's cabinet.

Before Congress adjourned on May 13 each party held a caucus of congressmen and selected its candidates for president and vice-president. Each party declared that it would support its two candidates equally, although it must have been clear that the result might be a tie. The Federalists decided on Adams and C. C. Pinckney; the Republicans declared for Jefferson and Burr.

Hamilton's mind was already busy on a scheme for defeating Adams. "For my individual part," he said on May 10, "my mind is made up. I will never more be responsible for him [Adams] by my direct support, even though the consequences should be the election of *Jefferson*." Each would sink the government, he added, but Jefferson as an opponent could be fought openly, while Adams must be indorsed by the party.[2]

In the situation, there were two ways in which the Federalists might defeat Adams and carry the elec-

[1] John Adams, *Works*, IX., 88, 99, 100.
[2] Hamilton, *Works* (Hamilton's ed.), VI., 436, 437, 441, 446.

tion: some of the devoted Hamilton electors in New York or elsewhere might fail to vote according to the caucus agreement, and that would give Pinckney the larger vote; another way would be that in South Carolina, where the Republicans had a strong following, the electors might be induced to go for a southern ticket and vote for Pinckney and Jefferson, a situation which would leave the former with the whole Federalist vote and weaken Adams by those votes which were thrown to Jefferson. It is probable that both of these schemes were in Hamilton's mind early in the campaign. The first was rendered futile by the loss of New York to his party and by the vigilance of the Adams supporters in New England; and the second was attempted in South Carolina, but failed through the loyalty of the Federalists and through the unwillingness of Pinckney himself to enter into such a trick.

Two advanced skirmishes in the spring of 1800 showed what the result might be in the autumn. In Pennsylvania the Republicans had just elected the governor and the lower house of the assembly. The law for choosing presidential electors was recently expired, and the Republicans brought in a bill to make the choice by districts. The Federalist Senate refused to accept this compromise, and held out for an election by the legislature; so that they prevented the enactment of any law on the subject. The result was that the electoral vote of the state was likely to be lost entirely in the coming autumn.

When that time came the Senate held stubbornly to their original purpose, and the Republicans were forced to make a compromise by which the fifteen votes of Pennsylvania were divided, seven going for the Federalists and eight for the Republicans. By this means the latter gained one vote for their candidates, and in the uncertainty of the moment they were prone to believe that even that much might decide the election.[1]

New York yielded the party of Jefferson more comfort. Here the electors were chosen by the legislature, and that body was elected in the spring. Strong efforts were made by each side to carry this important point. In May the news spread over the country that the Republicans had been successful, and this assured twelve Republican electors in the fall. The victors could not restrain their joy. One of them declared that the result was solely due to "the intervention of the Supreme Power and our friend Burr, the agent." Of the useful efforts of this agent there can be no doubt.[2]

As the summer passed, there was much whispering among the friends of Hamilton. Adams suspected them, and talked freely to his friends about the Massachusetts Hamiltonians, to whom he applied the term "Essex Junto," because a number of them lived in the county of that name. It was, however, an old term revived. He said openly that they were

[1] Schouler, *United States*, I., 463, 481.
[2] Adams, *Gallatin*, 241.

a British faction, and the Republican press repeated the term, probably to his satisfaction.

These expressions were repeated to Hamilton, and he made them his excuse for dealing a blow to his rival which was far out of proportion to the offence. He wrote a pamphlet against Adams, to circulate among Federalists in New England and Maryland, but he must have known that it would be impossible to conceal it from the rest of the world. Many of the best men in his party advised against his project, but he gave no heed. He was reminded that it was a violation of the decision of the caucus, but that moved him not. August 1 he wrote Adams a cool but polite note alluding to the latter's charges and asking him to deny or affirm them. He received no reply, and on October 1 he wrote again.[1] In his clear and cutting style he denounced the charges against him as "a base, wicked, and cruel calumny," and then he distributed his pamphlet. It was sent to his close friends, but extracts from it appeared almost immediately in the Republican papers, and he was forced to publish an authentic edition.[2]

Hamilton sought to make it appear that he acted solely from motives of defence; but it did not require fifty-three pages to prove that he was not of a British faction. Neither was it necessary for such a purpose to review at length Adams's political

[1] Hamilton, *Works* (Hamilton's ed.), VI., 449, 470.
[2] See Hamilton, *Writings* (Lodge's ed.), VI., 391–444.

career. Hamilton felt that an attack was necessary for the defence of his own faction : "Unless we give our reasons in one form or another," he said to Wolcott about the time he wrote first to Adams, the Adamsites and Republicans combining will "completely run us down in public opinion." [1]

The blow had been much heralded among his intimates, who said that it would crush the president ; but it fell short of that effect. The author could not let his arm swing fully, lest he should plainly commit party treason ; nor was it prudent to attack the policy of peace with France, for it clearly had the approval of the people. Although the attack injured Adams, it did far more harm to Hamilton ; for both contemporaries and posterity have considered it an ill-advised and angry utterance.

The returns from the autumn elections came duly to hand. They showed that Adams had all of the 39 New England votes and that Pinckney had 38 of them. The one vote which the latter lacked was thrown away on Jay, by an elector from Rhode Island, lest by some trickery Adams should be left in the lurch. Besides these, the Federalists had 10 votes from New Jersey and Delaware, the 7 which had been promised from Pennsylvania, 5 of Maryland's 10, and 4 of North Carolina's 12. All these were cast equally for Adams and Pinckney, and the totals were thus 65 and 64. As it turned out, the success of Hamilton's scheme in South Carolina

[1] Hamilton, *Works* (Hamilton's ed.), VI., 449.

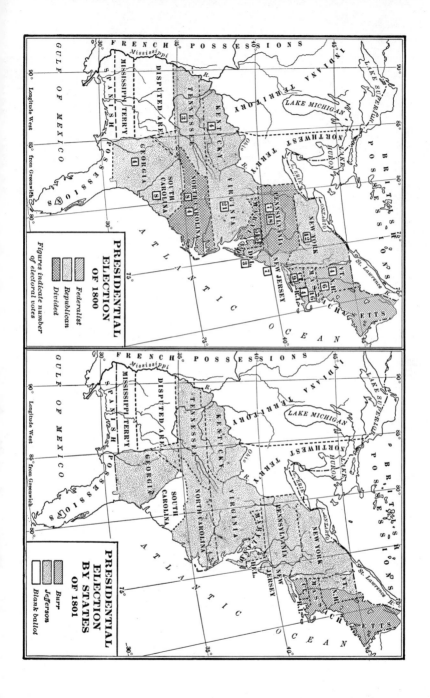

PRESIDENTIAL
ELECTION
OF 1800

Federalist
Republican
Divided

Figures indicate number
of electoral votes

PRESIDENTIAL
ELECTION
BY STATES
OF 1801

Burr
Jefferson
Blank ballot

would not have carried Pinckney into the first place.

Jefferson and Burr each got the rest of the vote, 73 in all. New York gave 12, Maryland 5, Pennsylvania 8, Virginia 21, North Carolina 8, Kentucky 4, Tennessee 3, South Carolina 8, and Georgia 4.[1] Jefferson and Burr thus had equal votes, and the election was thrown into the House, where it must be decided by the states, each voting through its representation as a unit. The Federalists controlled the majority of the states in the House, and thus it happened that they must at last elect the president, but he must be one of the Republican candidates.

In a Federalist caucus it was decided to vote for Burr. This was due to a long prejudice against Jefferson, and to a notion that Burr would be the more manageable. He protested formally against a sacrifice of his colleague on the ticket, but he did not take the positive tone to be expected in the situation from a man of high honor. February 11, 1801, the House took its first ballot by states. Four New England votes went for Burr, as did those of South Carolina and Delaware. The Vermont and Maryland delegations were equally divided. North Carolina's contained an equal number of Federalists and Republicans, but one of the former considered it his duty to vote for Jefferson in accordance with the well-known wish of his state. The same was true of the one Federalist representative who cast

---

[1] Lalor, *Cyclop. of Polit. Science*, II., 54.

the vote of Georgia.   Thus it happened that Jefferson had eight of the sixteen votes, and needed only one more to be president.[1]

This situation, which had been foreseen by both parties, produced much discussion in the country. Many wild rumors were afloat about the designs of the Federalists in order to defeat the evident wishes of the country.   It was reported that they would prevent any election at all and thrust the presidency on Marshall, secretary of state.   The Republicans formed a plan to surround the wilderness capital with militia in order to prevent fraud and hold the government till a new constitutional convention, called by Jefferson and Burr jointly, could meet. Monroe, then governor of Virginia, was feverishly anxious lest he should fail to execute his part in this programme.[2]

Conditions were really not so alarming as the Republicans supposed.   Hamilton had been for some weeks at work to prevent the election of Burr, whose unprincipled nature he well knew.   To Bayard, of Delaware, and to others, he wrote in the strongest terms against this "Cataline of America," as he called him.[3]   Much as he distrusted Jefferson, he saw that he was far more reliable than the trickster whom he had encountered on many occasions

---

[1] Lalor, *Cyclop. of Polit. Science*, I., 806–808.
[2] Jefferson, *Writings* (Ford's ed.), VII., 491; Monroe, *Writings*, III., 256, 258.
[3] Hamilton, *Works* (Hamilton's ed.), VI., 419–424.

in New York politics. Bayard and three of his
friends agreed that Burr should not be president.
They satisfied themselves that Jefferson would make
no wholesale removals of Federalists from the lower ranks of the civil service, where the Federalists
abounded, and on February 17, the ballot being the
thirty-sixth, they brought the contest to an end.
Bayard voted a blank; the one Federalist from
Vermont refused to vote, and his colleague cast the
vote of the state for Jefferson; two of the Federalists
of the Maryland delegation voted blanks, and that
gave the state to their opponents. Jefferson thus
received ten votes, which was one more than necessary to elect him.

In the last weeks of their power, the Federalists
committed one of the most damaging of their acts
of foolish party manipulation. There had been for
some time a desire to reorganize the federal court
system, and a bill to that end failed in the session of
1799–1800. It was desired to create special circuit
judges, and to relieve the justices of the supreme
court from serving in that capacity. The reform
was regarded as inevitable, and the defeated Federalists were alarmed lest the Republicans should
accomplish it and fill the offices thereby created.
Senator Gunn, of New Jersey, to Hamilton spoke
the purpose of his party when he said of his scheme:
"If neglected by the Federalists, the ground will be
occupied by the enemy the very next session of
Congress, and, sir, we shall see ——— and many

other scoundrels placed on the seat of justice." [1]
A law was accordingly passed, February 13, 1801,
creating sixteen new judges and increasing the number of marshals, attorneys, and clerks. It was hotly denounced by the Republicans as an abuse of
party power, and there can be no doubt that its
adoption was from an unworthy motive, although
it is not clear that the particular reform aimed at in
the agitation of the preceding years was unnecessary.
The judiciary act of 1801 vied in the popular mind
with the alien and sedition laws as the best evidence
of the unfitness of the Federalists to administer the
government. [2]

One of Adams's last acts was to appoint Marshall
chief-justice of the supreme court. It was a very
important step; for the loose constructionists were
just coming into a long period of control in the
executive and legislative departments of the government; and for thirty-four years Marshall remained at the head of the judiciary. [3] Firm Federalist and pre-eminent jurist, he was a continual
check on the opposing school, and in many important respects gave the national government cohesive
strength and practical efficiency.

In the exciting events of the winter of 1800–1801
Adams received but little popular attention; he

---

[1] Hamilton, *Works* (Hamilton's ed.), VI., 483.

[2] Farrand, *Judiciary Act of 1801* (*Am. Hist. Rev.*, V., 682).

[3] Cf. Babcock, *Am. Nationality* (*Am. Nation*, XIII.), chap.
xviii.

was neglected by friend and enemy. Deeply disgusted at the result of the election, he sought nothing but the retirement of his New England home. For Jefferson he felt a peculiar repugnance. March 3 found him busily signing the commissions of the appointees under the new judiciary act. It was no small task, and the night was far gone before he completed it. Early in the following morning he entered his carriage, and ere the citizens of Washington had risen from their slumbers he had driven rapidly from the scene of his rival's triumph.

The downfall of Federalism came because the party had outlived its usefulness. Its function of giving strength to the Union in the early days of "the experiment" had been performed. It was the party of the superior classes, of men who were supposed not to be influenced by passions and who had strong purposes and conservative instincts. It had solved the problems of the effective organization of a new government; but other questions were now at hand concerning internal affairs. Should the people be trusted with a large share of government? The Federalists recoiled at the prejudice and violence of the masses, declaring that incompetence could not be trusted. They sought to restrain the violent; they expressed open contempt; and they developed a party selfishness which they wished others to believe was patriotism. They fell into factions and dreamed mad dreams of expansion, till at last they gave the masterly leader of men who opposed them an opportunity to organize a majority of the people against their supremacy. So much did they bring into contempt the idea of government by the superior classes, that no capable politician since 1800 has dared to place his cause on any other ground than the will of the people.

CHAPTER XX

CRITICAL ESSAY ON AUTHORITIES

BIBLIOGRAPHICAL AIDS

VALUABLE information on the history of Washington's and Adams's administrations will be found in Justin Winsor, *Narrative and Critical History of America* (8 vols., 1884–1889), VIII., 294–336; Channing and Hart, *Guide to the Study of American History* (1896), an excellent list of secondary works and of the more necessary documents; J. N. Larned, *Literature of American History, a Bibliographical Guide* (1902), a co-operative work by a number of the best scholars in American history; although opinions may differ about some of the books, the work constitutes the best body of criticism so far made on our historical literature. Specialists should consult Richardson and Morse, *Writings on American History, 1902* (1904), "an attempt at an exhaustive bibliography of books and articles," which, it is announced, will be continued annually. For references on foreign relations, Albert Bushnell Hart, *A Trial Bibliography of American Diplomacy* (*American Historical Review*, VI., 848), reprinted in his *Foundations of American Foreign Policy* (1901), will be helpful. For public documents, consult A. W. Greely, *Public Documents of the First to the Fourteenth Congress* (*Senate Exec. Docs.*, 56 Cong., 1 Sess., No. 428). For references on Hamilton, see P. L. Ford, *Bibliotheca Hamiltoniana* (1886); and on Jefferson, see R. H. Johnston, *Bibliography of Jefferson*, announced to accompany A. A. Lipscomb's new edition of Jefferson's works.[1] A body of specific references on

[1] See below, p. 302.

political and diplomatic history will be found in Albert Bushnell Hart, *Hand-book of the History, Diplomacy, and Government of the United States* (1903), §§ 19c, 19d, 20e.

GENERAL SECONDARY WORKS

Richard Hildreth, *History of the United States* (6 vols., 1849–1852)—vols. IV. and V. deal with the period of the Federalists. The work is accurate for the time at which it was written, but dull, and partial to the Federalists. A better book is James Schouler, *History of the United States under the Constitution* (6 vols., 1880–1899), vol. I. dealing with the years 1783–1801. It is marked by good judgment and truthfulness, but the treatment is rather too chronological for clearness. J. B. McMaster, *History of the People of the United States from the Revolution to the Civil War* (5 vols., published, 1883–1903)—parts of vols. I. and II. deal with the years 1789–1801; it is full of sprightly incident, but it lacks the tone of strong and informing narrative, and gives the impression of seeking the *bizarre*. George Tucker, *History of the United States* (4 vols., 1856–1858)—the period of the Federalists falls in vols. I. and II.; it lacks breadth of view and leans strongly to Jefferson. J. C. Hamilton, *History of the Republic of the United States as Traced in the Writings of Alexander Hamilton* (7 vols., 4th ed., 1879)—it is a defence of Hamilton against Jefferson, Adams, Madison, and others; but it contains many valuable letters; Winsor calls it "the essential store-house for the student of Hamilton."

In smaller compass are the following valuable works of a general nature: the contributions of Alexander Johnston, in J. J. Lalor, *Cyclopædia of Political Science* (3 vols.), republished in *American Political History* (ed. by J. A. Woodburn, 2 vols., 1905); Woodrow Wilson, *A History of the American People* (5 vols., 1902)—although it is in several volumes, less than seventy pages are given to the Federalist period; Timothy Pitkin, *Political and Civil History of the United States* [1763–1797] (2 vols., 1828); F. A. Walker, *The Making of the Nation* (1895); and George Gibbs, *Memoirs of the Administrations of Washington and Adams* (2 vols., 1846), a work biased in itself, but exceedingly valuable because it contains the correspondence of Oliver Wolcott.

Valuable works in special fields are: Edward S. Maclay, *History of the United States Navy* (3 vols., rev. ed., 1898–1901); Edward S. Maclay, *History of American Privateers* (1899); J. R. Spears, *History of Our Navy* (5 vols., 1897–1898); Edward Stanwood, *History of the Presidency* (1898), fair and accurate, and contains some necessary documents; J. P. Gordy, *History of Political Parties in the United States* (2 vols., rev. ed., 1904), clear and fair in treatment, and much better than the first edition; Thomas Cooper, *Consolidation* [account of parties from 1787, extreme state-rights view] (2d ed., 1830).

SOURCES IN GENERAL

Much first-hand material is included in the public documents and works of statesmen described below. The material in these works and in other repositories is made available through Channing and Hart, *Guide to the Study of American History*, §§ 157–166; Justin Winsor, *Narrative and Critical History*, VII., VIII.; W. E. Foster, *References to the History of Presidential Administrations* (1885). A collection of illustrative extracts and documents are: Albert Bushnell Hart, *American History told by Contemporaries* (4 vols., 1897–1901), III., pts. ii.–v.; William Mac-Donald, *Select Documents Illustrative of the History of the United States, 1776–1861* (1898); Francis Wharton, *State Trials of the United States during the Administrations of Washington and Adams* (1849); C. D. Hazen, *Contemporary American Opinion of the French Revolution* (1897).

PUBLIC DOCUMENTS

The laws of the period are found in Richard Peters [ed.], *The Public Statutes at Large of the United States of America*

(8 vols., 1845).   The public laws are in vols. I.–V., private laws in vol. VI., Indian treaties in vol. VII., and foreign treaties in vol. VIII.   The debates in Congress, 1789–1801, are in *The Annals of Congress* (1834–1851), vols. I.–X., and in T. H. Benton, *Abridgment of the Debates of Congress, 1789–1850* (10 vols., 1857–1863).   The early proceedings of the Senate were recorded very briefly; but the gap is tolerably well supplied for the first Congress by William Maclay, *Journal, 1789–1791* (1900).   It must be remembered that the reports of the early debates were warped by party feeling, and from this even the *Annals* cannot escape.   For the journals of Congress, see *The Legislative Journal of the Senate* (5 vols., 1820–1821), *The Executive Journal of the Senate* (3 vols., 1829), and *The Journal of the House of Representatives* (9 vols., 1826).

The many public documents connected with the work of the executive departments were printed in a series known as *State Papers and Public Documents* (10 vols., 3d ed., 1819); but these are superseded by the folio series: *American State Papers; Documents Legislative and Executive* (38 vols., 1832–1861).   For Washington's and Adams's administrations the important volumes are those on *Foreign Relations* (vols. I. and II.), *Finance* (vol. I.), *Military Affairs* (vol. I.), *Naval Affairs* (vol. I.), *Indian Affairs* (vol. I.), *Public Lands* (vol. I.), and *Miscellaneous* (vol. I.). They contain reports of public officers, documents sent to Congress by the executive, foreign correspondence, etc.   A work of constant reference badly arranged is James D. Richardson, *Messages and Papers of the Presidents, 1789–1897* (10 vols., 1897).

WRITINGS AND BIOGRAPHIES OF STATESMEN

The state papers, private correspondence, diaries, and occasional autobiographical fragments of the leading statesmen are excellent sources of information.   Manuscript material of this kind is in the library of Congress, Washington, D. C., as follows: *Washington Manuscripts* (333 vols.),

Jefferson Manuscripts (135 vols.), *Madison Manuscripts* (75 vols.), *Alexander Hamilton Manuscripts* (64 vols.), and *Monroe Manuscripts* (22 vols.). Of these the government has published calendars of the Jefferson, Madison, and Monroe collections. Relatively, only a small part of these writings have been included in the various printed editions of the works of these men.

GEORGE WASHINGTON.—Two collections of his papers have been published: Worthington C. Ford, editor, *Writings of George Washington* (14 vols., 1889–1893), and Jared Sparks, editor, *Writings of George Washington* (12 vols., 1837). Ford's edition is modern and thoroughly satisfactory. Benson J. Lossing, editor, *Diary of George Washington, 1789–1791* (1840), contains material relating to the presidential vacation tours. A somewhat similar work is W. S. Baker, *Washington after the Revolution, 1784–1799* (1898), a calendar showing where Washington was on each day during the period indicated.

Of the many lives of Washington the most valuable for the period of his presidency are: John Marshall, *Life of George Washington* (5 vols., 1804–1807), an able but thoroughly Federalist book; Jared Sparks, *Life of George Washington* (1837); Washington Irving, *Life of George Washington* (5 vols., 1855–1859), in many respects still the best biography of Washington, but lacking in modern scholarship; Woodrow Wilson, *George Washington* (1897), readable, judicious, human, but too short for the student; P. L. Ford, *The True George Washington* (1896), various phases of the subject's life are described; G. W. P. Custis, *Recollections of Washington* (1860, edited by B. J. Lossing), many traditions; B. F. Hough, *Washingtoniana, etc.* (2 vols., rev. ed., 1865), collected descriptions of Washington's funeral and memorials; H. C. Lodge, *George Washington* (2 vols., 1889), readable and reliable; W. C. Ford, *George Washington* (2 vols., 1900), very painstaking and reliable; Richard Rush, *Washington in Domestic Life* (1857), chiefly letters from Washington to Lear, his secretary from 1790–1798; M. L. Weems, *Life of George Washington* (1800, and seventy other editions till 1891), largely mythical, but very widely circulated.

ALEXANDER HAMILTON.—His writings were first published by his son John C. Hamilton, *Works of Alexander Hamilton* (7 vols., 1850–1851), still an excellent edition, but somewhat supplanted by H. C. Lodge, *The Works of Alexander Hamilton* (9 vols., 1895–1896, and the federal edition, 12 vols., 1904). Several contemporary controversial pamphlets relating to Hamilton have been reprinted by the Hamilton Club of New York, among them John Williams (Anthony Pasquin), *The Life of Hamilton* and *The Hamiltoniad;* Alexander Hamilton, *Observations on Certain Documents* (1797), the "Reynolds Pamphlet"; and the anonymous *Letters to Alexander Hamilton, King of the Feds*.

The biographies of Hamilton include John T. Morse, Jr., *Life of Alexander Hamilton* (2 vols., 1876); Henry Cabot Lodge, *Alexander Hamilton* (1882), a clear and readable book, but, like Morse's, too enthusiastic for Hamilton; William G. Sumner, *Alexander Hamilton* (1890), thinks Hamilton's financial services are usually overstated; John C. Hamilton, *The Life of Alexander Hamilton* (2 vols., 1834), a family affair; and James A. Hamilton, *Reminiscences* (1869), in which the son makes a defence of the father.

THOMAS JEFFERSON.—Four editions of Jefferson's writings have appeared: J. T. Randolph, editor, *Memoirs, Correspondence, and Miscellanies of Thomas Jefferson* (4 vols., 1829, 1830); H. A. Washington, editor, *Writings of Thomas Jefferson* (9 vols., 1853–1854); Paul L. Ford, editor, *Writings of Thomas Jefferson* (10 vols., 1892–1899); and A. A. Lipscomb, editor, *The Writings of Thomas Jefferson* (in progress, 10 vols., published, 1903–1905). Of these three editions, Ford's will be most useful to students and others. H. B. Tompkins, *Bibliotheca Jeffersoniana* (1887), is an unsatisfactory bibliography of Jefferson, but R. H. Johnston announces one to appear in Lipscomb's edition of the *Writings* which promises to be better.

The important biographies of Jefferson are: George

Tucker, *Life of Thomas Jefferson* (2 vols., 1837), partial to Jefferson, but clear and readable; H. S. Randall, *Life of Thomas Jefferson* (3 vols., 1858), able and exhaustive, but not judicial in tone; John T. Morse, Jr., *Thomas Jefferson* (1883), readable and generally correct, deals chiefly with Jefferson's political career; James Parton, *Life of Thomas Jefferson* (2 vols., 1874), has Parton's well-known qualities, vivacity, incident, and lack of political grasp; Sarah N. Randolph, *Domestic Life of Thomas Jefferson* (1871), an intimate view by a relative; C. de Witt, *Thomas Jefferson, Étude historique sur la démocratie américaine* (1861), a good political essay; Theodore Dwight, *Character of Thomas Jefferson as Exhibited in His Writings* (1839), strong adverse criticism.

JAMES MADISON.—His works were published by order of Congress as *Letters and Other Writings of James Madison* (4 vols., 1865), but a better edition, edited by Gaillard Hunt, is now being printed. Henry D. Gilpin, editor, *The Papers of James Madison* (3 vols., 1840–1852), does not reach the national period. Of biographies, the largest, William C. Rives, *Life and Times of James Madison* (3 vols., 1859–1868), is full of information, apologetic and diffuse, and ends with March 4, 1797. A more scholarly and satisfactory work is Gaillard Hunt, *Life of James Madison* (1902); Sidney Howard Gay, *James Madison* (1884), is Federalist in tone and fails to understand its subject.

JAMES MONROE.—Stanislas H. Hamilton, editor, *Writings of James Monroe* (7 vols., 1898–1903), presents Monroe's important papers. No good biography of Monroe is published. Daniel C. Gilman, *James Monroe in His Relation to the Public Service* (1883), is inadequate; and the same may be said of John Quincy Adams, in *Lives of Madison and Monroe* (1850).

JOHN ADAMS.—His important papers and a strong but apologetic biography are contained in Charles Francis Adams, editor, *The Works of John Adams, . . . with a Life by the Author* (10 vols., 1850–1856). A later biography, and an excellent one, is John T. Morse, Jr., *John Adams* (1885).

MINOR STATESMEN.—The lives and papers of various other leaders of the period afford valuable information. Of them the following works are valuable though usually apologetic: C. R. King, *Life and Correspondence of Rufus King* (6 vols., 1894–1900), very important because of King's ability and influence among the Federalists, chiefly correspondence; H. P. Johnston, *Correspondence and Public Papers of John Jay* (4 vols., 1890–1893); William Jay, *Life of John Jay* (2 vols., 1833); George Pellew, *John Jay* (1890); Seth Ames, editor, *Works of Fisher Ames* (2 vols., 1857), a brilliant man of whom too few papers have been preserved; William Wirt Henry, *Life, Correspondence, and Speeches of Patrick Henry* (3 vols., 1891), a good book, and valuable for affairs in Virginia; Moses Coit Tyler, *Patrick Henry* (1887), carefully and fairly written; William Wirt, *Sketches of the Life and Character of Patrick Henry* (1818, and many other editions), long a very popular book, but superseded in recent years; Henry Adams, editor, *Writings of Albert Gallatin* (3 vols., 1879); Henry Adams, *Life of Albert Gallatin* (1879), a model biography; J. A. Stevens, *Albert Gallatin* (1884), readable, fair, and informing; J. T. Austin, *Life of Elbridge Gerry* (2 vols., 1828–1829), defends Gerry's conduct in France in 1798; Kate Mason Rowland, *Life of George Mason* (2 vols., 1892); A. B. Magruder, *John Marshall* (1885), inadequate for the subject; Anne C. Morris, editor, *Diary and Letters of Gouverneur Morris* (2 vols., 1888), important and highly interesting; Theodore Roosevelt, *Gouverneur Morris* (1888), an interesting and appreciative biography; Octavius Pickering and C. W. Upham, *Life of Timothy Pickering* (4 vols., 1867–1875), contains letters and other important information about the "Essex Junto"; *Historical Index to the Pickering Papers* (1896), a calendar of the fifty-seven manuscript volumes of papers in possession of the Massachusetts History Society, in the society's *Collections*, 6th series, vol. VIII.; J. C. Amory, *Life of James Sullivan, with Selections from His Writings* (2 vols., 1859), biography of a much-hated Massachusetts Republican; William Sullivan, *Fa-*

miliar Letters on Public Characters and Public Events, 1783–1815 (1834), caustic Federalist sketches; General James Wilkinson, *Memoirs of My Own Time* (3 vols., 1816), absolutely untrustworthy but suggestive on western history; C. B. Todd, editor, *Life and Letters of Joel Barlow* (1886), throws light on the Scioto Land Company and on our relations with the Barbary States; Moncure D. Conway, *Omitted Chapters of History Disclosed in the Life and Papers of Edmund Randolph* (1888), fails to prove that Randolph was a much-abused man; Moncure D. Conway, *Life of Thomas Paine* (2 vols., 1892); Conway has also edited *Writings of Thomas Paine* (4 vols., 1894–1896); see also, William Garrott Brown, *Oliver Ellsworth* (1905).

DIPLOMATIC RELATIONS

W. H. Trescott, *Diplomatic History of the Administrations of Washington and Adams* (1857), clear and fair, but not brilliant; Theodore Lyman, *Diplomacy of the United States, 1778–1826* (2d ed., 2 vols., 1828), creditable but out of date; Eugene Schuyler, *American Diplomacy and the Furtherance of Commerce* (1886), a useful outline; *Treaties and Conventions Concluded between the United States and Other Powers since July 4, 1776* (1886), an official publication of the texts; Freeman Snow, *Treaties and Topics in American Diplomacy* (1894), handy for students—besides the texts it gives convenient résumés; John W. Foster, *A Century of American Diplomacy* (1900), popular and scrappy; Worthington C. Ford, *The United States and Spain in 1790* (1890), a good monograph.

RELATIONS WITH GREAT BRITAIN

J. Franklin Jameson, editor, *Letters of Phineas Bond, British Consul at Philadelphia, to the Foreign Office* (Am. Hist. Assoc., *Report*, 1896, p. 513, 1897, p. 454); Tench Coxe, *Examination of the Conduct of Great Britain Respecting Neutrality since 1791* (1808); and A. C. McLaughlin, *Western Posts and British Debts* (Am. Hist. Assoc., *Report* 1894, p. 413).

RELATIONS WITH FRANCE

Among essential sources are the collections and articles by Frederick J. Turner, under the following titles: *Correspondence of the French Ministers to the United States, 1791–1797* (Am. Hist. Assoc., *Report* 1903, II.), taken from the French public archives; *Documents on the Relations of France to Louisiana* (*Am. Hist. Rev.*, III., 490); *The Origin of Genêt's Projected Attack on Louisiana and the Floridas* (*ibid.*, III., 650); *France and the United States in the Mississippi Valley* (*ibid.*, X., 249); *Carondelet on the Defence of Louisiana, 1794* (*ibid.*, II., 474); *The Mangourit Correspondence in Respect to Genêt's Projected Attack upon the Floridas, 1793–1794* (Am. Hist. Assoc., *Report* 1897, p. 569); H. E. Bourne, editor, *Correspondence of the Comte de Moustier with the Comte de Montmorin, 1787–1789* (*Am. Hist. Rev.*, VIII., 709, IX., 86); *Correspondence of George Rogers Clark and Genêt, 1793–1794* (Am. Hist. Assoc., *Report* 1896, p. 930); W. R. Shepherd, *Wilkinson and the Beginning of the Spanish Conspiracy* (*Am. Hist. Rev.*, IX., 490); W. R. Shepherd, editor, *Papers Bearing on James Wilkinson's Relations with Spain, 1788–1789* (*ibid.*, IX., 748); L. Goldsmith, *Exposition of the Conduct of France towards America, Illustrated by Cases Decided in the Council of Prizes* (1810); Alfred T. Mahan, *Influence of Sea Power on the French Revolution and Empire* (2 vols., 1898), see vol. I., 122–161.

SOCIAL CONDITIONS

Many Europeans visited America about the close of the eighteenth century and published their observations of society there. These books of travel are the chief source of information about the society of the period. For the student the best are: J. P. Brissot de Warville, *New Travels in the United States of America* [1788] (1791, 1792), a French republican who desired to show his countrymen how free government succeeded in America; enthusiasm warped his judgment, but for actual observations he is

reliable; François Alexandre Frédéric, duc de Rochefoucauld-Liancourt, *Travels through the United States, 1795–1797*
(2 vols., 1799, London ed.), full of economic and social
facts, but the author hardly understood American life;
Isaac Weld, *Travels through the States of North America and
Canada, 1795–1797* (2 vols., 1799), very popular when
published, and still valuable for its description of manners;
John Bernard, *Retrospections of America* [1797–1811] (1887),
full of incident; John Davis, *Travels of Four and a Half
Years in the United States* [1798–1802] (1803), of little
value; P. Campbell, *Travels in the Interior Inhabited Parts
of North America, 1791–1792* (1793), good for customs in
New York and Canada and for an account of St. Clair's
defeat; Timothy Dwight, *Travels in New England and New
York* [1796–1815] (4 vols., 1821–1822), one of the best of our
books of travel, marked by accurate observation and good
judgment.　A good description of society about 1800 will
be found in Henry Adams, *History of the United States* (9
vols., 1889–1891), I., chaps. i.–vi.　For social life in New
York and Philadelphia, see R. W. Griswold, *The Republican
Court* (1864).

SLAVERY

M. S. Locke, *Anti-Slavery in America . . . 1619–1808*
(1901), is an excellent piece of research.　It is well sup-
plemented by W. E. B. du Bois, *Suppression of the Slave-
Trade* (1896), which is scholarly and clear.　Among other
works the most useful are: J. C. Ballagh, *History of Slavery
in Virginia* (1902); Jeffrey R. Brackett, *The Negro in
Maryland* (1889); John S. Bassett, *History of Slavery in
the State of North Carolina* (*Johns Hopkins University
Studies*, 1899); J. C. Hurd, *The Law of Freedom and Bondage in the United States* (2 vols., 1858–1862); W. F. Poole,
Anti-Slavery Opinions before the Year 1800 (1887); G. W.
Williams, *History of the Negro Race in America* (1883);
Mary Tremaine, *Slavery in the District of Columbia* (Uni-
versity of Nebraska, *Seminary Papers*); and F. A. Ogg,

Jay's Treaty and the Slavery Interests of the United States (Am. Hist. Assoc., *Report* 1901, p. 273).

ECONOMIC CONDITIONS

Few books deal with our economic history at this early period. Of the statistical works the most useful are: Timothy Pitkin, *A Statistical View of the Commerce of the United States* (1817, 1835), a reliable work; and Adam Seybert, *Statistical Annals of the United States of America, 1789–1818* (1818). See also Tench Coxe, *View of the United States of America* (1794, 1795), by the commissioner of the revenue. For financial history the best books are: Davis R. Dewey, *Financial History of the United States* (1903), a valuable compendium with a short bibliography; W. G. Sumner, *History of Banking in the United States* (1896), generally considered the best work on the subject; W. G. Sumner, *History of American Currency* (1874, 1876), sketchy though widely used; John J. Knox, *History of Banking in the United States* (1900), accurate and clear; M. St. C. Clarke and D. A. Hall, *Legislative and Documentary History of the Bank of the United States* (1832), contains the documents relating to the first United States bank; Jonathan Elliot, editor, *The Funding System of the United States and Great Britain* (1845), *House Executive Documents*, 28 Cong., 1 Sess., No. 15. On public lands a useful though discursive authority is Thomas Donaldson, *The Public Domain, Its History, with Statistics* (1881), in *Report* of the Public Land Commission for 1881.

INDUSTRIAL HISTORY

Two good brief books are: Edwin E. Sparks, *The Expansion of the American People* (1900); Katherine Coman, *Industrial History of the United States* (1905). Works on special topics are: J. L. Bishop, *History of American Manufactures* (3 vols., 1864–1867), a popular work which contains many facts not easily found elsewhere; W. R. Bagnall, *Textile Industries of the United States* (vol. I., 1893), is a very reliable work, only one volume of which has been issued. Mr. Bagnall has also written *Samuel Slater and the Early Development of Cotton Manufacture in the United States* (1890); Samuel Batchelder, *Introduction and Early Progress of Cotton Manufacture in the United States;* and *The Correspondence of Eli Whitney Relative to the Invention of the Cotton-Gin (Am. Hist. Rev.*, 1897, p. 90), have valuable information on cotton. On the iron industry, see J. M. Swank, *History of the Manufacture of Iron in All Ages* (rev. ed., 1892), and B. F. French, *History of the Iron Trade in the United States, 1621–1857* (1858).

THE KENTUCKY AND VIRGINIA RESOLUTIONS

Convenient texts in *American History Leaflets*, No. 15; E. D. Warfield, *The Kentucky Resolutions of 1798* (1887), presents narrative history of Kentucky resolutions and makes briefer mention of those of Virginia. Frank M. Anderson, *Contemporary Opinion of the Virginia and Kentucky Resolutions (Am. Hist. Rev.*, V., 45, 225) is a good discussion. In this connection A. C. McLaughlin, *Social Compact and Constitutional Construction (Am. Hist. Rev.*, V., 467), is suggestive. See also Jonathan Elliot, *Journal and Debates of the Federal Convention* (1830), IV., App., 357–388, for replies of some of the states, the Virginia resolutions of 1799 – 1800, and Madison's letter on nullification, 1830. E. P. Powell, *Nullification and Secession in the United States* (1897), has a chapter on the resolutions of 1798; and C. W. Loring, *Nullification, Secession, Webster's Argument and the Kentucky and Virginia Resolutions* (1893), combats the theory that nationality is a growth.

THE DEVELOPMENT OF THE WEST

A good treatment is Justin Winsor, *The Westward Movement . . . 1763–1798* (1897). A book full of natural force and interest is Theodore Roosevelt, *The Winning of the*

West (4 vols., 1889–1896). Other works of value are: Burke Aaron Hinsdale, *The Old Northwest* (1888, 1889); F. A. Ogg, *The Opening of the Mississippi* (1904); C. H. Haskins, *The Yazoo Land Companies* (Am. Hist. Assoc., *Papers*, V., 395); G. L. Rives, *Spain and the United States in 1795* (*Am. Hist. Rev.*, IV., 62); A. C. McLaughlin, *The Western Posts and British Debts* (Am. Hist. Assoc., *Report* 1894, p. 413); and Arthur St. Clair, *Narrative of the Campaign against the Indians, 1791* (2 vols., 1882). Much valuable material on the early history of the west is to be found in state histories of which the best are: KENTUCKY—Butler's (1834), Collins's (2 vols., 1874), Connelly's (1889), Marshall's (2 vols., 1884), and Shaler's (1885); OHIO—Atwater's (1838), Black's (1888), and King's (1888); TENNESSEE — Haywood's (1823, 1891), Phelan's (1888), and Goodpasture's (1900); ALABAMA — Pickett's (1823, 1900) and Brewer's (1872); MISSISSIPPI — Claiborne's (vol. I., 1880), Lowry and McCardle's (1893), and Riley's (1900); LOUISIANA—Gayarré's (4 vols., 1854, 1856, 1885), Martin's (2 vols., 1827, 1882), and Fortier's (4 vols., 1904).

POLITICAL AFFAIRS

The following are valuable: A. D. Morse, *Causes and Consequences of the Party Revolution of 1800* (Am. Hist. Assoc., *Report* 1894, p. 531); A. D. Morse, *The Politics of John Adams* (*Am. Hist. Rev.*, IV., 292); Max Farrand, *The Judiciary Act of 1801* (*ibid.*, V., 682); *South Carolina in the Presidential Election of 1800* (*ibid.*, IV., 111), letters from C. C. Pinckney to Jefferson; Carl R. Fish, *The Civil Service and the Patronage* (1905), an excellent monograph; Gaillard Hunt, *Office-Seeking during Washington's Administration* (*Am. Hist. Rev.*, I., 270); Gaillard Hunt, *Office-Seeking during John Adams's Administration* (*ibid.*, II., 241); and G. P. Fisher, *Jefferson and the Social Compact Theory* (Am. Hist. Assoc., *Report* 1893, p. 163); C. H. Kerr, *Origin and Development of the United States Senate* (1895).

THE WHISKEY INSURRECTION

Two contemporary accounts of the insurrection were published: William Findley, *History of the Insurrection in the Four Western Counties of Pennsylvania* (1796), a very good narrative; and H. H. Brackenridge, *Incidents of the Insurrection* (1795). H. M. Brackenridge, *History of the Western Insurrection* (1859), is a fair and rather full presentation from the stand-point of the participants. Townsend Ward, *Insurrection of 1794 in the Western Counties of Pennsylvania* (Pennsylvania Hist. Soc., *Memoirs*, VI.), contains some more modern information. Official papers relating to the affair are to be found in *Annals of Congress*, 4 Cong., 2791 – 2868; and in *American State Papers*, *Military Affairs*, I.

INDEX